SLOW COOKER COOKBOOK

Top 500 Recipes For Everyday
Crock Pot Cooking At Home

Sarah Dixon

ISBN: 979-8865326335

Warning-Disclaimer

The purpose of this book is to educate and entertain. The author or publisher does not guarantee that anyone following the techniques, suggestions, tips, ideas, or strategies will become successful. The author and publisher shall have neither liability or responsibility to anyone with respect to any loss or damage caused, or alleged to be caused, directly or indirectly by the information contained in this book.

CONTENTS

SNACKS & APPETIZERS 52

CHICKEN RECIPES 66

PORK RECIPES 94

FISH AND SEAFOOD 104

MEATLESS RECIPES 110

DESSERTS 136

INTRODUCTION

Welcome to the world of slow cooking, where convenience meets culinary delight. In this cookbook, I invite you to embark on a delicious journey through the realm of the humble yet versatile slow cooker. As we delve into the aromatic, mouthwatering, and utterly comforting world of slow-cooked cuisine, you'll discover that great flavors don't always require hours of active kitchen time.

The slow cooker, often affectionately called a "crockpot," is an unsung hero in the modern kitchen. It allows you to create incredible meals with minimal effort, turning simple ingredients into gastronomic masterpieces. Whether you're a busy professional seeking to savor a home-cooked meal at the end of a hectic day or a culinary enthusiast eager to explore new tastes, this recipe book is your trusted companion.

This Slow Cooker Cookbook has a collection of the Top 500 carefully curated recipes that cover a wide range of cuisines, from comfort foods to some more exotic dishes. You'll find recipes that suit every palate, dietary preference, and occasion. Whether you're hosting a family gathering, preparing weekday dinners, or simply looking to expand your culinary repertoire, our recipes will help you create memorable, mouthwatering meals with ease.

TOP 5 REASONS WHY THE SLOW COOKER IS AMAZING

1. **Convenience**. You can prepare your ingredients in the morning, set the cooker, and then leave it to work its magic throughout the day. This hands-off approach is perfect for busy individuals and families, as it allows you to come home to a hot, ready meal without the need for constant supervision.

2. **Time Savings**: Slow cookers are excellent time-savers. You can cook tough cuts of meat and legumes that would normally require hours of simmering or braising, all while you're away doing other things. This is especially useful for preparing meals in advance or when you have a busy schedule.

3. **Flavor Development**: Slow cooking allows flavors to meld and intensify over an extended period. The low, consistent heat helps to break down tough fibers in meat, resulting in incredibly tender and flavorful dishes. It's a great way to infuse your meals with deep, complex tastes.

4. **Energy Efficiency:** Slow cookers are generally energy-efficient. They use less electricity compared to running an oven or stovetop for hours on end. This can help reduce your bills and is more environmentally friendly.

5. **Versatility:** Slow cookers are versatile appliances that can be used to prepare a wide variety of dishes, from soups and stews to roasts, curries, and even desserts. They accommodate different dietary preferences and can be adapted to suit specific recipes and tastes.

Step-by-Step Guide to Using a Slow Cooker:

1. **Select Your Recipe:** Choose a slow cooker recipe and gather all the ingredients.
2. **Prepare Ingredients:** Chop vegetables, trim meat, and measure out spices and liquids as needed. Sauté the food if necessary.
3. **Layer Ingredients:** Place ingredients in the slow cooker following the recipe's order. You can brown meat or sauté ingredients beforehand if desired.
4. **Set Temperature and Time:** Select the appropriate heat setting (Low or High) and cooking time based on the recipe you are cooking. Low is best for longer cooking, while on High is better for shorter ones.
5. **Lid On, Walk Away:** Securely place the lid on the slow cooker and avoid frequently opening it. Let the slow cooker do its job as you go about your day.
6. **Check for Doneness:** As you approach the suggested cooking time, grab a thermometer (in applicable) and ensure meats are properly cooked. Vegetables should be tender, and flavors should be well-developed.
7. **Serve and Enjoy:** Make sure you have turned off the slow cooker, then carefully remove the lid, and serve your delicious meal. Be cautious when handling the hot cooker and steam.
8. **Clean Up:** Unplug the slow cooker and let it cool. Remove the insert and clean it according to the manufacturer's instructions. Most slow cooker inserts are dishwasher safe for easy cleanup.

CONCLUSION

The beauty of slow cooking lies in its simplicity. You may need to sauté some of the ingredients and then, just toss them into the pot, set the timer, and let the magic happen while you go about your day. The result? Tender meats, perfectly cooked vegetables, and rich, complex flavors that develop over hours of gentle simmering. With our step-by-step instructions and expert tips, you'll master the art of slow cooking in no time.

So, dust off that crockpot and get ready to explore a world of culinary delights.

Happy slow cooking!

BREAKFAST

1. Perfectly Steamed Eggs

Serves: 6 | Total Time: 2 hours 45 minutes

INGREDIENTS

6 large eggs
1 tbsp white vinegar

DIRECTIONS

Arrange the eggs in a single layer at the bottom of your Slow Cooker without stacking. Cover the eggs with enough water and add the vinegar. Cover the cooker and cook for 2 ½ hours on High. Gently transfer the eggs to a bowl of ice water to cool for at least 10 minutes and halt the cooking process. Serve the eggs sliced into wedges.

2. Cinnamon Spice Oatmeal Bliss

Serves: 4 | Total Time: 3 hours 15 minutes

INGREDIENTS

2 tbsp coconut oil, melted
1 egg
¾ cup milk
2 cups quick-cooking oats
½ cup maple syrup
1 tsp baking powder
½ tsp salt

DIRECTIONS

Grease your Slow Cooker with melted coconut oil. In a medium bowl, beat the egg with salt. Add the milk, oats, maple syrup, and baking powder. Mix well. Pour the mixture into the cooker. Cover and cook on Low for 3 hours or until tender. Serve up this maple-infused oat delight for a warm and comforting breakfast!

3. Herb Spinach-Mushroom Frittata

Serves: 4 | Total Time: 3 hours 20 minutes

INGREDIENTS

1 tbsp olive oil
6 large eggs
2 tbsp whole milk
1 cup mushrooms, sliced
1 cup spinach, torn
2 green onions, sliced
1 tsp thyme
Salt and pepper to taste
1 cup shredded mozzarella

DIRECTIONS

Grease a baking dish with olive oil. In a large bowl, beat the eggs. Stir in salt, pepper, whole milk, mushrooms, spinach, green onions, mozzarella, and thyme. Pour the mixture into the baking dish. Place the dish in your Slow Cooker. Cover and cook on Low for 3 hours or until set. Turn off the cooker and allow the frittata to cool for 10 minutes. Serve this savory herb frittata sliced into wedges for a delightful brunch or dinner option.

4. Savory Sausage and Spinach Breakfast Bake

Serves: 4 | Total Time: 4 hours 15 minutes

INGREDIENTS

1 (1-lb) package frozen hash browns
8 oz turkey sausage, crumbled
1 tbsp olive oil
⅓ cup spinach, finely chopped
4 large eggs
½ cup almond milk
Salt and pepper to taste
½ cup salsa
1 cup shredded pepper jack cheese

DIRECTIONS

Heat avocado oil over medium heat in a skillet and cook the turkey sausage until browned. Transfer it to your Slow Cooker. Whisk together eggs, almond milk, salt, and pepper in a large bowl. Pour the egg mixture into the slow cooker. Add hash browns, spinach, salsa, and cheese. Stir to combine.

Cover with the lid and cook on Low for 4 hours or until the potatoes are tender and the eggs are set. Wake up to the aroma of this delightful breakfast bake and enjoy a flavorful start to your day!

5. Gruyère Breakfast Casserole

Serves: 6 | Total Time: 4 hours 15 minutes

INGREDIENTS

1 tbsp butter, melted
6 large eggs
½ cup whole milk
1 lb Swiss cheese, grated
Salt and pepper to taste
2 tbsp fresh chives, chopped

DIRECTIONS

Grease your Slow Cooker with melted butter. Whisk together the eggs, whole milk, grated Swiss cheese, chopped chives, salt, and pepper in a medium bowl. Pour the mixture into the slow cooker. Cover and cook on Low for 4 hours until the eggs are set. Turn off the cooker and let the flavors meld for a few minutes before serving. Dive into this Swiss harmony breakfast casserole!

6. Creamy Parmesan-Spinach Oatmeal

Serves: 6 | Total Time: 7 hours 15 minutes

INGREDIENTS

3 cups steel-cut oatmeal
1 sweet onion, peeled and minced
4 cups chicken broth
1 cup milk
1 tsp dried basil leaves
½ tsp dried rosemary leaves
Salt and black pepper to taste
¾ cup grated Parmesan cheese
2 cups chopped baby spinach
2 tbsp chopped fresh parsley

DIRECTIONS

Combine the oatmeal, onion, broth, milk, basil, rosemary, salt, and pepper in your slow cooker. Cover and cook on low for 6 to 7 hours or until the oatmeal is tender. Stir in the Parmesan cheese, spinach, and parsley, and let stand, covered, for another 5 minutes. Stir well and serve.

7. Cheesy Breakfast Strata

Serves: 6 | Total Time: 4 hours 15 minutes

INGREDIENTS

1 tbsp butter, melted
3 bread slices, cubed
1 ½ cups shredded cheddar
4 oz turkey sausage, crumbled
6 large eggs
3 cups milk
½ tsp mustard powder
Salt and pepper to taste

DIRECTIONS

Grease your Slow Cooker with melted butter. Add the bread cubes, cheddar, and crumbled turkey sausage. Stir to combine. Whisk together the eggs, almond milk, mustard powder, salt, and pepper in a bowl. Pour the egg mixture over the bread mixture in the cooker. Cover and cook on Low for 4 hours. Turn off the cooker and let it rest for 10 minutes before serving. Delight in this comforting and cheesy breakfast strata!

8. Hearty Mushroom and Kale Frittata

Serves: 6 | Total Time: 4 hours 15 minutes

INGREDIENTS

1 tbsp avocado oil
4 eggs, beaten
2 cups mushroom slices
1 cup almond milk
1 cup shredded cheddar
3 cups kale, chopped
2 tbsp chives, finely chopped
Salt and pepper to taste

DIRECTIONS

Grease your Slow Cooker with avocado oil. In a large bowl, combine beaten eggs, almond milk, cheddar cheese, kale, mushrooms, chives, salt, and pepper. Stir until well combined. Pour the mixture into the slow cooker. Cover with the lid and cook on Low for 3-4 hours. Once done, allow the frittata to rest for 15 minutes before serving.

9. Berry-Infused Quinoa Breakfast Bowl

Serves: 4 | Total Time: 8 hours 15 minutes

INGREDIENTS

1 cup quinoa
2 cups water
2 cups oat milk
½ teaspoon sea salt
½ tsp ground cinnamon
½ tsp ground ginger
¼ tsp vanilla extract
½ cup fresh raspberries

DIRECTIONS

Place the quinoa, water, oat milk, sea salt, cinnamon, ginger, and vanilla in your Slow Cooker. Stir well to combine.

Cover the cooker and cook on Low for 8 hours. Stir in the fresh raspberries just before serving. Wake up to the delightful aroma and savor the deliciousness of this berry-infused quinoa breakfast bowl!

10. Blueberry Coconut Quinoa

Serves: 4 | Total Time: 3 hours 15 minutes

INGREDIENTS

¾ cup quinoa, rinsed
¼ cup shredded coconut
1 tbsp honey
1 (13.5-oz) can coconut milk
2 cups fresh blueberries
1 tsp orange zest

DIRECTIONS

Mix the quinoa, shredded coconut, orange zest, and honey in your Slow Cooker. Pour the coconut milk over the quinoa. Cover and cook on Low for 3 hours. Fluff the quinoa with a fork, then scoop it into serving bowls. Top with fresh blueberries for a burst of sweetness and enjoy this delightful and nutritious breakfast option.

11. Citrus-Infused Coconut Porridge

Serves: 6 | Total Time: 8 hours 5 minutes

INGREDIENTS

4 cups oat milk
3 cups apple juice
2 ¼ cups coconut flour
1 tsp ground cinnamon
¼ cup agave syrup
1 tsp orange zest

DIRECTIONS

Place oat milk, apple juice, coconut flour, cinnamon, orange zest, and agave syrup in your Slow Cooker. Stir well to combine. Cover and cook on Low for 8 hours. Wake up to the delightful aroma of this citrus-infused coconut porridge and serve a warm and comforting bowl.

SOUPS AND STEWS

12. Mushroom & Quinoa Beef Soup

Serves: 6 | Total Time: 8 hours 15 minutes

INGREDIENTS

1 ½ lb beef chuck roast, cut into bite-size pieces
6 cups mushroom broth
1 tbsp sun-dried tomato paste
2 cups frozen mirepoix
¾ cup quinoa
1 ½ cups sliced mushrooms
1 bay leaf
1 tsp onion powder
1 tsp roasted garlic flakes
1 tsp dried rosemary
Salt and black pepper to taste

DIRECTIONS

In your Slow Cooker, combine all the ingredients, giving it a gentle stir to ensure an even mix. Secure the lid and set the Slow Cooker on Low for 8 hours, allowing the flavors to meld. Remove and discard the bay leaf before serving. Dish out this mushroom-infused delight and savor the flavors!

13. Hearty Potato & Bacon Soup

Serves: 6 | Total Time: 1 hour 45 minutes

INGREDIENTS

1 lb potatoes, peeled, cubed
6 bacon slices, chopped
1 sweet onion, chopped
1 carrot, diced
1 celery stalk, diced
1 tbsp olive oil
2 cups chicken stock
Salt and black pepper to taste

DIRECTIONS

In a skillet, heat olive oil over medium heat. Add bacon and cook until crispy. Set aside on paper towels to drain excess grease. Combine in your Slow Cooker the bacon, sweet onion, potatoes, carrot, celery, stock, salt and pepper. Cover with the lid and cook on High for 1 hour and 15 minutes. Remove the lid. Blend the soup until smooth with an immersion blender. Garnish with the reserved crispy bacon. Serve hot and enjoy!

14. Hearty Bean and Veggie Soup

Serves: 6 | Total Time: 4 hours 15 minutes

INGREDIENTS

1 can (15 oz) black beans
1 can (15 oz) kidney beans
1 cup diced tomatoes
1 yellow onion, chopped
1 garlic clove, minced
1 zucchini, diced
1 bell pepper, sliced
1 sweet potato, diced
1 lemon, juiced
1 cucumber, peeled and sliced
2 tbsp chopped parsley
½ tsp paprika
½ tsp coriander powder
2 cups vegetable broth
1 tbsp avocado oil
Salt and black pepper to taste

DIRECTIONS

Heat avocado oil in a skillet over medium heat. Saute onion, sweet potato, garlic, and zucchini for 5 minutes until softened. Transfer the mixture to your Slow Cooker. Add bell pepper, paprika, coriander powder, vegetable broth, black beans, kidney beans, tomatoes, 2 cups of water, salt, and pepper.

Cover and cook on Low for 4 hours. When ready, uncover, ladle into bowls, and garnish with parsley and cucumber. Squeeze lemon juice on top and enjoy your flavorful veggie stew!

15. Mediterranean Chicken and Lentil Soup

Serves: 6 | Total Time: 6 hours 15 minutes

INGREDIENTS

1 lb chicken breasts
1 cup green lentils
1 yellow onion, finely sliced
2 cloves garlic, finely minced
5 cups low-sodium chicken broth
2 egg yolks
¼ cup Greek yogurt
½ tsp dried basil
Salt and black pepper to taste

DIRECTIONS

Combine onion, lentils, chicken, garlic, and broth in your slow cooker. Cook on Low for 6 hours. Shred the chicken and return it to the slow cooker. In a bowl, whisk egg yolks, Greek yogurt, and basil. Stir into the slow cooker. Season with salt and pepper. Enjoy!

16. Velvety Autumn Bisque

Serves: 6 | Total Time: 4 hours 15 minutes

INGREDIENTS

2 cups butternut squash, cubed
2 parsnips, cubed
1 celery root, peeled, cubed
1 sweet potato, peeled and cubed
1 sweet onion, chopped
2 garlic cloves, minced
¼ tsp ground coriander
2 tbsp olive oil
2 cups vegetable broth
Salt and black pepper to taste
1 pinch nutmeg

DIRECTIONS

In a skillet over medium heat, warm olive oil. Sauté sweet onion and garlic for 2-3 minutes until softened. Transfer to your Slow Cooker. Add parsnip, butternut squash, celery root, sweet potato, 3 cups of water, vegetable broth, nutmeg, ground coriander, salt, and black pepper to the Slow Cooker. Cover with the lid and cook for 4 hours on Low. Once done, remove the lid and use an immersion blender to blend until smooth. Serve.

17. Savory White Bean and Root Vegetable Blend

Serves: 6 | Total Time: 4 hours 15 minutes

INGREDIENTS

1 can (15 oz) navy beans
1 red onion, chopped
2 garlic cloves, minced
½ rutabaga, peeled, cubed
1 turnip, diced
2 cups vegetable broth
3 cups almond milk
1 tbsp grapeseed oil
½ tsp dried rosemary
Salt and black pepper to taste

DIRECTIONS

Heat grapeseed oil in a skillet over medium heat. Sauté red onion, garlic, rutabaga, and turnip for 5 minutes until softened. Transfer the mixture to your Slow Cooker. Add navy beans, vegetable broth, almond milk, dried rosemary, salt, and pepper. Cover and cook on Low for 4 hours. Once done, use an immersion blender to achieve a creamy consistency, and serve this delightful blend of white beans and root vegetables. Enjoy the rich flavors!

18. Ham & Vegetable Bean Soup

Serves: 6 | Total Time: 2 hours 15 minutes

INGREDIENTS

1 can (15 oz) cannellini beans, drained and rinsed
4 oz ham, diced
1 sweet onion, chopped
2 garlic cloves, minced

1 yellow bell pepper, diced
1 carrot, diced
1 cup diced tomatoes
1 tbsp olive oil
2 cups vegetable broth
Salt and black pepper to taste

DIRECTIONS

In a skillet, heat olive oil over medium heat. Add diced ham and cook for 2 minutes until lightly browned. Add onion and garlic; cook for another 2 minutes until softened. Transfer the ham mixture to the Slow Cooker. Add bell pepper, carrot, tomatoes, and cannellini beans. Pour in broth, 3 cups water, salt and pepper. Cover and cook on High for 2 hours until vegetables are tender. Remove the lid and stir the soup gently. Serve warm.

19. Meaty Bean Soup

Serves: 6 | Total Time: 3 hours 15 minutes

INGREDIENTS

1 can (15 oz) pinto beans
2 bacon slices, chopped
4 pork sausages, sliced
1 sweet onion, chopped
1 garlic clove, chopped
½ tsp dried rosemary
½ tsp dried thyme
1 potato, diced
1 celery stalk, sliced
1 can diced tomatoes
6 cups chicken stock
Salt and black pepper to taste

DIRECTIONS

In a skillet over medium heat, cook bacon until crisp for 2-3 minutes and transfer to the Slow Cooker. Add in sweet onion, garlic, rosemary, thyme, pork sausages, potato, celery, diced tomatoes, pinto beans, chicken stock, salt, and pepper. Cover with the lid and cook on High for 3 hours. Remove the lid and serve hot. Enjoy!

20. Turkey & Chickpea Soup

Serves: 6 | Total Time: 6 hours 15 minutes

INGREDIENTS

1 can (15 oz) chickpeas
2 turkey breasts, cubed
1 shallot, chopped
1 carrot, diced
1 parsnip, diced
1 celery stalk, sliced
1 red bell pepper, diced
1 can diced tomatoes
2 cups chicken stock
2 tbsp olive oil
2 cups water
1 tsp dried Italian herbs
2 oz Parmesan shavings
Salt and black pepper to taste

DIRECTIONS

In a skillet, heat the oil over medium heat and brown turkey for 2 minutes, then transfer it to the Slow Cooker. Add in shallot, carrot, parsnip, celery, bell pepper, chickpeas, diced tomatoes, chicken stock, water, Italian herbs, salt, and pepper. Cook on Low heat for 6 hours. Garnish with Parmesan shavings to serve.

21. Creamy Rustic Soup

Serves: 6 | Total Time: 6 hours 15 minutes

INGREDIENTS

4 potatoes, peeled and cubed
1 can (15 oz) sweet corn
1 celery stalk, sliced
2 shallots, chopped
½ tsp dried thyme
Salt and black pepper to taste

DIRECTIONS

In your Slow Cooker, combine shallots, cubed potatoes, celery, sweet corn, chicken stock, salt, pepper, and dried thyme. Pour in 6 cups of water, cover, and cook on Low for 6 hours. After cooking, reserve a small portion of corn and then blend the soup until smooth. Ladle into bowls and top with the reserved corn to serve.

22. Creamy Broccoli Bliss Soup

Serves: 6 | Total Time: 9 hours

INGREDIENTS

½ tsp smoked paprika
2 cups vegetable broth
1 lb sweet potatoes, peeled
1 golden beet, diced
2 shallots, minced
1 tsp roasted garlic powder
¼ tsp dried oregano
Salt and black pepper to taste
1 lb broccoli florets
½ cup Gouda cheese, shredded
½ cup almond milk
1 tbsp olive oil

DIRECTIONS

In your Slow Cooker, combine the broth, sweet potatoes, beet, shallots, garlic powder, and oregano. Season with salt and pepper. Cover and cook on Low for 8 hours. Once cooked, transfer the soup to a blender and blend until velvety smooth. Add three-quarters of the broccoli and pulse a few times to reach your preferred consistency.

Return the blended mixture to the Slow Cooker. Stir in Gouda cheese, almond milk, and olive oil. Add the remaining broccoli and cover. Cook on High for 20-25 minutes until everything is warmed through. Sprinkle with smoked paprika. Ladle into bowls and savor the creamy bliss of this delightful broccoli soup!

23. Spicy Tomato Fiesta Soup

Serves: 6 | Total Time: 6 hours 15 minutes

INGREDIENTS

1 can (15 oz) black beans
1 yellow onion, diced
1 garlic clove, minced
1 parsnip, diced
1 celery stalk, sliced
1 red bell pepper, diced
1 yellow bell pepper, diced
1 jalapeno, chopped
2 tbsp olive oil
1 tsp dried thyme
½ tsp dried basil
½ tsp dried oregano
1 tsp Cajun seasoning
2 tbsp chopped cilantro
4 cups chicken stock
1 cup tomato paste
2 cups water
Salt and black pepper to taste

DIRECTIONS

Heat olive oil in a skillet over medium heat. Sauté yellow onion, garlic, parsnip, and bell peppers for 5 minutes until softened, stirring frequently. Transfer the sautéed mixture to your Slow Cooker. Add celery, jalapeño, thyme, basil, oregano, Cajun seasoning, chicken stock, tomato paste, water, black beans, salt, and black pepper. Cover with the lid and cook for 6 hours on Low. After cooking, stir in cilantro and serve immediately.

24. Lemon Herb Chicken and Artichoke Soup

Serves: 4 | Total Time: 5 hours 15 minutes

INGREDIENTS

1 cup marinated artichoke hearts, chopped
2 boneless, skinless chicken thighs, cubed
2 tbsp fresh oregano
4 cups chicken broth
¼ tsp honey
¼ tsp onion powder
¼ tsp lemon pepper seasoning
¼ tsp ground coriander
¼ tsp garlic powder
¼ tsp black pepper
¼ cup white wine vinegar
1 onion, coarsely chopped
1 cup dry white wine
3 potatoes, roughly diced
5 baby carrots, diced
Juice of 1 lemon
3 garlic cloves, minced

DIRECTIONS

Place all the ingredients into your slow cooker. Stir to combine them. Cover and cook the soup on high for 1 hour, then adjust the setting to low and continue cooking for an additional 4 hours. Before serving, gently break the chicken thighs into bite-size pieces. Enjoy.

25. Southwest Bean & Corn Soup

Serves: 6 | Total Time: 4 hours 15 minutes

INGREDIENTS

2 cups cooked white beans
½ cup canned sweet corn
1 red onion, chopped
2 red bell peppers, diced
1 garlic clove, minced
½ tsp chili powder
½ tsp cumin powder
1 lb butternut squash cubes
2 tbsp olive oil
4 cups vegetable broth
2 tbsp tomato paste
1 bay leaf
1 thyme sprig
Salt and black pepper to taste

DIRECTIONS

In a skillet, heat olive oil over medium heat. Add chopped onion and cook for 2 minutes until softened. Transfer it to your Slow Cooker among bell peppers, garlic, chili powder, cumin powder, butternut squash, white beans, sweet corn, vegetable broth, tomato paste, bay leaf, thyme sprig, salt, and pepper. Cover with the lid and cook for 4 hours on Low, allowing the flavors to meld together. Remove the lid and stir gently. Serve immediately.

26. Classic French Onion Soup

Serves: 6 | Total Time: 1 hour 45 minutes

INGREDIENTS

4 sweet onions, thinly sliced
6 cups vegetable broth
2 tbsp butter
1 tsp brown sugar
1 tbsp olive oil
1 tbsp balsamic vinegar
Salt and black pepper to taste
1 thyme sprig
1 rosemary sprig
Toasted baguette slices for serving
2 tbsp grated Parmesan cheese

DIRECTIONS

In a skillet over medium heat, melt butter and oil. Add onions and cook for 10-12 minutes, stirring occasionally until caramelized. Stir in brown sugar and cook for an additional 2 minutes. Transfer the caramelized onions to your Slow Cooker and add in vegetable broth, balsamic vinegar, thyme, rosemary, salt, and pepper.

Cover with the lid and cook on High for 1 hour and 30 minutes. When done, remove the lid and discard thyme and rosemary sprigs. Top the soup with toasted baguette slices and grated cheese. Serve and enjoy!

27. Festive Garbanzo Bean Pozole with Pork

Serves: 6 | Total Time: 6 hours 15 minutes

INGREDIENTS

2 can (15 oz) garbanzo beans
1 lb pork tenderloin, cubed
1 sweet onion, chopped
2 garlic cloves, chopped
1 red bell pepper, diced
1 can sweet corn
1 cup diced tomatoes
1 jalapeno pepper, chopped
2 limes, juiced
1 tbsp olive oil
½ tsp cumin powder
½ tsp dried oregano
½ tsp dried basil
¼ tsp chili powder
4 cups chicken stock
2 cups water
Salt and black pepper to taste

DIRECTIONS

In a skillet over medium heat, heat oil and brown pork for 5 minutes on all sides. Transfer to the Slow Cooker. Add in sweet onion, garlic, cumin, oregano, basil, chili powder, garbanzo beans, sweet corn, tomatoes, jalapeño, bell pepper, chicken stock, water, salt, and pepper. Cover with lid and cook on Low for 6 hours. After cooking, remove the lid and mix in lime juice. Serve immediately.

28. Sausage & Zucchini Herb Soup

Serves: 6 | Total Time: 2 hours 15 minutes

INGREDIENTS

2 zucchini, cubed
2 peeled potatoes, cubed
1 lb Italian sausages, sliced
2 celery stalks, sliced
2 yellow bell peppers, diced
2 carrots, sliced
1 shallot, chopped
2 cups chicken broth
2 tbsp chopped fresh basil
1 tsp dried thyme
¼ tsp garlic powder
Salt and black pepper to taste
1 tbsp grated Parmesan cheese

DIRECTIONS

In your Slow Cooker, combine Italian sausages, celery, zucchini, potatoes, bell peppers, carrots, shallot, chicken broth, basil, thyme, garlic powder, salt, and pepper. Cook for 2 hours on High. Ladle the soup into bowls and sprinkle with grated Parmesan before serving. Enjoy!

29. Tomato Lentil & Ham Soup

Serves: 6 | Total Time: 1 hour 45 minutes

INGREDIENTS

4 oz ham, diced
1 cup dried lentils, rinsed
1 carrot, diced
1 celery stalk, sliced
1 shallot, chopped
½ cup crushed tomatoes
1 ½ cups vegetable broth
½ tsp dried thyme
½ tsp smoked paprika
1 tbsp olive oil
2 cups water
Salt and black pepper to taste

DIRECTIONS

In your Slow Cooker, combine olive oil, ham, carrot, celery, shallot, thyme, smoked paprika, lentils, water, crushed tomatoes, vegetable broth, salt, and pepper. Cover with the lid and cook for 1 hour and 30 minutes on High. Once done, check the lentils for tenderness. If they're cooked to your liking, serve the stew immediately. Enjoy!

30. Beef Sausage & Split Pea Soup

Serves: 6 | Total Time: 6 hours 15 minutes

INGREDIENTS

1 sweet onion, chopped
2 carrots, diced
1 cup split peas, rinsed
4 beef sausages, sliced
1 celery stalk, diced
1 garlic clove, chopped
1 red chili, chopped
1 lime, juiced
½ tsp dried thyme
2 tbsp tomato paste
2 tbsp chopped parsley
Salt and black pepper to taste

DIRECTIONS

In your Slow Cooker, combine split peas, sausages, onion, carrots, celery, garlic, red chili, thyme, tomato paste, salt, and pepper. Pour in 6 cups of water to the mixture. Cover with the lid and cook for 6 hours on Low. When done, remove the lid, stir in lime juice and parsley, and let it sit for a few minutes. Serve warm. Enjoy!

31. Spicy Beef & Bean Soup

Serves: 6 | Total Time: 7 hours 15 minutes

INGREDIENTS

1 can (15 oz) kidney beans
1 can (15 oz) cannellini beans
1 lb beef stew meat, cubed
1 onion, chopped
1 garlic clove, chopped
1 cup canned corn

1 cup tomato sauce
1 cup dark beer
4 cups water
2 cups beef stock
1 avocado, sliced
½ cup sour cream
2 tbsp taco seasoning
1 jalapeno pepper, chopped
1 tbsp olive oil
Salt and black pepper to taste

DIRECTIONS

Heat olive oil in a skillet over medium heat. Sauté onion, beef stew meat, and garlic and cook for 2 minutes. Transfer the mixture to your Slow Cooker among kidney beans, cannellini beans, corn, tomato sauce, dark beer, taco seasoning, jalapeño, water, beef stock, salt, and pepper. Cover with the lid and cook for 6 hours on Low. When done, serve the stew in bowls and top with sour cream and avocado slices.

32. Vegetable and Chicken Rice Soup

Serves: 6 | Total Time: 7 hours 15 minutes

INGREDIENTS

2 red bell peppers, diced
1 celery stalk, sliced
1 sweet onion, chopped
2 chicken breasts, cubed
1 cup butternut squash diced
1 zucchini, diced
1 can diced tomatoes
4 cups water
2 cups chicken stock
⅔ cup white rice, rinsed
2 tbsp olive oil
Salt and black pepper to taste

DIRECTIONS

Warm olive oil in a skillet over medium heat. Cook chicken for 5 minutes until golden on all sides. Transfer it to your Slow Cooker. Add in squash, bell peppers, celery, onion, zucchini, tomatoes, water, chicken stock, rice, salt, and pepper. Cover with the lid and cook for 7 hours on Low. After cooking, remove the lid and serve. Enjoy!

33. Spicy Tilapia Soup

Serves: 6 | Total Time: 6 hours 15 minutes

INGREDIENTS

1 chipotle pepper, chopped
1 carrot, diced
1 sweet onion, chopped
1 red bell pepper, diced
1 celery stalk, diced
1 cup diced tomatoes
1 lime, juiced
2 tilapia fillets, cubed
3 tbsp olive oil
2 tbsp chopped parsley
Salt and black pepper to taste

DIRECTIONS

Warm olive oil in a skillet over medium heat and cook onion for 2 minutes until softened. Transfer it to your Slow Cooker. Add in bell pepper, chipotle, carrot, celery, tomatoes, lime juice, tilapia, parsley, 6 cups of water, salt, and pepper. Cover with the lid and cook for 6 hours on Low. After cooking, remove the lid and serve. Enjoy!

34. Kale and Sausage Soup

Serves: 6 | Total Time: 7 hours 15 minutes

INGREDIENTS

1 can diced tomatoes
1 smoked sausage, sliced
1 sweet onion, chopped
1 kale head, shredded
2 tbsp tomato paste
6 cups beef stock
1 thyme sprig
1 lemon, juiced
Salt and black pepper to taste

DIRECTIONS

In your Slow Cooker, combine smoked sausage, onion, kale, tomato paste, tomatoes, beef stock, salt, pepper, and thyme. Cover and cook on Low for 7 hours. Once done, stir in lemon juice and serve warm. Enjoy!

35. Beef and Kale Soup

Serves: 6 | Total Time: 7 hours 30 minutes

INGREDIENTS

1 can (15 oz) diced tomatoes
½ lb beef stew meat, cubed
1 sweet onion, chopped
1 carrot, grated
1 lb kale, shredded
2 cups beef stock
2 cups water
2 tbsp olive oil
½ tsp cumin seeds
Salt and black pepper to taste

DIRECTIONS

In a skillet over medium heat, warm olive oil and sear beef stew meat for 5-6 minutes on all sides until browned. Transfer it to your Slow Cooker. Add in onion, carrot, kale, tomatoes, beef stock, water, cumin seeds, salt, and pepper. Cover with the lid and cook for 7 hours on Low. After cooking, remove the lid and serve warm. Enjoy!

36. Kidney Bean Soup

Serves: 6 | Total Time: 6 hours 15 minutes

INGREDIENTS

1 can (15 oz) kidney beans
1 shallot, chopped
1 carrot, diced
2 jalapeno peppers, minced
2 cups vegetable stock
4 cups water
1 tbsp olive oil
½ tsp chili powder
½ tsp cumin powder
½ cup diced tomatoes
Salt and black pepper to taste

DIRECTIONS

In your Slow Cooker, mix olive oil, shallot, carrot, jalapeño, vegetable stock, kidney beans, water, chili powder, cumin, tomatoes, salt, and pepper. Cover with the lid and cook for 6 hours on Low. After cooking, remove the lid and serve topped with sour cream. Enjoy!

37. Vegetable Barley Soup

Serves: 6 | Total Time: 6 hours 15 minutes

INGREDIENTS

2 cups chard, chopped
1 shallot, chopped
1 garlic clove, chopped
1 carrot, diced
1 celery stalk, diced
2 yellow bell peppers, diced
2 peeled tomatoes, diced
2 cups vegetable stock
2 tbsp olive oil
1 tsp dried oregano
1 tsp dried basil
⅔ cup pearl barley
1 lime, juiced
Salt and black pepper to taste

DIRECTIONS

In a skillet over medium heat, warm olive oil and sauté shallot, garlic, carrot, celery, and bell peppers for 5 minutes until softened. Transfer to your Slow Cooker among tomatoes, vegetable stock, oregano, basil, barley, 4 cups of water, chard, lime juice, salt, and pepper. Cover with the lid and cook for 6 hours on Low. Serve immediately.

38. Ground Beef & Corn Soup

Serves: 6 | Total Time: 6 hours 15 minutes

INGREDIENTS

1 cup sweet corn
1 shallot, chopped
½ lb ground beef
1 can (15 oz) black beans
1 can diced tomatoes
1 jalapeno pepper, chopped

2 garlic cloves, chopped
2 tbsp olive oil
½ tsp chili powder
½ tsp cumin powder
½ tsp coriander seeds
Salt and black pepper to taste
2 cups chicken stock
1 lime, juiced

DIRECTIONS

In a skillet, warm olive oil over medium heat. Cook ground beef for 5 minutes until no longer pink, stirring often. Transfer it to your Slow Cooker. Add in black beans, tomatoes, corn, shallot, jalapeño, garlic, chili powder, cumin, coriander, chicken stock, 3 cups of water, salt, and pepper. Cover and cook on Low for 6 hours. After cooking, remove the lid, stir in lime juice, and serve hot. Enjoy!

39. Awesome White Soup

Serves: 6 | Total Time: 2 hours 15 minutes

INGREDIENTS

10 oz cauliflower florets
2 peeled sweet potatoes, cubed
2 shallots, chopped
2 garlic cloves, chopped
½ tsp dried basil
½ tsp dried thyme
2 tbsp olive oil
3 cups vegetable broth
3 cups water
Salt and black pepper to taste

DIRECTIONS

In a skillet, warm olive oil over medium heat. Sauté shallots and garlic until softened, about 2-3 minutes. Transfer to your Slow Cooker. Add in cauliflower, sweet potatoes, vegetable broth, water, basil, thyme, salt, and pepper. Cover and cook for 2 hours on High. After cooking, blend the soup until creamy. Serve and enjoy.

40. Lima Bean Soup with Bacon

Serves: 6 | Total Time: 7 hours 15 minutes

INGREDIENTS

4 cups frozen lima beans
2 shallots, chopped
2 bacon slices, chopped
2 carrots, diced
2 peeled sweet potatoes, cubed
1 celery stalk, sliced
1 can diced tomatoes
2 cups chicken stock
4 cups water
1 bay leaf
Salt and black pepper to taste
1 tbsp chopped parsley

DIRECTIONS

In your Slow Cooker, combine bacon, lima beans, shallots, carrots, sweet potatoes, celery, tomatoes, chicken stock, water, bay leaf, salt, and pepper. Cover and cook on Low for 7 hours. When ready, remove the lid. Divide between bowls and serve topped with parsley. Enjoy!

41. Smoked Corn Soup

Serves: 4 | Total Time: 5 hours 30 minutes

INGREDIENTS

2 bacon slices, chopped
3 cups frozen corn
4 cups vegetable broth
1 shallot, chopped
1 garlic clove, chopped
2 tbsp olive oil
¼ tsp smoked paprika
Salt and black pepper to taste

DIRECTIONS

In a skillet, heat olive oil over medium heat and sauté garlic, shallot, and bacon; cook until golden brown. Transfer to your Slow Cooker. Add corn, vegetable broth, smoked paprika, salt, and pepper. Cover and cook for 5 hours on Low. Once ready, blend the soup until smooth with an immersion blender before serving. Enjoy!

42. Chipotle Turkey Soup

Serves: 6 | Total Time: 6 hours 30 minutes

INGREDIENTS

½ can (2 oz) chipotle chiles, chopped
1 can (15 oz) diced tomatoes
1 can (15 oz) sweet corn
2 shallots, chopped
2 garlic cloves, chopped
1 turkey breast, diced
6 cups chicken stock
1 tbsp olive oil
½ tsp cumin powder
½ tsp chili powder
1 bay leaf
Salt and black pepper to taste

DIRECTIONS

Warm olive oil in a skillet over medium heat and sauté shallots, garlic, and turkey for 5 minutes. Transfer the mixture to your Slow Cooker. Add in chipotle chiles, tomatoes, corn, stock, cumin powder, chili, bay leaf, salt, and pepper. Cover with the lid and cook for 6 hours on Low. After cooking, remove the bay leaf and serve. Enjoy!

43. Creamy Daikon & Leek Soup

Serves: 6 | Total Time: 6 hours 15 minutes

INGREDIENTS

4 peeled daikon, cubed
2 tbsp olive oil
2 leeks, sliced
1 tbsp all-purpose flour
2 cups vegetable stock
½ cup coconut milk
1 thyme sprig
Salt and black pepper to taste

DIRECTIONS

In a skillet over medium heat, warm olive oil and sauté leeks for 5 minutes until softened. Add in flour and cook for 1 more minute. Transfer it to your Slow Cooker and add in vegetable stock, 4 cups of water, daikon, thyme, salt, and pepper. Cover with the lid and cook for 6 hours on Low. After cooking, remove the thyme sprig. Stir in coconut milk and blend the soup with an immersion blender until creamy. Serve hot and enjoy!

44. Italian Sausage and Bean Soup

Serves: 6 | Total Time: 6 hours 30 minutes

INGREDIENTS

1 can diced tomatoes
1 can white beans
½ lb Italian sausages, sliced
1 sweet onion, chopped
2 garlic cloves, chopped
1 red bell pepper, diced
1 zucchini, diced
2 tbsp chopped parsley
½ tsp dried oregano
½ tsp dried basil
¼ cup dry white wine
2 cups chicken stock
½ cup short pasta
Salt and black pepper to taste

DIRECTIONS

Combine sausages, onion, garlic, bell pepper, zucchini, oregano, basil, tomatoes, beans, wine, 3 cups of water, and chicken stock in your Slow Cooker. Cover and cook for 1 hour on High. Stir in pasta, salt, and pepper and cook for another 5 hours on High. After cooking, remove the lid and serve topped with parsley. Enjoy!

45. Beef and Beet Soup

Serves: 6 | Total Time: 8 hours 15 minutes

INGREDIENTS

2 peeled sweet potatoes, cubed
1 sweet onion, chopped
1 lb beef stew meat, cubed
2 beets, peeled and cubed
1 can diced tomatoes
2 tbsp tomato paste

2 tbsp olive oil
1 cup vegetable stock
½ tsp cumin seeds
1 tsp red wine vinegar
1 tsp honey
½ tsp dried dill
1 tsp dried parsley
Salt and black pepper to taste

DIRECTIONS

In a skillet over medium heat, warm olive oil and cook beef stew meat for 2-3 minutes until golden on all sides. Transfer it to your Slow Cooker among beets, tomatoes, sweet potatoes, onion, tomato paste, 5 cups of water, vegetable stock, cumin seeds, vinegar, honey, dill, parsley, salt, and pepper. Cover with the lid and cook for 8 hours on Low. After cooking, remove the lid and serve immediately. Enjoy!

46. Curried Veggie Chowder

Serves: 6 | Total Time: 8 hours 15 minutes

INGREDIENTS

1 can (15 oz) sweet corn
2 peeled potatoes, cubed
1 onion, chopped
2 garlic cloves, chopped
4 cups vegetable broth
½ jalapeño pepper, chopped
1 ½ cups coconut milk
¼ tsp ground cumin
Salt and black pepper to taste

DIRECTIONS

In your Slow Cooker, combine onion, garlic, vegetable broth, sweet corn, potatoes, jalapeño pepper, coconut milk, ground cumin, salt, and pepper. Cover and cook for 8 hours on Low. Serve immediately. Enjoy!

47. Vegetable Minestrone Soup

Serves: 6 | Total Time: 6 hours 15 minutes

INGREDIENTS

4 sun-dried tomatoes, chopped
2 carrots, diced
2 celery stalks, diced
2 garlic cloves, chopped
1 onion, chopped
2 peeled tomatoes, diced
2 tbsp tomato paste
1 zucchini, cubed
1 cup green peas
2 cups chicken broth
2 cups water
1 tsp dried oregano
1 thyme sprig
1 can red kidney beans, rinsed
1 cup small pasta
Salt and black pepper to taste
2 tbsp chopped fresh basil
Grated Parmesan for serving

DIRECTIONS

In your Slow Cooker, combine sun-dried tomatoes, carrots, celery, garlic, onion, tomatoes, tomato paste, zucchini, green peas, broth, water, oregano, thyme, kidney beans, pasta, salt, and pepper. Cover and cook for 6 hours on Low. When done, remove the lid and stir in fresh basil. Serve warm, topped with grated Parmesan cheese. Enjoy!

48. Cheesy Broccoli Soup

Serves: 6 | Total Time: 3 hours 15 minutes

INGREDIENTS

1 (10.5-oz) can condensed cream of mushroom soup
1 head broccoli, cut into florets
2 peeled potatoes, cubed
1 onion, chopped
½ cup grated Parmesan cheese
1 tbsp olive oil
Salt and black pepper to taste

DIRECTIONS

In a skillet, heat olive oil over medium heat and sauté onion for 2 minutes. Transfer to your Slow Cooker. Add in broccoli, potatoes, cream of mushroom soup, 3 cups of water, salt, and pepper. Cover and cook for 3 hours on High. Blend the soup until smooth with an immersion blender. Serve topped with Parmesan cheese. Enjoy!

49. Veggie Soup with Beef

Serves: 6 | Total Time: 7 hours 15 minutes

INGREDIENTS

2 peeled potatoes, cubed
½ lb beef stew meat, cubed
1 celery stalk, sliced
1 sweet onion, chopped
1 carrot, sliced
1 garlic clove, chopped
5 oz broccoli florets
1 cup diced tomatoes
2 tbsp olive oil
½ tsp dried basil
2 cups beef stock
Salt and black pepper to taste

DIRECTIONS

In a skillet over medium heat, warm olive oil and sear beef stew meat for 2-3 minutes on all sides. Transfer it to your Slow Cooker. Add in celery, onion, carrot, garlic, broccoli, potatoes, tomatoes, basil, beef stock, 4 cups of water, salt, and pepper. Cover with the lid and cook for 7 hours on Low. Serve immediately. Enjoy!

50. Beef Stroganoff Soup

Serves: 6 | Total Time: 8 hours 15 minutes

INGREDIENTS

1 (10.5-oz) can condensed cream of celery soup
2 lb beef stew meat, cubed
1 onion, chopped
1 cup mushrooms, sliced
2 tbsp all-purpose flour
2 tbsp olive oil
4 cups beef broth
1 cup water
½ cup sour cream
Salt and black pepper to taste

DIRECTIONS

Season beef stew meat with salt and pepper, and coat with flour. Warm olive oil in a skillet over medium heat. Cook beef for 2-3 minutes on all sides. Transfer to your Slow Cooker. Add onion, celery soup, mushrooms, broth, water, sour cream, salt, and pepper. Cover and cook for 8 hours on Low. Serve immediately. Enjoy!

51. Chicken Pasta Soup

Serves: 6 | Total Time: 8 hours 15 minutes

INGREDIENTS

1 (10.5-oz) can condensed cream of chicken soup
1 cup frozen mixed vegetables (peas, carrots, corn)
6 oz farfalle pasta
2 chicken breasts, cubed
2 tbsp all-purpose flour
2 shallots, chopped
1 celery stalk, sliced
Salt and black pepper to taste

DIRECTIONS

Season chicken breasts with salt, pepper, and coat with flour. Place seasoned chicken, shallots, celery, cream of chicken soup, frozen mixed vegetables, 6 cups of water, and farfalle pasta in your Slow Cooker. Cover and cook for 8 hours on Low. Serve warm and enjoy!

52. Creamy Pumpkin and Spice Soup

Serves: 6 | Total Time: 5 hours 15 minutes

INGREDIENTS

1 (½ lb) peeled pumpkin, cubed
1 shallot, chopped
2 sweet potatoes, sliced
1 celery stalk, chopped
2 garlic cloves, chopped
2 cups chicken stock
1 thyme sprig
2 tbsp olive oil
½ cinnamon stick

1-star anise
½ tsp cumin powder
¼ tsp chili powder
Salt and black pepper to taste

DIRECTIONS

Heat olive oil in a skillet over medium heat and sauté shallot, sweet potatoes, celery, and garlic until softened. Transfer the mixture to the Slow Cooker among pumpkin, stock, 4 cups of water, thyme, salt, pepper, cinnamon, star anise, cumin, and chili powder. Cover with the lid and cook for 5 hours on Low. After cooking, discard cinnamon, thyme, and star anise. Blend the soup with an immersion blender until smooth. Serve hot.

53. Harvest Pumpkin Soup

Serves: 6 | Total Time: 3 hours 30 minutes

INGREDIENTS

2 sweet potatoes, peeled and cubed
1 shallot, chopped
2 carrots, sliced
2 oranges, juiced
1 tsp orange zest
6 cups vegetable stock
1 bay leaf
2 tbsp olive oil
1 tsp pumpkin seed oil
2 tbsp pumpkin seeds
½ cinnamon stick
Salt and black pepper to taste

DIRECTIONS

In a skillet over medium heat, warm olive oil and sauté shallot and carrots for 2-3 minutes. Transfer it to your Slow Cooker among sweet potatoes, orange juice, orange zest, vegetable stock, bay leaf, salt, pepper, and cinnamon stick. Cover with the lid and cook for 2 hours on High. Then, cook for 1 hour on Low. After cooking, remove the cinnamon stick and bay leaf. Using an immersion blender, blend until smooth. Ladle into bowls, drizzle with pumpkin seed oil and top with pumpkin seeds. Enjoy!

54. Sausage Soup with Vegetables

Serves: 6 | Total Time: 6 hours 15 minutes

INGREDIENTS

1 sweet onion, chopped
2 carrots, diced
½ lb kielbasa sausages, sliced
½ lb Swiss chard, torn
1 parsnip, diced
1 garlic clove, chopped
2 red bell peppers, diced
2 peeled sweet potatoes, cubed
2 cups vegetable broth
4 cups water
1 lemon, juiced
Salt and black pepper to taste

DIRECTIONS

In your Slow Cooker, combine sausages, onion, carrots, parsnip, garlic, bell peppers, sweet potatoes, vegetable broth, water, chard, lemon juice, salt, and pepper. Cover and cook for 6 hours on Low. Serve immediately. Enjoy!

55. Vegetable Root Soup with Rice

Serves: 6 | Total Time: 6 hours 30 minutes

INGREDIENTS

2 carrots, sliced
1 onion, chopped
1 celery stalk, sliced
1 turnip, chopped
1 cup diced tomatoes
¼ cup brown rice, rinsed
2 peeled potatoes, sliced
1 celery root, cubed
2 cups vegetable stock
4 cups water
1 lemon, juiced
Salt and black pepper to taste

DIRECTIONS

Combine onion, carrots, celery, turnip, potatoes, celery root, stock, water, tomatoes, brown rice, lemon juice, salt, and pepper in your Slow Cooker. Cover with the lid and cook for 6 hours on Low. Serve warm. Enjoy!

56. Bean and Sausage Soup with Cabbage

Serves: 6 | Total Time: 6 hours 15 minutes

INGREDIENTS

1 yellow bell pepper, diced
1 can (15 oz) white beans
½ lb kielbasa sausages, sliced
1 onion, chopped
1 carrot, diced
1 parsnip, diced
1 cup diced tomatoes
½ lb cabbage, shredded
2 cups chicken stock
½ tsp dried thyme
½ tsp dried rosemary
Salt and black pepper to taste

DIRECTIONS

Combine sausages, onion, carrot, parsnip, bell pepper, beans, tomatoes, cabbage, chicken stock, 4 cups of water, thyme, rosemary, salt, and pepper in your Slow Cooker. Cover with the lid and cook for 6 hours on Low. Remove the lid and serve immediately. Enjoy!

57. Creamy Cheese Cauliflower Soup

Serves: 6 | Total Time: 4 hours 15 minutes

INGREDIENTS

1 (10.5-oz) can condensed mushroom soup
10 oz cauliflower florets
1 peeled potato, cubed
1 shallot, chopped
2 garlic cloves, chopped
2 tbsp olive oil
½ tsp dried thyme
1 cup grated Gruyère cheese
Salt and black pepper to taste

DIRECTIONS

Heat olive oil in a skillet over medium heat and sauté shallot and garlic for 5 minutes until softened. Transfer it to the Slow Cooker. Add cauliflower, potato, mushroom soup, 4 cups of water, thyme, Gruyère cheese, salt, and pepper. Cover and cook for 4 hours on Low. After cooking, blend the soup with an immersion blender until smooth and creamy. Serve and enjoy!

58. Bean Soup with Smoky Turkey

Serves: 6 | Total Time: 6 hours 15 minutes

INGREDIENTS

2 cans (15-oz) cannellini beans
1 red bell pepper, diced
1 onion, chopped
1 garlic clove, chopped
1 celery stalk, diced
1 cup diced smoked turkey
2 cups chicken stock
2 tbsp olive oil
2 tbsp chopped cilantro
Salt and black pepper to taste

DIRECTIONS

Heat olive oil in a skillet over medium heat and sauté onion, garlic, celery, and bell pepper for 5 minutes until softened. Transfer the mixture to the Slow Cooker. Add smoked turkey, cannellini beans, chicken stock, 4 cups of water, salt, and pepper. Cover and cook for 6 hours on Low. Before serving, top with chopped cilantro. Enjoy!

59. Rustic Tomato Soup

Serves: 6 | Total Time: 7 hours 15 minutes

INGREDIENTS

1 (14.5-oz) can fire-roasted tomatoes, chopped
2 peeled sweet potatoes, cubed
1 lb ground turkey
2 shallots, chopped

1 carrot, sliced
2 cups chopped okra
½ cup green peas
½ cup sweet corn
2 tbsp olive oil
4 cups vegetable broth
2 cups water
1 lemon, juiced
Salt and black pepper to taste

DIRECTIONS

In a skillet, heat olive oil over medium heat and sear ground turkey for 2-3 minutes, stirring often. Transfer to your Slow Cooker. Add shallots, carrot, tomatoes, okra, green peas, sweet potatoes, corn, vegetable broth, water, lemon juice, salt, and pepper. Cover and cook for 7 hours on Low. Serve immediately and enjoy!

60. Basil Tilapia Soup

Serves: 6 | Total Time: 4 hours 15 minutes

INGREDIENTS

1 lb tilapia fillets, cubed
1 red bell pepper, diced
1 shallot, chopped
1 garlic clove, chopped
1 celery stalk, sliced
1 carrot, sliced
1 parsnip, sliced
½ tsp dried thyme
½ tsp dried basil
2 cups milk
4 cups water
1 lemon, juiced
1 tsp lemon zest
Salt and black pepper to taste

DIRECTIONS

Combine shallot, garlic, celery, carrot, parsnip, bell pepper, thyme, basil, milk, water, lemon juice, and lemon zest in the Slow Cooker. Cover with the lid and cook for 1 hour on High. Add tilapia, salt, and pepper to the mixture and continue cooking for 3 hours on Low. Serve immediately. Enjoy!

61. Asparagus and Shrimp Soup

Serves: 6 | Total Time: 2 hours 15 minutes

INGREDIENTS

1 bunch of asparagus, chopped
6 oz shrimp, cooked
1 onion, chopped
3 garlic cloves, minced
1 celery stalk, sliced
1 carrot, chopped
1 cup green peas
2 cups chicken stock
4 cups water
1 tbsp olive oil
Salt and black pepper to taste

DIRECTIONS

Heat olive oil in a skillet over medium heat and sauté shallot, garlic, and celery for 2 minutes until softened. Transfer it to the Slow Cooker. Add asparagus, carrot, green peas, chicken stock, water, salt, and pepper. Cover and cook on High for 2 hours. After cooking, blend the soup with an immersion blender until creamy. Serve topped with cooked shrimp.

62. Spicy Pumpkin and Kale Soup

Serves: 4 | Total Time: 6 hours 30 minutes

INGREDIENTS

2 cups pumpkin cubes
1 sweet onion, chopped
1 red bell pepper, diced
½ green chili, chopped
2 tbsp olive oil
4 cups vegetable stock
1 bunch kale, shredded
½ tsp ground cumin
Salt and black pepper to taste

DIRECTIONS

Combine onion, bell pepper, green chili, olive oil, pumpkin, vegetable stock, water, kale, ground cumin, salt, and pepper in your Slow Cooker. Cover with the lid and cook for 6 hours on Low. Serve immediately. Enjoy!

63. Herby Ham and Vegetable Soup

Serves: 4 | Total Time: 8 hours 30 minutes

INGREDIENTS

2 carrots, sliced
2 lb peeled sweet potatoes, cubed
2 cups diced ham
1 onion, chopped
1 garlic clove, chopped
1 leek, sliced
1 celery stalk, sliced
½ tsp dried thyme
½ tsp dried parsley
2 cups vegetable stock
2 cups water
Salt and black pepper to taste

DIRECTIONS

Combine ham, onion, garlic, leek, celery, carrots, sweet potatoes, thyme, parsley, stock, water, salt, and pepper in your Slow Cooker.Cover with the lid and cook for 8 hours on Low. Serve hot and enjoy!

64. Sweet Potato Soup with Bacon

Serves: 6 | Total Time: 6 hours 30 minutes

INGREDIENTS

4 peeled sweet potatoes, cubed
4 bacon slices, chopped
1 celery stalk, sliced
2 cups chicken stock
1 bay leaf
4 leeks, sliced
1 tbsp olive oil
¼ tsp cayenne pepper
¼ tsp smoked paprika
1 thyme sprig
1 rosemary sprig
Salt and black pepper to taste

DIRECTIONS

In a skillet over medium heat, warm olive oil. Add bacon and cook until crisp. Add leeks and cook for 5 minutes until softened. Transfer the mixture to the Slow Cooker. Add celery, sweet potatoes, chicken stock, 4 cups of water, bay leaf, cayenne pepper, smoked paprika, thyme, rosemary, salt, and pepper. Cover with the lid and cook for 6 hours on Low. Serve warm and enjoy!

65. Red Quinoa Soup

Serves: 6 | Total Time: 6 hours 30 minutes

INGREDIENTS

4 roasted red bell peppers, chopped
½ cup white quinoa, rinsed
½ cup tomato paste
1 shallot, chopped
1 garlic clove, chopped
2 cups vegetable stock
4 cups water
½ tsp dried thyme
½ tsp dried parsley
1 pinch cayenne pepper
Salt and black pepper to taste

DIRECTIONS

Combine shallot, garlic, roasted red bell peppers, tomato paste, stock, water, quinoa, thyme, parsley, cayenne pepper, salt, and pepper in your Slow Cooker. Cover with the lid and cook for 6 hours on Low. Serve and enjoy!

66. Red Bean and Barley Soup

Serves: 6 | Total Time: 3 hours 15 minutes

INGREDIENTS

½ cup barley, rinsed
1 can (15 oz) red beans
2 shallots, chopped
1 carrot, diced
½ peeled sweet potato, diced
1 can diced tomatoes
4 cups water
2 cups chicken stock
½ tsp cayenne pepper
Salt and black pepper to taste
2 tbsp chopped cilantro
Sour cream for serving

DIRECTIONS

Combine shallots, carrots, sweet potato, diced tomatoes, barley, red beans, water, chicken stock, cayenne pepper, salt, and pepper in your Slow Cooker. Cover with the lid and cook for 3 hours on High. When done, remove the lid and serve the soup topped with sour cream and cilantro. Enjoy!

67. Turkey and Potato Soup

Serves: 4 | Total Time: 3 hours 30 minutes

INGREDIENTS

2 large sweet peeled potatoes, cubed
1 ½ cups diced turkey
1 sweet onion, chopped
1 cup butternut squash, diced
1 celery stalk, diced
1 parsnip, diced
2 cups chicken stock
2 cups water
1 bay leaf
1 thyme sprig
Salt and black pepper to taste

DIRECTIONS

In your Slow Cooker, combine turkey, onion, squash, celery, parsnip, sweet potatoes, chicken stock, water, bay leaf, thyme, salt, and pepper. Cover with the lid and cook for 3 hours on High. Serve warm and enjoy!

68. Tomato Dumpling Soup

Serves: 4 | Total Time: 8 hours 15 minutes

INGREDIENTS

2 shallots, chopped
2 garlic cloves, chopped
2 lb peeled tomatoes, cubed
1 cup pumpkin, cubed
1 peeled celery root, cubed
1 egg
2 cups vegetable stock
2 tbsp olive oil
1 tsp olive oil
4 tsp all-purpose flour
½ tsp dried thyme
½ tsp dried parsley
½ red chili, sliced
1 tbsp brown sugar
1 tsp balsamic vinegar
Salt and black pepper to taste

DIRECTIONS

In a skillet, warm olive oil over medium heat and sauté shallot and garlic until softened for 5 minutes and transfer to the Slow Cooker. Add in tomatoes, pumpkin, celery, vegetable stock, 2 cups of water, thyme, parsley, red chili, brown sugar, vinegar, salt, and pepper. Cover with the lid and cook for 6 hours on Low. After 6 hours, remove the lid and blend the soup with an immersion blender until smooth.

Mix egg, olive oil, flour, and salt in a bowl. Form small dumplings from the mixture and place them into the soup. Cover with the lid and cook for an additional 2 hours on Low. Serve immediately.

69. Red Pepper Corn Chowder

Serves: 6 | Total Time: 8 hours 15 minutes

INGREDIENTS

1 red bell pepper, diced
2 peeled sweet potatoes, cubed
1 shallot, chopped
2 cups frozen sweet corn
6 cups chicken stock
2 tbsp olive oil
¼ tsp cayenne pepper
¼ tsp cumin powder
Salt and black pepper to taste

DIRECTIONS

Heat olive oil in a skillet, sauté shallot until soft, then transfer to the Slow Cooker. Add bell pepper, sweet potatoes, corn, chicken stock, cayenne pepper, cumin, salt, and pepper. Cover and cook on Low for 8 hours. Blend the cooked mixture until smooth using a blender. Serve warm.

70. Asparagus Tortellini Soup

Serves: 4 | Total Time: 6 hours 15 minutes

INGREDIENTS

1 (10.5-oz) can condensed cream of asparagus soup
½ lb asparagus, diced
7 oz cheese tortellini
1 shallot, chopped
1 garlic clove, chopped
4 cups chicken stock
½ tsp dried thyme
½ tsp dried parsley
1 cup evaporated milk
Salt and black pepper to taste

DIRECTIONS

Combine shallot, garlic, asparagus, asparagus soup, chicken stock, thyme, parsley, milk, cheese tortellini, salt, and pepper in your Slow Cooker. Cover with the lid and cook for 6 hours on Low. Serve warm.

71. Vegetable Medley Curry

Serves: 6 | Total Time: 6 hours 30 minutes

INGREDIENTS

10 oz broccoli florets
2 peeled sweet potatoes, cubed
½ head cabbage, shredded
2 peeled tomatoes, diced
1 sweet onion, chopped
4 garlic cloves, chopped
2 tbsp olive oil
1 tsp grated ginger
1 cup green peas
2 tbsp red curry paste
6 cups vegetable stock
½ lemongrass stalk, crushed

DIRECTIONS

Warm the olive oil in a skillet over medium heat and sauté onion and garlic for 5 minutes. Add ginger and curry paste, cook for 2 more minutes, then transfer to the Slow Cooker. Add in broccoli, sweet potatoes, cabbage, tomatoes, green peas, vegetable stock, and lemongrass. Cook for 6 hours on Low. Serve immediately.

72. Beef and Pinto Bean Soup

Serves: 6 | Total Time: 7 hours 30 minutes

INGREDIENTS

2 cans (15 oz) pinto beans
1 lb ground beef
1 yellow bell pepper, diced
2 carrots, diced
1 celery stalk, diced
1 parsnip, diced
2 tbsp olive oil
½ tsp chili powder
Salt and black pepper to taste

DIRECTIONS

Warm olive oil over medium heat and sear ground beef for 5 minutes in a skillet, stirring frequently, then transfer to the Slow Cooker. Add in bell pepper, carrots, celery, parsnip, pinto beans, chicken stock, 6 cups of water, chili powder, salt, and pepper. Cover with the lid and cook for 7 hours on Low. When done, remove the lid and serve.

73. Zesty Mushroom Soup

Serves: 6 | Total Time: 8 hours 30 minutes

INGREDIENTS

1 lb mushrooms, chopped
2 peeled sweet potatoes, cubed
2 peeled oranges, diced
1 sweet onion, chopped
1 garlic clove, chopped
1 yellow bell pepper, diced
2 tbsp olive oil
1 zucchini, cubed
2 cups vegetable stock
1 lemon, juiced
1 tbsp chopped dill
4 cups water
½ cup tomato sauce
Salt and black pepper to taste

DIRECTIONS

In a skillet, warm olive oil over medium heat and sauté onion, garlic, and bell pepper until softened, about 5 minutes. Transfer the sautéed mixture to your Slow Cooker. Add mushrooms, zucchini, sweet potatoes, oranges, vegetable stock, water, tomato sauce, salt, and pepper. Cover and cook on Low for 8 hours. After cooking, remove the lid, stir in lemon juice and dill. Serve chilled and enjoy!

74. Sweet Potato and Broccoli Curry

Serves: 4 | Total Time: 7 hours 30 minutes

INGREDIENTS

2 sweet peeled potatoes, cubed
8 oz broccoli florets
1 sweet onion, chopped
2 garlic cloves, chopped
1 tsp grated ginger
2 tbsp green curry paste
2 tbsp olive oil
¼ tsp chili powder
1 cup coconut milk
3 cups vegetable stock
Salt and black pepper to taste
½ lemongrass stalk

DIRECTIONS

In a skillet, warm olive oil over medium heat and sauté onion, garlic, ginger, and curry paste for 2-3 minutes until softened. Transfer the sautéed mixture to your Slow Cooker. Add broccoli, sweet potatoes, chili powder, coconut milk, stock, lemongrass, salt, and pepper. Cover and cook for 7 hours on Low. After cooking, remove the lid, discard the lemongrass, and blend the mixture with an immersion blender until smooth. Serve and enjoy!

75. Autumn Soup

Serves: 6 | Total Time: 6 hours 15 minutes

INGREDIENTS

1 can diced tomatoes
1 can (15 oz) white beans
2 cups pumpkin cubes
2 shallots, chopped
2 garlic cloves, chopped
1 red chili, chopped
2 tbsp olive oil
¼ tsp grated ginger
½ cinnamon stick
¼ tsp ground coriander
2 tbsp tomato paste
3 cups vegetable stock
1 bay leaf
Salt and black pepper to taste

DIRECTIONS

Warm olive oil over medium heat and sauté shallots, garlic, ginger, and red chili in a skillet for 3-4 minutes. Transfer the sautéed mixture to your Slow Cooker. Add tomato paste, tomatoes, white beans, pumpkin, vegetable stock, bay leaf, cinnamon stick, ground coriander, salt, and pepper. Cover with the lid and cook for 6 hours on Low. After cooking, remove the lid, discard the bay leaf and cinnamon stick, and serve. Enjoy!

76. Simple Slow Cooker Fish Stew

Serves: 4 | Total Time: 6 hours 30 minutes

INGREDIENTS

1 lb hake fillets, cubed
2 peeled sweet potatoes, cubed
1 shallot, chopped
2 garlic cloves, chopped
1 red bell pepper, diced
1 carrot, diced
1 fennel bulb, sliced
1 cup diced tomatoes
1 celery stalk, sliced
½ lemon, juiced
1 tbsp chopped parsley
Salt and black pepper to taste

DIRECTIONS

Combine shallot, garlic, bell pepper, carrot, fennel, tomatoes, vegetable stock, sweet potatoes, celery, lemon juice, 4 cups of water, salt, and pepper in your Slow Cooker. Cook for 1 hour on High. After 1 hour, add hake fillets to the Slow Cooker. Cover again and cook for an additional 5 hours on Low. Top with parsley and serve.

77. Savory Beef & Pearl Barley Soup

Serves: 6 | Total Time: 6 hours 15 minutes

INGREDIENTS

1 lb stewing beef, cubed
1 sweet onion, chopped
1 carrot, sliced
1 parsnip, sliced
2 peeled tomatoes, diced
2 cups beef stock
2 tbsp olive oil
¾ cup pearl barley
½ tsp dried thyme
Salt and black pepper to taste
Chopped fresh parsley for garnish

DIRECTIONS

In a skillet over medium heat, warm olive oil. Sear the beef and cook for 5-6 minutes, on all sides and transfer it to your Slow Cooker. Add in onion, carrot, parsnip, tomatoes, stock, barley, thyme, salt, and pepper and stir. Cook on Low for 6 hours. Garnish with chopped fresh parsley to serve.

78. Slow-Cooked Beef and Sweet Onion Soup

Serves: 6 | Total Time: 7 hours 15 minutes

INGREDIENTS

1 ½ lb beef chuck, cubed
1 sweet onion, chopped
1 garlic clove, chopped
2 carrots, sliced
1 celery stalk, sliced
1 parsnip, diced
1 can diced tomatoes
1 cup beef stock
1 cup red wine
2 tbsp olive oil
1 bay leaf
Salt and black pepper to taste

DIRECTIONS

In a skillet over medium heat, heat oil and brown beef chuck for 5 minutes on all sides. Transfer to the Slow Cooker and add in sweet onion, garlic, carrots, celery, tomatoes, beef stock, red wine, parsnip, 4 cups of water, bay leaf, salt, and pepper. Cover with the lid and cook on Low for 7 hours. Discard the bay leaf. Serve immediately.

79. Flavorful Lentil Soup with Bacon

Serves: 6 | Total Time: 4 hours 15 minutes

INGREDIENTS

1 cup dried lentils, rinsed
1 carrot, diced
4 bacon slices, chopped
1 sweet onion, chopped
2 garlic cloves, chopped
1 celery stalk, sliced
1 potato, diced
1 cup diced tomatoes
2 cups chicken stock
1 tbsp apple cider vinegar
2 tbsp chopped parsley
1 tsp curry powder
¼ tsp ground ginger
Salt and black pepper to taste

DIRECTIONS

In a skillet over medium heat, crisp bacon for 2-3 minutes and transfer to the Slow Cooker. Add in sweet onion, garlic, lentils, carrot, celery, potato, tomatoes, stock, 4 cups of water, curry powder, ginger, salt, and pepper. Cover and cook on Low for 4 hours. Once done, remove the lid, stir in apple cider vinegar and parsley. Serve hot.

80. Beefy Tomato Soup

Serves: 6 | Total Time: 8 hours 15 minutes

INGREDIENTS

2 slices bacon, chopped
2 lb beef roast, cubed
2 sweet onions, chopped
1 can diced tomatoes
1 cup tomato sauce
2 cups beef stock

3 cups water
1 tbsp olive oil
2 sprigs thyme
1 sprig rosemary
Salt and black pepper to taste

DIRECTIONS

In a skillet over medium heat, crisp bacon for 2-3 minutes. Add in beef roast and cook for 5 minutes on all sides. Transfer the mixture to the Slow Cooker. Add in onions, tomatoes, tomato sauce, stock, 3 cups of water, olive oil, thyme, rosemary, salt, and pepper. Cover and cook on Low for 8 hours. Remove the herb sprigs and serve.

81. Creamy Potato and Bacon Soup

Serves: 6 | Total Time: 6 hours 30 minutes

INGREDIENTS

1 (10.5-oz) can condensed cream of chicken soup
2 peeled potatoes, cubed
6 bacon slices, chopped
1 sweet onion, chopped
1 ½ cups heavy cream
1 tbsp chopped parsley
Salt and black pepper to taste

DIRECTIONS

In a skillet over medium heat, crisp the bacon for 2-3 minutes. Transfer it to your Slow Cooker, leaving the bacon fat in the skillet. In the same skillet, sauté sweet onion until translucent and slightly caramelized. Transfer it to the Slow Cooker. Add in potatoes, chicken soup, heavy cream, salt, and pepper and stir well. Cook on Low for 4 hours. Once ready, stir the parsley and continue cooking on Low for an additional 2 hours. Serve and enjoy

82. Creamy Three-Bean Soup

Serves: 6 | Total Time: 4 hours 30 minutes

INGREDIENTS

1 can (15 oz) black beans
1 can (15 oz) cannellini beans
1 can (15 oz) garbanzo beans
2 sweet onions, chopped
2 garlic cloves, minced
2 red bell peppers, diced
2 carrots, diced
2 cups chicken stock
1 cup diced tomatoes
2 tbsp olive oil
1 lime, juiced
½ cup sour cream
2 tbsp chopped parsley
Salt and black pepper to taste

DIRECTIONS

In a skillet over medium heat, sauté sweet onions, garlic, bell pepper, and carrots in olive oil for 5 minutes. Transfer the mixture to the Slow Cooker and add in black beans, cannellini beans, garbanzo beans, chicken stock, tomatoes, salt, and pepper. Pour in 4 cups of water, cover with the lid, and cook on Low for 4 hours. When done, remove the lid and stir in lime juice. Serve topped with a dollop of sour cream and chopped parsley.

83. Corn, Potato, and Ham Chowder

Serves: 6 | Total Time: 4 hours 15 minutes

INGREDIENTS

1 (10.5-oz) can condensed cream of chicken soup
4 peeled sweet potatoes, cubed
1 cup diced ham
1 cup sweet corn
1 sweet onion, chopped
1 tbsp olive oil
½ tsp smoked paprika
½ tsp dried thyme
Salt and black pepper to taste

DIRECTIONS

In your Slow Cooker, mix olive oil, onion, cream of chicken soup, 4 cups of water, sweet potatoes, ham, sweet corn, smoked paprika, dried thyme, salt, and pepper. Cover and cook for 4 hours on High. Serve warm and enjoy!

84. Chili Vegetable Soup

Serves: 6 | Total Time: 7 hours 15 minutes

INGREDIENTS

½ lb cannellini beans, rinsed
1 sweet onion, chopped
2 tomatoes, diced
1 yellow bell pepper, diced
2 carrots, diced
1 parsnip, diced
1 celery stalk, diced
2 cups chicken stock
4 cups water
2 tbsp tomato paste
½ tsp cumin powder
¼ tsp chili powder
1 bay leaf
Salt and black pepper to taste
2 tbsp chopped cilantro
½ cup sour cream

DIRECTIONS

In your Slow Cooker, combine cannellini beans, chicken stock, water, sweet onion, carrots, parsnip, celery, bell pepper, tomatoes, tomato paste, cumin powder, chili powder, bay leaf, salt, and pepper. Cover with the lid and cook on Low for 7 hours. When done, remove the lid and stir in cilantro. Serve topped with sour cream.

85. Sweet Butternut Squash Soup

Serves: 6 | Total Time: 2 hours 15 minutes

INGREDIENTS

1 lb butternut squash cubes
1 shallot, chopped
2 garlic cloves, minced
2 tbsp curry paste
1 tbsp honey
1 tsp Worcestershire sauce
1 tbsp olive oil
½ tsp grated ginger
2 cups vegetable broth
1 cup coconut milk
1 tbsp tomato paste
Salt and black pepper to taste

DIRECTIONS

In a skillet over medium heat, sauté shallot, garlic, ginger, and curry paste for 1 minute and transfer it to the Slow Cooker. Add in butternut cubes, Worcestershire sauce, honey, broth, coconut milk, tomato paste, salt, and pepper. Pour in 2 cups of water, cover, and cook on High for 2 hours. After cooking, remove the lid and blend the soup with an immersion blender until smooth. Serve hot, garnished with a drizzle of coconut milk and fresh cilantro.

86. Zesty Seafood Soup

Serves: 6 | Total Time: 6 hours 15 minutes

INGREDIENTS

½ lb fresh shrimps, peeled and deveined
½ lb haddock fillets, cubed
1 sweet onion, chopped
1 fennel bulb, thinly sliced
4 garlic cloves, minced
4 peeled tomatoes, diced
1 bay leaf
1 cup dry white wine
½ cup seafood broth
Juice of 1 lime
2 tbsp olive oil
1 tsp dried oregano
1 tsp dried basil
1 pinch chili powder
Salt and black pepper to taste

DIRECTIONS

In a skillet over medium heat, warm olive oil and sauté onion, fennel, and garlic for 5 minutes until softened. Transfer the mixture to your Slow Cooker. Add in wine, broth, tomatoes, bay leaf, oregano, basil, chili, salt, and pepper and stir well. Cook on High for 1 hour. Add the haddock, shrimps, and lime juice and stir. Cook for an additional 5 hours on Low. When done, remove the bay leaf. Serve immediately.

87. Pancetta & Beef Stew

Serving Size: 6 | Total Time: 8 hours 10 minutes

INGREDIENTS

1 tbsp olive oil
2 lb beef stew meat, cubed
8 oz pancetta, chopped
2 cups beef broth
4 mushrooms, sliced
2 carrots, chopped
1 onion, diced
2 garlic cloves, minced
Salt and pepper to taste

DIRECTIONS

In a skillet over medium heat, warm olive oil. Add pancetta and fry for 5 minutes until crispy. Stir in beef, onion, carrots, garlic, and mushrooms. Sauté for 5-6 minutes. Season with salt and pepper.

Transfer the mixture to your Slow Cooker and pour in the broth. Stir well to combine. Cook on Low for 8 hours. Serve warm and enjoy!

88. Hot Shredded Turkey Stew

Serving Size: 6 | Total Time: 8 hours 10 minutes

INGREDIENTS

2 lb boneless, skinless turkey breast
4 cups vegetable broth
2 cups frozen mirepoix
3 tbsp harissa paste
1 tsp garlic powder
½ tsp dried thyme
4 russet potatoes, peeled and diced
1 cup frozen peas
Salt and pepper to taste

DIRECTIONS

Combine broth, mirepoix, harissa paste, garlic powder, thyme, salt, and pepper in your Slow Cooker. Stir to combine. Add potatoes and turkey to the mixture. Cook on Low for 8 hours.

After cooking, transfer the potatoes to a plate. Mash two of them with a fork and cut the remaining into cubes. Add the potatoes back to the cooker.

Place the turkey on a cutting board and shred it with two forks. Return it to the Slow Cooker. Stir to combine. Add frozen peas and let them rest for 5 minutes until heated through. Serve warm and enjoy!

89. Veggie & Seafood Stew

Serving Size: 6 | Total Time: 8 hours 15 minutes

INGREDIENTS

6 oz boneless, skinless haddock fillet, cut into 1-inch pieces
6 oz boneless, skinless tilapia fillet, cut into 1-inch pieces
8 oz cremini mushrooms, halved
8 oz mussels, cleaned and debearded
4 cups chicken stock
1 lb pearl onions, peeled
3 Roma tomatoes, chopped
1 celeriac bulb, cubed
1 fennel bulb, chopped
2 celery stalks, chopped
3 carrots, chopped
Salt and pepper to taste
1 lemon, juiced and zested
1 tbsp flour
8 oz cooked crab meat
2 tbsp chopped dill

DIRECTIONS

Combine pearl onions, mushrooms, tomatoes, celeriac, fennel, celery, carrots, salt, and pepper in your Slow Cooker. Pour in 3 cups of chicken stock. Cover and cook on Low for 7 ½ hours.

Add lemon juice, remaining stock, and flour to your Slow Cooker. Add haddock, tilapia, crab meat, and mussels. Set the Slow Cooker to High and cook for 30 minutes. Top the stew with dill and lemon zest. Serve and enjoy!

90. Hearty Lentil and Vegetable Stew

Serves: 6 | Total Time: 6 hours 30 minutes

INGREDIENTS

STEW:

1 cup green lentils, rinsed
1 cup brown lentils, rinsed
1 shallot, finely chopped
2 celery stalks, sliced
2 carrots, diced
1 red bell pepper, diced
1 can (14 oz) diced tomatoes
1 bay leaf
4 cups vegetable broth
Salt and black pepper to taste

TOPPING:

2 fresh tomatoes, diced
3 garlic cloves, minced
1 tbsp olive oil
2 tbsp fresh basil, chopped
Salt and black pepper to taste

DIRECTIONS

Combine the green and brown lentils, shallot, celery, carrots, red bell pepper, canned tomatoes, bay leaf, broth, salt, and pepper in your Slow Cooker. Stir everything together. Cover and cook for 6 hours on Low.

In a bowl, combine garlic, basil, fresh diced tomatoes, salt, pepper, and olive oil to create the topping mixture. Serve topped with the prepared topping mixture. Enjoy your delicious and nutritious lentil stew!

91. Creamy Mushroom Beef Stew

Serving Size: 4 | Total Time: 8 hours 15 minutes

INGREDIENTS

2 lb beef chuck roast, cut into bite-size pieces
2 yellow onions, cut into very thin half-moons
1 lb cremini mushrooms, sliced
1 tsp paprika
2 garlic cloves, pressed
1 cup beef broth
1 ½ cups sour cream
1 tbsp all-purpose flour
2 tbsp dry white wine
2 cups cooked egg noodles
Salt and pepper to taste

DIRECTIONS

Place onions, garlic, mushrooms, and beef in your Slow Cooker. Sprinkle with paprika, salt, and pepper. Pour the beef broth and white wine over the top. Cover and cook on Low for 8 hours.

In a small bowl, whisk together flour and sour cream. Stir the sour cream mixture into the stew. Set the slow cooker to High and cook with the lid off for 8-10 minutes until the sauce thickens. Serve the beef stew over cooked egg noodles. Enjoy!

92. Chicken and Broccoli Stew

Serves: 6 | Total Time: 6 hours 15 minutes

INGREDIENTS

1 (10.5-oz) can of condensed cream chicken soup
½ head broccoli, cut into florets
3 chicken breasts, cubed
2 potatoes, cubed
1 celery stalk, sliced
1 shallot, sliced
1 ½ cups chicken broth
2 tbsp olive oil
Salt and pepper to taste
2 tbsp parsley, chopped

DIRECTIONS

Warm the olive oil in a pan over medium heat and sear the chicken for 2-3 minutes until golden on all sides. Transfer it to your Slow Cooker. Add condensed cream of chicken soup, celery, shallot, broccoli, potatoes, chicken broth, salt, and pepper. Cover with the lid and cook for 6 hours on Low. Top with parsley and serve warm. Enjoy!

93. Harvest Vegetable Medley Stew

Serving Size: 6 | Total Time: 8 hours 15 minutes

INGREDIENTS

1 acorn squash, peeled and seeds removed, cubed
4 cups vegetable stock
1 tbsp cornstarch
1 lb baby carrots
1 lb parsnips, chopped
1 sweet potato, cubed
8 shallots, quartered
4 garlic cloves, minced
2 tbsp olive oil
1 tsp dried sage
1 tsp dried thyme
Salt and pepper to taste
2 tbsp chopped parsley

DIRECTIONS

Whisk together cornstarch and vegetable stock in your Slow Cooker. Add acorn squash, baby carrots, parsnips, sweet potato, shallots, garlic, olive oil, sage, thyme, salt, and pepper. Cover and cook on Low for 8 hours. Just before serving, sprinkle the stew with chopped parsley. Enjoy!

94. Rustic Tomato and Cannellini Bean Stew

Serves: 6 | Total Time: 6 hours 30 minutes

INGREDIENTS

1 can (28 oz) diced tomatoes
1 tsp Worcestershire sauce
1 red onion, chopped
2 garlic cloves, chopped
1 ½ cups cannellini beans, soaked
3 cups vegetable broth
1 bay leaf
1 rosemary sprig
Salt and pepper to taste

DIRECTIONS

Combine tomatoes, Worcestershire sauce, red onion, garlic, cannellini beans, broth, bay leaf, rosemary, salt, and pepper in your Slow Cooker. Stir to combine. Cover with the lid and cook for 6 hours on Low. Serve immediately.

95. Cozy Chicken and Wine Mushroom Stew

Serves: 6 | Total Time: 6 hours 30 minutes

INGREDIENTS

4 garlic cloves, minced
4 cups sliced cremini mushrooms
6 chicken thighs
1 large onion, chopped
½ cup red wine
1 cup chicken broth
1 thyme sprig
Salt and pepper to taste

DIRECTIONS

Combine garlic, cremini mushrooms, chicken thighs, onion, red wine, broth, thyme, salt, and pepper in your Slow Cooker. Cover with the lid and cook for 6 hours on Low. Serve hot and enjoy!

96. Fragrant Chicken Stew

Serves: 6 | Total Time: 8 hours 15 minutes

INGREDIENTS

1 ½ cups apple cider
1 whole chicken, cut into pieces
1 tsp dried rosemary
1 tsp dried basil
1 tsp coriander powder
Salt and pepper to taste

DIRECTIONS

Dust chicken pieces with dried rosemary, basil, coriander powder, salt, and pepper. Place the seasoned chicken into your Slow Cooker and pour in apple cider. Cover with the lid and cook for 8 hours on Low. Serve.

97. Coconut Thai Turkey Stew

Serves: 6 | Total Time: 4 hours 15 minutes

INGREDIENTS

2 turkey breasts, cut into strips
2 red bell peppers, sliced
2 heirloom tomatoes, diced
2 cups shiitake mushrooms, sliced
2 zucchinis, sliced
4 garlic cloves, minced
1 lemongrass stalk, sliced
1 tbsp red Thai curry paste
1 cup coconut milk
½ cup chicken broth
Salt and pepper to taste

DIRECTIONS

Combine turkey, zucchini, bell peppers, tomatoes, shiitake mushrooms, garlic, lemongrass, curry paste, coconut milk, chicken broth, salt, and pepper in your Slow Cooker. Cover with the lid and cook for 4 hours on Low. Serve.

98. Citrus-Infused Lamb and Date Stew

Serving Size: 6 | Total Time: 8 hours 20 minutes

INGREDIENTS

2 lb boneless leg of lamb, cut into 1-inch pieces
Juice and zest of 1 lemon
1 tbsp flour
2 onions, chopped
2 carrots, chopped
1 (14-oz) can diced tomatoes
1 cup chopped dried apricots
1 tsp garlic powder
1 tsp ground ginger
1 tsp ground coriander
½ tsp red pepper flakes
Salt and pepper to taste
3 tbsp chopped cilantro

DIRECTIONS

Whisk together lemon juice, lemon zest, and flour in your Slow Cooker. Add lamb, onions, carrots, tomatoes, apricots, garlic powder, ginger, ground coriander, red pepper flakes, salt, and pepper. Cover and cook on Low for 8 hours. Just before serving, sprinkle the stew with chopped cilantro. Enjoy!

99. Rustic Pork and Potato Stew

Serving Size: 6 | Total Time: 8 hours

INGREDIENTS

1 ½ lb boneless pork loin roast, cut into 1-inch pieces
3 leeks (white part only), chopped
1 yellow onion, chopped
1 lb peeled sweet potatoes, cubed
4 cups chicken broth
1 tsp dried rosemary
¾ tsp dried thyme
Salt and pepper to taste
3 tbsp all-purpose flour
3 tbsp butter, melted

DIRECTIONS

Mix pork, leeks, onion, sweet potatoes, chicken broth, rosemary, thyme, salt, and pepper in your Slow Cooker. Cover and cook on Low for 7 hours.

In a small bowl, whisk together flour and melted butter. Stir the mixture into the slow cooker. Cover and set to High. Let the stew thicken for about 30 minutes. Ladle the stew into bowls and serve hot. Enjoy!

100. Smoky Chicken and Poblano Stew

Serving Size: 6 | Total Time: 8 hours 10 minutes

INGREDIENTS

1 ½ lb boneless, skinless chicken thighs, cut into 1-inch pieces
1 (16-oz) can fire-roasted diced tomatoes

2 chopped poblano peppers
2 oz pancetta, chopped
8 oz cremini mushrooms, chopped
1 onion, chopped
2 carrots, chopped
1 cup chicken broth
2 garlic cloves, pressed
1 tsp smoked paprika
Salt and pepper to taste
1 tsp cayenne pepper
2 tbsp chopped cilantro

DIRECTIONS

Combine chicken thighs, poblano peppers, pancetta, cremini mushrooms, fire-roasted diced tomatoes, onion, carrots, broth, garlic, smoked paprika, cayenne pepper, salt, and pepper in your Slow Cooker. Cover and cook on Low for 8 hours. Top with cilantro before serving. Enjoy!

101. Turkey and Sweet Potato Stew

Serves: 6 | Total Time: 3 hours 15 minutes

INGREDIENTS

2 lb peeled sweet potatoes, cubed
2 turkey breasts, cubed
2 shallots, chopped
2 tbsp olive oil
½ tsp cumin powder
½ tsp garlic powder
1 pinch of cinnamon powder
1 ½ cups chicken broth
Salt and pepper to taste

DIRECTIONS

In a pan over medium heat, warm olive oil and sear turkey and shallots for 5 minutes until turkey is lightly browned. Transfer the mixture to your Slow Cooker. Add sweet potatoes, cumin powder, garlic powder, cinnamon powder, chicken broth, salt, and pepper. Cover with the lid and cook for 3 hours on High. Serve warm. Enjoy!

102. Earthy Mushroom Medley Stew

Serving Size: 4 | Total Time: 8 hours 15 minutes

INGREDIENTS

4 Portobello mushrooms, chopped
4 oz Shiitake mushrooms, sliced
4 oz cremini mushrooms, quartered
8 oz button mushrooms, quartered
4 cups vegetable stock
1 tbsp porcini powder
½ tbsp flour
1 tbsp Dijon mustard
2 carrots, chopped
1 red onion, chopped
1 tsp dried parsley
1 tsp garlic powder
Salt and pepper to taste
Pinch of red pepper flakes
2 tbsp chopped chives

DIRECTIONS

Combine Portobello mushrooms, Shiitake, cremini, button mushrooms, carrots, onion, garlic powder, salt, pepper, and red pepper flakes in your Slow Cooker. Whisk vegetable stock in a bowl with porcini powder, flour, and Dijon mustard. Pour the mixture into the Slow Cooker. Cook on Low for 8 hours. Sprinkle with chopped chives. Enjoy!

103. Chicken and Vegetable Stew

Serves: 6 | Total Time: 8 hours 30 minutes

INGREDIENTS

3 chicken breasts, cubed
1 onion, chopped
2 carrots, sliced
2 celery stalks, sliced
2 ripe tomatoes, diced
1 can (15 oz) kidney beans, rinsed
1 cup tomato sauce
4 potatoes, cubed
2 tbsp olive oil
1 tsp dried thyme
½ tsp smoked paprika
Salt and pepper to taste

DIRECTIONS

Add olive oil, chicken, onion, carrots, celery, tomatoes, kidney beans, tomato sauce, potatoes, 2 cups of water, thyme, smoked paprika, salt, and pepper in your Slow Cooker. Stir to combine. Cook for 8 hours on Low. Serve.

104. Chicken Stew with Spinach & Sweet Potatoes

Serves: 6 | Total Time: 6 hours 30 minutes

INGREDIENTS

6 chicken thighs, boneless
3 cups spinach, chopped
2 sweet potatoes, cubed
¼ cup chopped cilantro
¼ cup chopped parsley
1 cup vegetable stock
2 tbsp olive oil
¼ tsp cumin powder
¼ tsp chili powder
¼ tsp paprika
Salt and pepper to taste

DIRECTIONS

Warm olive oil in a pan over medium heat. Sear the chicken until golden brown on all sides, about 6-8 minutes. Transfer to the Slow Cooker. Add cilantro, parsley, spinach, sweet potatoes, vegetable stock, cumin powder, chili powder, paprika, salt, and pepper. Cover with the lid and cook for 6 hours on Low. Serve warm and enjoy!

105. Mediterranean Lamb and Olive Stew

Serves: 6 | Total Time: 6 hours 15 minutes

INGREDIENTS

2 lamb thighs, boneless
4 garlic cloves, minced
1 shallot, chopped
¼ cup dry white wine
1 can (28 oz) diced tomatoes
½ cup pitted black olives, halved
12 pitted Kalamata olives, halved
2 tbsp tomato paste
½ cup tomato sauce
2 tbsp olive oil
¼ tsp smoked paprika
Salt and pepper to taste

DIRECTIONS

Combine olive oil, lamb thighs, garlic, shallot, white wine, tomato paste, tomato sauce, smoked paprika, diced tomatoes, black olives, and Kalamata olives in your Slow Cooker. Season with salt and pepper. Mix well. Cover with the lid and cook for 6 hours on Low. Serve immediately and enjoy!

106. Coconut Chicken & Broccoli Stew

Serves: 6 | Total Time: 6 hours 30 minutes

INGREDIENTS

½ head broccoli, cut into florets
1 can (15-oz) chickpeas
2 red bell peppers, diced
2 cups fresh spinach, torn
2 chicken breasts, cubed
1 cup tomato sauce
1 cup coconut cream
1 cup chicken stock
2 tbsp olive oil
1 tsp turmeric powder
Salt and pepper to taste

DIRECTIONS

Sprinkle chicken breasts with turmeric, salt, and pepper. Warm olive oil in a pan over medium heat and sear the chicken for 2-3 minutes until golden brown. Transfer to the Slow Cooker. Add broccoli, chickpeas, bell peppers, tomato sauce, coconut cream, stock, and spinach. Season with salt and pepper. Cook for 6 hours on Low. Serve.

107. Spicy Cajun Rice Bowl

Serving Size: 6 | Total Time: 8 hours 20 minutes

INGREDIENTS

2 (14-oz) cans fire-roasted diced tomatoes
1 lb shrimp, peeled and deveined
1 lb andouille sausage, sliced
2 cups chicken stock
1 green bell pepper, chopped
1 red bell pepper, chopped
2 large carrots, chopped

1 onion, chopped
2 jalapeño peppers, minced
1 tsp smoked paprika
1 tsp garlic powder
1 tsp Cajun seasoning blend
Salt and black pepper to taste
1 cup basmati rice
⅛ tsp cayenne pepper

DIRECTIONS

In your Slow Cooker, combine shrimp, sausage, fire-roasted diced tomatoes, chicken stock, bell peppers, carrots, onion, jalapeños, paprika, garlic powder, Cajun seasoning, salt, black pepper, rice, and cayenne pepper. Cover and cook on Low for 8 hours. Serve hot and enjoy!

108. Spicy Beef and Vegetable Stew

Serves: 6 | Total Time: 8 hours 15 minutes

INGREDIENTS

1 lb baby carrots
1 lb beef chuck, cubed
1 large onion, chopped
4 garlic cloves, minced
½ cup tomato juice
2 tbsp olive oil
1 tsp sesame oil
3 tbsp soy sauce
1 tsp hot chili paste
1 cup diced tomatoes
Salt and pepper to taste
Cooked brown rice for serving

DIRECTIONS

Warm olive oil in a pan over medium heat and sear beef for 2-3 minutes until golden on all sides. Transfer the cooked beef to your Slow Cooker. Add sesame oil, baby carrots, onion, garlic, tomato juice, soy sauce, chili paste, tomatoes, salt, and pepper. Cook for 8 hours on Low. Serve the stew over cooked brown rice. Enjoy!

109. Mushroom Stew with Cheesy Chicken

Serves: 6 | Total Time: 6 hours 15 minutes

INGREDIENTS

2 chicken breasts, cubed
2 garlic cloves, minced
1 shallot, chopped
4 cups cremini mushrooms, sliced
1 cup shredded mozzarella cheese
1 cup vegetable stock
2 tbsp olive oil
1 thyme sprig
Salt and pepper to taste

DIRECTIONS

Warm olive oil in a pan over medium heat and sear chicken for 5 minutes until golden brown on all sides. Transfer to the Slow Cooker. Add garlic, shallot, sliced cremini mushrooms, mozzarella cheese, vegetable stock, thyme, salt, and pepper. Cover with the lid and cook for 6 hours on Low. Stir gently before serving. Enjoy!

110. Tuscan-Inspired Pork Stew

Serves: 6 | Total Time: 6 hours 15 minutes

INGREDIENTS

1 lb porcini mushrooms, chopped
2 lb pork shoulder, cubed
6 garlic cloves, minced
2 shallots, chopped
2 carrots, sliced
1 parsnip, diced
½ cup red wine
1 cup marinara sauce
10 pitted green olives, sliced
1 celery stalk, sliced
½ cup fire-roasted tomatoes
1 tbsp olive oil
2 bay leaves
1 thyme sprig
Salt and pepper to taste

DIRECTIONS

Heat olive oil in a pan over medium heat and brown pork on all sides, then transfer to your Slow Cooker. Add garlic, shallots, carrots, parsnip, mushrooms, ½ cup of water, wine, marinara sauce, olives, celery, fire-roasted tomatoes, bay leaves, thyme, salt, and pepper. Cover and cook on Low for 6 hours. Serve hot and enjoy!

111. Colorful Chicken Pepperonata

Serving Size: 6 | Total Time: 8 hours 20 minutes

INGREDIENTS

1 yellow bell pepper, chopped
1 green bell pepper, chopped
1 red bell pepper, chopped
1 onion, chopped
2 (14-oz) cans diced tomatoes
¼ cup capers, drained
2 tsp Italian seasoning
1 tsp garlic powder
Salt and pepper to taste
Pinch of red pepper flakes
1 tbsp cornstarch
8 chicken thighs
¼ cup chopped fresh basil
7 oz pitted green olives
2 tbsp fresh parsley, chopped

DIRECTIONS

Combine bell peppers, onion, tomatoes, capers, Italian seasoning, garlic powder, salt, pepper, and red pepper flakes in your Slow Cooker. Stir to combine. In a small bowl, whisk together ¾ cup of water and cornstarch.

Pour the mixture into the Slow Cooker. Top the vegetable mixture with chicken thighs, pressing them gently into the vegetables. Cook on Low for 8 hours. Just before serving, sprinkle the dish with fresh basil and parsley. Enjoy!

112. Crispy Chicken Stew

Serves: 6 | Total Time: 6 hours 30 minutes

INGREDIENTS

6 chicken thighs, boneless and skinless, cut into chunks
6 bacon slices, chopped
1 sweet onion, chopped
2 garlic cloves, minced
2 large carrots, sliced
2 celery stalks, sliced
1 cup sweet corn
2 cups sliced cremini mushrooms
¼ cup dry white wine
1 cup chicken broth
½ cup heavy cream
1 thyme sprig
Salt and pepper to taste

DIRECTIONS

In a pan over medium heat, cook bacon until crispy. Transfer to the Slow Cooker. Add chicken, onion, garlic, carrots, celery, corn, mushrooms, wine, broth, heavy cream, thyme, salt, and pepper. Cook for 6 hours on Low.

113. Chicken & Chickpea Stew

Serves: 6 | Total Time: 8 hours 15 minutes

INGREDIENTS

2 sweet potatoes, peeled and cubed
2 carrots, sliced
6 chicken thighs
1 celery stalk, sliced
1 onion, chopped
4 garlic cloves, chopped
1 can (15 oz) chickpeas, rinsed
½ tsp ground cumin
½ tsp dried thyme
1 can fire-roasted tomatoes
1 cup chicken broth
Salt and pepper to taste

DIRECTIONS

Combine sweet potatoes, carrots, chicken thighs, celery, onion, garlic, chickpeas, cumin, thyme, fire-roasted tomatoes, broth, salt, and pepper in your Slow Cooker. Cook for 8 hours on Low. Serve immediately. Enjoy!

114. Slow-Cooked Soy Glazed Chicken

Serves: 6 | Total Time: 8 hours 15 minutes

INGREDIENTS

½ cup tomato sauce
6 bone-in, skinless chicken thighs
½ cup soy sauce
2 tbsp brown sugar
½ tsp chili flakes

DIRECTIONS

Combine tomato sauce, chicken thighs, soy sauce, brown sugar, and chili flakes in your Slow Cooker. Cover with the lid and cook for 8 hours on Low. Serve warm and enjoy!

115. Farmer Stew

Serves: 6 | Total Time: 6 hours 30 minutes

INGREDIENTS

2 lb potatoes, cubed
2 ripe tomatoes, diced
6 bacon slices, chopped
2 lb beef chuck, cubed
1 chorizo sausage, sliced
1 onion, finely chopped
2 garlic cloves, chopped
2 red bell peppers, diced
1 tbsp tomato paste
2 cups beef broth
2 bay leaves
1 tbsp olive oil
¼ tsp cayenne pepper
Salt and pepper to taste

DIRECTIONS

Warm olive oil in a pan over medium heat. Add bacon and cook until crispy. Add beef chunks and cook for 2-3 minutes until golden on all sides. Transfer everything to your Slow Cooker. Add chorizo slices, onion, garlic, bell peppers, tomatoes, potatoes, tomato paste, beef broth, bay leaves, cayenne pepper, salt, and pepper. Cover with the lid and cook for 6 hours on Low. Serve hot and enjoy!

116. Herbed Beef Stew

Serves: 6 | Total Time: 7 hours 15 minutes

INGREDIENTS

2 ripe tomatoes, diced
2 zucchinis, cubed
2 lb beef sirloin, cubed
1 sweet onion, chopped
4 garlic cloves, minced
4 red bell peppers, diced
1 cup fire-roasted tomato sauce
2 tbsp olive oil
2 tbsp tomato paste
½ cup fresh orange juice
1 tsp dried oregano
½ tsp dried basil
Salt and pepper to taste
1 bay leaf
1 thyme sprig

DIRECTIONS

Warm olive oil in a pan over medium heat and sear the beef for 5 minutes until golden on all sides. Transfer it to your Slow Cooker. Add onion, garlic, tomatoes, zucchini, bell peppers, fire-roasted tomato sauce, tomato paste, orange juice, oregano, basil, bay leaf, thyme, salt, and pepper. Cook for 7 hours on Low. Serve warm.

117. Homemade Pork Stew

Serves: 6 | Total Time: 6 hours 30 minutes

INGREDIENTS

2 red apples, peeled and cubed
1 ½ lb sweet potatoes, cubed
2 ripe tomatoes, cubed
2 lb pork shoulder, cubed
4 garlic cloves, chopped
1 large onion, chopped
1 lb acorn squash cubes
1 carrot, sliced
1 cup chicken stock
2 tbsp olive oil
1 tsp dried thyme
1 tsp dried sage
2 bay leaves
Salt and pepper to taste

DIRECTIONS

Heat olive oil in a pan over medium heat and brown pork on all sides and transfer to your Slow Cooker. Add garlic, onion, acorn squash, apples, carrots, sweet potatoes, tomatoes, thyme, sage, bay leaves, chicken stock, salt, and pepper. Cover and cook on Low for 6 hours. Serve hot and enjoy!

118. Chicken Stew with Caramelized Onions

Serves: 6 | Total Time: 6 hours 30 minutes

INGREDIENTS

2 chicken thighs, cubed
4 bacon slices, chopped
2 red bell peppers, sliced
3 large onions, sliced
1 celery stalk, sliced
¼ cup dry white wine
1 can fire-roasted tomatoes
2 tbsp olive oil
Salt and pepper to taste

DIRECTIONS

Heat olive oil in a pan over medium heat and cook bacon until crispy. Add onions and cook for 10 minutes until soft and caramelized. Transfer to your Slow Cooker. Add chicken, celery, bell peppers, wine, tomatoes, salt, and pepper. Cover and cook on Low for 6 hours. Serve hot and enjoy!

119. Beefy Root Vegetable Stew

Serves: 6 | Total Time: 7 hours 15 minutes

INGREDIENTS

1 ½ lb beef chuck roast, cubed
1 onion, chopped
1 celery stalk, sliced
2 parsnips, sliced
4 potatoes, cubed
1 cup diced tomatoes
1 ½ cups beef stock
2 tbsp olive oil
2 tbsp all-purpose flour
1 bay leaf
1 thyme sprig
Salt and pepper to taste

DIRECTIONS

Coat beef with flour. Heat olive oil in a pan and brown the beef for 5 minutes. Transfer to your Slow Cooker. Add onion, celery, parsnips, potatoes, tomatoes, stock, bay leaf, thyme, salt, and pepper. Cook on Low for 7 hours.

120. Spicy Beef & Bean Stew

Serves: 6 | Total Time: 8 hours 30 minutes

INGREDIENTS

2 sweet potatoes, peeled and cubed
1 can (15 oz) black beans
1 large zucchini, cubed
2 lb beef chuck, cubed
1 large onion, chopped
2 carrots, sliced
1 cup frozen corn
1 cup diced tomatoes
1 cup green peas
1 ½ cups beef stock
½ tsp paprika
1 tsp dried thyme
1 tsp jerk seasoning
Salt and pepper to taste

DIRECTIONS

Combine beef, onion, carrots, black beans, zucchini, sweet potatoes, corn, tomatoes, green peas, paprika, thyme, jerk seasoning, beef stock, salt, and pepper in your Slow Cooker. Mix well. Cover with the lid and cook for 8 hours on Low. Drizzle with sour cream before serving, if desired. Enjoy!

121. Crunchy Beef Stew

Serves: 6 | Total Time: 5 hours 15 minutes

INGREDIENTS

2 carrots, sliced
8 oz bread croutons
1 lb stewing beef, cubed
1 shallot, chopped
2 garlic cloves, chopped
1 can fire-roasted tomatoes
1 poblano pepper, chopped
1 cup beef stock
1 cup chopped mushrooms
2 celery stalks, chopped
2 tbsp olive oil
Salt and pepper to taste

DIRECTIONS

Heat olive oil in a pan over medium heat. Cook the beef for 4-6 minutes until golden on all sides. Transfer the meat to your Slow Cooker. Add shallot, garlic, tomatoes, poblano pepper, stock, mushrooms, celery, carrots, salt, and pepper. Scatter with bread croutons. Cover and cook for 5 hours on Low. Serve hot and enjoy!

122. Lentil Stew with Sausages

Serves: 6 | Total Time: 6 hours 15 minutes

INGREDIENTS

1 chipotle pepper in adobo sauce, chopped
1 onion, finely chopped
2 carrots, diced
1 lb pork sausages, sliced
1 celery stalk, diced
2 garlic cloves, chopped
1 cup red lentils
1 cup green lentils
1 can (14 oz) diced tomatoes
3 cups chicken broth
2 tbsp chopped fresh cilantro
1 tbsp tomato paste
Salt and pepper to taste

DIRECTIONS

Combine sausages, onion, carrots, celery, garlic, red lentils, green lentils, diced tomatoes, tomato paste, chicken broth, chipotle pepper, salt, and pepper in your Slow Cooker. Stir well to combine. Cover with the lid and cook for 6 hours on Low. Remove the bay leaf and sprinkle with fresh cilantro to serve. Enjoy!

123. Wild Pork Stew with Chorizo

Serves: 6 | Total Time: 3 hours 15 minutes

INGREDIENTS

1 chorizo link, chopped
1 can (15 oz) red beans, rinsed
1 red onion, chopped
1 lb pork shoulder, cubed
1 cup green peas
½ cup frozen sweet corn
½ cup wild rice, rinsed
1 tbsp olive oil
1 ½ cups chicken broth
Salt and pepper to taste
Lemon wedges for serving

DIRECTIONS

In a pan over medium heat, warm olive oil. Add the pork shoulder cubes and cook for 8-10 minutes, stirring occasionally, until browned. Transfer to your Slow Cooker. Add in chorizo, red beans, red onion, green peas, frozen sweet corn, wild rice, chicken broth, salt, and pepper. Cover with the lid and cook for 3 hours on High. When done, remove the lid and serve hot. Enjoy!

124. Smoked Potato Stew

Serves: 6 | Total Time: 6 hours 30 minutes

INGREDIENTS

2 sweet potatoes, peeled and cubed
1 lb Yukon gold potatoes, cubed
1 cup diced bacon
1 large onion, chopped
2 carrots, diced
1 celery stalk, diced
2 red bell peppers, diced
½ tsp ground cumin
½ tsp smoked paprika
1 can (14 oz) diced tomatoes
Salt and pepper to taste
2 cups chicken broth

DIRECTIONS

In a pan over medium heat, cook bacon until crispy. Transfer it to your Slow Cooker. Add onion, carrots, celery, bell peppers, sweet potatoes, potatoes, ground cumin, smoked paprika, tomatoes, salt, pepper, and chicken broth. Cover with the lid and cook for 6 hours on Low. Serve warm and enjoy!

125. Cajun-Style Beef Stew

Serves: 6 | Total Time: 6 hours 30 minutes

INGREDIENTS

1 ½ lb sweet potatoes, cubed
1 ½ lb beef sirloin, cubed
4 bacon slices, chopped
2 tbsp olive oil
1 tbsp Cajun seasoning
1 tsp smoked paprika
¼ tsp cayenne pepper
1 tbsp apple cider vinegar
Salt and pepper to taste

DIRECTIONS

Heat olive oil in a pan over medium heat and sear beef and bacon for 5 minutes until the meat begins to brown on all sides and the bacon is crispy. Transfer to your Slow Cooker. Add Cajun seasoning, smoked paprika, cayenne pepper, vinegar, sweet potatoes, salt, and pepper. Cover and cook for 6 hours on Low. Serve hot and enjoy!

126. Cheddar Mushroom & Beef Stew

Serves: 6 | Total Time: 5 hours 30 minutes

INGREDIENTS

2 large onions, sliced
1 ½ lb ground beef
1 carrot, grated
1 cup sliced mushrooms
2 tbsp olive oil
½ cup spicy tomato sauce
Salt and pepper to taste
2 cups shredded cheddar cheese

DIRECTIONS

Heat olive oil in a pan over medium heat and sauté the onions for 10 minutes until they caramelize. Transfer to your Slow Cooker. Add ground beef, grated carrot, mushrooms, spicy tomato sauce, salt, and pepper. Scatter shredded cheddar cheese on top. Cover and cook for 5 hours on Low. Serve hot and enjoy!

127. Effortless Pork Stew with Red Cole Slaw

Serves: 6 | Total Time: 4 hours 15 minutes

INGREDIENTS

1 small red cabbage head, shredded
1 large onion, chopped
4 garlic cloves, minced
1 ½ lb pork shoulder, cubed
2 tbsp olive oil
1 tbsp maple syrup
1 tsp smoked paprika
¼ cup apple cider vinegar
Salt and pepper to taste

DIRECTIONS

Combine red cabbage, pork cubes, olive oil, onion, garlic, maple syrup, smoked paprika, apple cider vinegar, salt, and pepper in your Slow Cooker. Stir well to mix all the ingredients. Cook for 4 hours on Low. Serve hot.

128. Marinara Beef & Vegetable Stew

Serves: 6 | Total Time: 7 hours 15 minutes

INGREDIENTS

2 red bell peppers, sliced
2 yellow bell peppers, sliced
2 lb beef chuck, cubed
1 cup marinara sauce
2 cups cherry tomatoes
1 thyme sprig
2 tbsp olive oil
1 tsp smoked paprika
Salt to taste

DIRECTIONS

Heat olive oil in a pan over medium heat and sear beef for 5 minutes until golden. Transfer to your Slow Cooker. Add bell peppers, marinara sauce, cherry tomatoes, thyme, smoked paprika, and salt. Cook for 7 hours on Low.

129. Picante Mixed Bean Stew with Pork

Serves: 6 | Total Time: 10 hours 15 minutes

INGREDIENTS

2 carrots, sliced
1 onion, chopped
1 lb dried navy beans, rinsed
1 cup red kidney beans, soaked
2 lb pork shoulder, cubed
½ cup diced bacon
1 celery stalk, sliced
1 can (14 oz) fire-roasted tomatoes
2 serrano peppers, chopped
1 ½ cups chicken broth
Salt and pepper to taste

DIRECTIONS

Combine pork, bacon, celery, carrots, onion, navy beans, red kidney beans, fire-roasted tomatoes, serrano peppers, broth, salt, and pepper in your Slow Cooker. Cook for 10 hours on Low. Serve hot and enjoy!

130. Savory Cannellini Bean Stew

Serves: 4 | Total Time: 4 hours 15 minutes

INGREDIENTS

1 shallot, chopped
1 garlic clove, chopped
1 lb pork tenderloin, cubed
1 can (15 oz) cannellini beans
1 cup diced tomatoes
2 thyme sprigs
2 tbsp olive oil
1 cup chicken stock
Salt and pepper to taste

DIRECTIONS

In a pan over medium heat, warm olive oil and sear pork for 2-3 minutes until golden brown on all sides. Transfer it to your Slow Cooker. Add cannellini beans, shallot, garlic, tomatoes, thyme, chicken stock, salt, and pepper. Cover with the lid and cook for 4 hours on Low. When done, remove the lid and serve warm. Enjoy!

131. Spicy Pork Stew

Serves: 6 | Total Time: 5 hours 15 minutes

INGREDIENTS

1 jar pickled jalapeño, chopped
2 lb pork shoulder, cubed
4 garlic cloves, chopped
1 large onion, chopped
1 cup beef broth
1 cup crushed tomatoes
2 tbsp olive oil
1 tsp chili powder
Salt and pepper to taste

DIRECTIONS

Heat olive oil in a pan over medium heat. Add pork and cook for 2-3 minutes until golden on all sides. Transfer to your Slow Cooker. Add jalapeño, garlic, onion, chili powder, beef broth, crushed tomatoes, salt, and pepper. Cover and cook for 5 hours on Low. Serve hot and enjoy!

132. Tomato Zucchini Stew

Serves: 4 | Total Time: 1 hour 45 minutes

INGREDIENTS

1 shallot, chopped
1 garlic cloves, minced
2 large zucchinis, cubed
2 ripe tomatoes, crushed
1 bay leaf
1 cup vegetable broth
1 tbsp olive oil
Salt and pepper to taste

DIRECTIONS

Combine olive oil, shallot, garlic, zucchini, tomatoes, bay leaf, broth, salt, and pepper in your Slow Cooker. Stir well to mix. Cover with the lid and cook for 1 hour and 45 minutes on High. Serve warm and enjoy!

133. Garden Vegetable Medley Stew

Serves: 6 | Total Time: 6 hours 30 minutes

INGREDIENTS

½ head cauliflower, cut into florets
1 carrot, sliced
1 sweet onion, chopped
4 garlic cloves, minced
2 red bell peppers, diced
2 tbsp olive oil
1 daikon, cubed
1 zucchini, cubed
2 grape tomatoes, halved
2 cups vegetable broth
1 bay leaf
Salt and pepper to taste

DIRECTIONS

Warm olive oil and sauté onion and garlic in a pan over medium heat for 2 minutes until softened. Transfer it to your Slow Cooker. Add cauliflower, bell peppers, carrot, daikon, zucchini, grape tomatoes, broth, bay leaf, salt, and pepper. Stir well to combine. Cover with the lid and cook for 6 hours on Low. Serve hot and enjoy!

134. Asian-Style Chicken Stew

Serves: 4 | Total Time: 4 hours 15 minutes

INGREDIENTS

2 chicken thighs, cut into strips
1 lb butternut squash, peeled and cubed
1 cup coconut milk
½ cup chicken stock
1-star anise
2 tbsp olive oil
½ cinnamon stick
¼ tsp ground turmeric
Salt and pepper to taste

DIRECTIONS

Combine chicken, olive oil, butternut squash, coconut milk, chicken stock, star anise, cinnamon stick, turmeric, salt, and pepper in your Slow Cooker. Mix well. Cover with the lid and cook for 4 hours on Low. When done, remove the cinnamon stick. Serve warm and enjoy!

135. Garlicky Beef Stew with Mushrooms

Serves: 6 | Total Time: 6 hours 15 minutes

INGREDIENTS

2 tbsp olive oil
4 garlic cloves, chopped
2 cups sliced mushrooms
2 lb beef chuck, cubed
½ cup red wine
2 tbsp all-purpose flour
2 tbsp Dijon mustard
1 thyme sprig
Salt and pepper to taste

DIRECTIONS

Sprinkle beef cubes with salt, pepper, and flour. Heat olive oil in a pan over medium heat and sear beef for 2-3 minutes until golden on all sides. Transfer to your Slow Cooker. Add garlic, sliced mushrooms, 1 cup of water, red wine, Dijon mustard, thyme, salt, and pepper. Cover and cook for 6 hours on Low. Serve hot and enjoy!

136. Fire-Roasted tomato and Black Bean Chili

Serves: 6 | Total Time: 7 hours 30 minutes

INGREDIENTS

2 tomatoes, diced
1 carrot, diced
2 red onions, chopped
2 garlic cloves, chopped
1 red bell pepper, diced
1 celery stalk, diced
1 cup fire-roasted tomatoes
2 tbsp marinara sauce
1 cup kidney beans, soaked
2 cups vegetable stock
1 cup water
1 bay leaf
1 thyme sprig
Salt and pepper to taste

DIRECTIONS

In your Slow Cooker, combine onions, garlic, bell pepper, carrot, celery, tomatoes, fire-roasted tomatoes, marinara sauce, kidney beans, vegetable stock, water, bay leaf, thyme, salt, and pepper. Cook for 7 hours on Low. Serve hot.

137. Stunning Red Beef Stew

Serves: 6 | Total Time: 5 hours 30 minutes

INGREDIENTS

2 lb baby potatoes, halved
2 carrots, diced
2 lb beef chuck, cubed
1 large onion, chopped
2 red bell peppers, diced
1 celery stalk, chopped
2 tbsp olive oil
1 cup beef broth
1 cup crushed tomatoes
1 bay leaf
1 rosemary sprig
Salt and pepper to taste

DIRECTIONS

Heat olive oil in a pan over medium heat. Add beef and cook for 2-3 minutes until golden on all sides. Transfer to your Slow Cooker. Add onion, bell peppers, carrots, celery, potatoes, beef broth, crushed tomatoes, bay leaf, rosemary, salt, and pepper. Cover and cook for 5 hours on Low. Serve hot and enjoy!

138. Meaty Bean Stew

Serves: 6 | Total Time: 7 hours 15 minutes

INGREDIENTS

1 ½ lb pork shoulder, cubed
2 sweet onions, chopped
4 bacon slices, chopped
½ lb dried navy beans
4 garlic cloves, chopped
1 tsp ground cumin
½ tsp ground coriander
1 tsp apple cider vinegar
2 cups chicken broth
Salt and pepper to taste

DIRECTIONS

Combine pork, onions, bacon, dried navy beans, garlic, cumin, ground coriander, apple cider vinegar, chicken broth, salt, and pepper in your Slow Cooker.Mix well. Cover and cook for 7 hours on Low. Serve hot and enjoy!

139. Slow Cooker Pork & Potato Stew

Serves: 6 | Total Time: 5 hours 15 minutes

INGREDIENTS

4 garlic cloves, minced
2 lb red potatoes, cubed
2 lb pork roast, cubed
1 celery stalk, sliced
1 sweet onion, sliced
1 leek, sliced
1 tbsp soy sauce
1 tbsp honey
1 tbsp dried rosemary
1 cup diced tomatoes
1 cup beef stock
1 tbsp Dijon mustard
1 tsp Worcestershire sauce
1 bay leaf
Salt and pepper to taste

DIRECTIONS

Combine pork roast, celery, onion, leek, garlic, potatoes, mustard, Worcestershire sauce, soy sauce, honey, rosemary, tomatoes, beef stock, bay leaf, salt, and pepper in your Slow Cooker. Cover and cook on Low for 5 hours. Serve.

SNACKS & APPETIZERS

140. Classic Buffalo Chicken Wings

Serves: 6 | Total Time: 7 hours 15 minutes

INGREDIENTS

½ cup buffalo sauce
½ cup spicy tomato paste
1 tsp garlic powder
1 tsp onion powder
½ tsp cayenne pepper
½ tsp smoked paprika
1 tbsp tomato paste
2 tbsp apple cider vinegar
1 tbsp Worcestershire sauce
1 cup sour cream
2 oz blue cheese, crumbled
3 lb chicken wings

DIRECTIONS

Combine buffalo sauce, spicy tomato sauce, vinegar, Worcestershire sauce, tomato paste, garlic powder, onion powder, cayenne pepper, smoked paprika, sour cream, and blue cheese in your Slow Cooker. Add chicken wings and toss until well coated. Cover with the lid and cook for 7 hours on Low. When done, remove the lid and serve with your favorite dipping sauce. Enjoy!

141. Dilly Baby Potatoes

Serves: 6 | Total Time: 2 hours 15 minutes

INGREDIENTS

3 lb baby potatoes
2 garlic cloves, chopped
2 green onions, sliced
¼ cup vegetable broth
Salt and black pepper to taste
2 tbsp fresh dill, chopped

DIRECTIONS

In your Slow Cooker, combine baby potatoes, garlic, green onions, salt, black pepper, and broth. Cover with the lid and cook for 2 hours on High. When done, remove the lid and serve topped with dill. Enjoy!

142. Smoky Cocktail Sausages

Serves: 4 | Total Time: 4 hours 10 minutes

INGREDIENTS

14 oz smoked cocktail sausages
½ cup honey
1 green onion, finely diced
½ cup ketchup

DIRECTIONS

Combine cocktail sausages, honey, green onion, and ketchup in your Slow Cooker. Stir to coat the sausages evenly with the sauce. Close the cooker lid and set the heat setting to Low. Cook for 4 hours, allowing the flavors to meld together. Serve on toothpicks and enjoy!

143. Stuffed Mushrooms in Marinara Sauce

Serves: 4 | Total Time: 4 hours 15 minutes

INGREDIENTS

8 large mushroom caps
1 cup marinara sauce
3 tbsp grated Parmesan cheese
Sea salt and pepper to taste
¼ lb ground beef sausage
1 clove garlic, finely diced
1/8 cup red onion, diced
2 tsp extra virgin olive oil
1 tbsp thyme, chopped

DIRECTIONS

In a skillet over medium heat, add olive oil, sauté garlic, and red onion until softened. Add in sausage and cook until browned. Transfer the mixture into a mixing bowl, then add the Parmesan cheese, salt, and pepper. Mix well. Carefully spoon the sausage mixture into the mushroom caps.

Pour the marinara sauce into your Slow Cooker. Place stuffed mushrooms into the pot, covering them with sauce. Cook on high for 4 hours. Serve topped with thyme and enjoy!

144. Crab Spread with Spinach

Serves: 6 | Total Time: 2 hours 15 minutes

INGREDIENTS

2 garlic cloves, chopped
1 lb fresh spinach, chopped
1 can crab meat, drained
2 shallots, chopped
2 jalapeno peppers, minced
1 cup grated Gruyère cheese
½ cup milk
1 cup Greek yogurt
1 cup cream cheese
1 cup grated Monterey Jack cheese
1 tbsp white wine vinegar

DIRECTIONS

In your Slow Cooker, combine crab meat, spinach, shallots, jalapeño peppers, Gruyère cheese, milk, Greek yogurt, cream cheese, Monterey Jack cheese, white wine vinegar, and garlic. Cover with the lid and cook for 2 hours on High. Serve warm or chilled, accompanied by vegetable sticks if desired. Enjoy!

145. Peach-Glazed Mini Meatballs

Serves: 6 | Total Time: 6 hours 30 minutes

INGREDIENTS

2 tbsp peach sauce
1 cup Buffalo sauce
½ cup tomato sauce
1 tsp red wine vinegar
Salt and pepper to taste
2 lb ground pork
1 lb ground beef
4 garlic cloves, minced
1 shallot, chopped
1 egg
¼ cup breadcrumbs
2 tbsp chopped parsley
1 tbsp chopped cilantro
½ tsp chili powder

DIRECTIONS

Combine peach sauce, Buffalo sauce, tomato sauce, vinegar, salt, and pepper in your Slow Cooker. Mix ground pork, beef, garlic, shallot, egg, breadcrumbs, parsley, cilantro, and chili powder in a bowl.Season with salt and pepper. Shape the mixture into mini meatballs and place them into the Slow Cooker pot. Cover and cook for 6 hours on Low. When done, remove the lid and serve with cocktail skewers. Enjoy!

146. Mediterranean Eggplant Dip

Serves: 6 | Total Time: 6 hours 15 minutes

INGREDIENTS

2 large eggplants
Salt and pepper to taste
4 tbsp lemon juice
1 tsp dried oregano
4 tbsp olive oil
6 cloves garlic, minced
½ cup plain yogurt
½ cup red onion, chopped
1 cup tomatoes, diced

DIRECTIONS

Use a fork to poke the eggplant, then place it in your Slow Cooker. Cover with the lid and cook on Low for 6 hours. Once ready, half the eggplant and spoon the pulp into a bowl. Mix the pulp with red onion, yogurt, tomatoes, garlic, olive oil, and oregano. Season with lemon juice, pepper, and salt. Serve and enjoy!

147. Turkey & Poblano Dip

Serves: 6 | Total Time: 4 hours 15 minutes

INGREDIENTS

1 lb ground turkey
2 shallots, chopped
2 tbsp olive oil
2 cups red salsa
1 cup cream cheese
2 cups grated Pepper Jack cheese
2 poblano peppers, minced
1 tbsp Worcestershire sauce
4 garlic cloves, minced
¼ cup chopped cilantro
Salt and pepper to taste

DIRECTIONS

In your Slow Cooker, combine ground turkey, olive oil, shallots, red salsa, cream cheese, grated Pepper Jack cheese, minced poblano peppers, Worcestershire sauce, minced garlic, and chopped cilantro. Sprinkle with salt and pepper to taste. Cover with the lid and cook for 4 hours on Low. Serve warm with tortilla chips. Enjoy!

148. Mustardy Gouda Dip with Bacon

Serves: 6 | Total Time: 4 hours 15 minutes

INGREDIENTS

1 onion, chopped
10 bacon slices, chopped
1 cup cream cheese
1 tsp Worcestershire sauce
1 tsp yellow mustard
1 cup grated Gouda cheese
½ cup milk
Salt and pepper to taste

DIRECTIONS

In your Slow Cooker, combine bacon, onions, Worcestershire sauce, mustard, cream cheese, Gouda cheese, and milk. Sprinkle with salt and pepper to taste. Cover with the lid and cook for 4 hours on Low. Enjoy!

149. Asparagus & Blue Cheese Dip

Serves: 6 | Total Time: 6 hours 15 minutes

INGREDIENTS

1 bunch asparagus, chopped
2 garlic cloves, chopped
2 onions, chopped
1 red chili, chopped
1 cup cream cheese
1 cup heavy cream
2 oz blue cheese, crumbled
2 tbsp chopped parsley

DIRECTIONS

In your Slow Cooker, combine onions, red chili, garlic, asparagus, cream cheese, heavy cream, and blue cheese. Cover with the lid and cook for 6 hours on Low. Stir in chopped parsley. Serve warm or chilled. Enjoy!

150. Spicy Creole Walnuts

Serves: 6 | Total Time: 2 hours 15 minutes

INGREDIENTS

2 lb raw, whole walnuts
¼ cup coconut oil
¼ cup honey
1 tbsp Creole seasoning
½ tsp red pepper flakes
Salt to taste

DIRECTIONS

Combine raw walnuts, coconut oil, honey, Creole seasoning, red pepper flakes, and a pinch of salt in your Slow Cooker. Cover with the lid and cook for 2 hours on High. When done, remove the lid and stir. Allow them to cool slightly before serving. Enjoy!

151. Thyme Bean Hummus with Golden Onions

Serves: 6 | Total Time: 8 hours 15 minutes

INGREDIENTS

1 lb cannellini beans, soaked
4 garlic cloves, minced
2 cups water
2 cups chicken stock
1 bay leaf
2 thyme sprigs
2 large onions, sliced
2 tbsp olive oil
Salt and pepper to taste

DIRECTIONS

In your Slow Cooker, combine cannellini beans, garlic, water, stock, bay leaf, and thyme sprigs. Cook for 8 hours on Low. When done, remove the lid, strain the beans, reserving ¼ cup, and discard bay leaf and thyme. Transfer the beans and reserved liquid to a blender. Blend until smooth. Season with salt and pepper. Transfer it to a bowl.

Warm olive oil in a skillet over medium heat. Add onions and cook for about 10 minutes until they caramelize, stirring occasionally. Spread the bean hummus in a serving dish. Top with caramelized onions. Enjoy!

152. Mexican Pork Casserole

Serves: 6 | Total Time: 6 hours 15 minutes

INGREDIENTS

1 red onion, chopped
2 lb ground pork
4 garlic cloves, minced
2 tbsp Mexican seasoning
1 tsp chili powder
1 can (14.5 oz) diced tomatoes
1 can (15 oz) sweet corn, drained
2 cups grated Monterey Jack cheese

DIRECTIONS

Put red onion, ground pork, garlic, Mexican seasoning, chili powder, tomatoes, corn, and Monterey Jack cheese in your Slow Cooker. Cover with the lid and cook for 6 hours on Low. Serve and enjoy!

153. Chorizo Cheese Dip

Serves: 6 | Total Time: 6 hours 15 minutes

INGREDIENTS

2 peeled tomatoes, diced
8 chorizo links, diced
1 chili pepper, chopped
1 cup cream cheese
2 cups grated Pepper Jack cheese
½ cup beer

DIRECTIONS

In your Slow Cooker, combine tomatoes, chorizo links, chili pepper, cream cheese, Pepper Jack cheese, and beer. Cover with the lid and cook for 6 hours on Low. When done, remove the lid and stir the dip well. Serve warm.

154. Honey-Glazed Wings

Serves: 6 | Total Time: 7 hours 15 minutes

INGREDIENTS

¼ cup honey
3 lb chicken wings
1 tsp garlic powder
1 tsp smoked paprika
2 tbsp balsamic vinegar
1 tbsp Dijon mustard
1 tsp Worcestershire sauce
½ cup tomato sauce
1 tsp salt

DIRECTIONS

In your Slow Cooker, mix chicken wings, honey, garlic powder, smoked paprika, balsamic vinegar, mustard, Worcestershire sauce, tomato sauce, and salt. Toss to coat the wings well. Cook for 7 hours on Low. Serve warm.

155. Sweet and Spicy Crab Spread

Serves: 6 | Total Time: 2 hours 15 minutes

INGREDIENTS

1 cup canned sweet corn
½ cup peach preserves
2 tbsp butter
2 red bell peppers, diced
2 serrano peppers, minced
1 cup sour cream
1 can crab meat, drained
1 tsp Worcestershire sauce
1 tsp hot sauce
1 cup grated Monterey Jack cheese

DIRECTIONS

In your Slow Cooker, combine butter, sweet corn, bell peppers, peach preserves, serrano peppers, sour cream, crabmeat, Worcestershire sauce, hot sauce, and Monterey Jack cheese. Cover with the lid and cook for 2 hours on Low. When done, remove the lid and serve the dip warm or chilled. Enjoy!

156. Wine & Swiss Cheese Fondue

Serves: 6 | Total Time: 2 hours 15 minutes

INGREDIENTS

2 cups grated Swiss cheese
4 tbsp butter
1 shallot, chopped
2 garlic cloves, minced
2 tbsp all-purpose flour
2 poblano peppers, minced
1 cup milk
1 cup white wine
Salt and pepper to taste

DIRECTIONS

In a skillet over medium heat, melt the butter. Add the shallot and garlic, and cook for 2 minutes. Stir in the flour and cook for 2 more minutes until it forms a paste. Pour in the milk and cook for 5 minutes, stirring often, until the mixture thickens. Transfer the mixture to your Slow Cooker. Add in poblano peppers, Swiss cheese, and white wine. Cover with the lid and cook for 2 hours on High. Stir the fondue well. Season with salt and pepper.

157. Artichokes with Crab Meat Stuffing

Serves: 6 | Total Time: 6 hours 15 minutes

INGREDIENTS

6 fresh artichokes
2 tbsp olive oil
2 cups crab meat, chopped
4 garlic cloves, minced
1 cup seasoned breadcrumbs
1 tbsp chopped fresh basil
¼ cup white wine
Salt and pepper to taste

DIRECTIONS

Prepare artichokes by cutting stems, trimming leaves, and cleaning the center. In a bowl, mix crab meat, garlic, olive oil, seasoned breadcrumbs, basil, salt, and pepper. Stuff each artichoke with the anchovy mixture. Place stuffed artichokes into your Slow Cooker. Pour white wine over the top. Cover and cook for 6 hours on Low.

158. Kalamata Beef Spread

Serves: 6 | Total Time: 6 hours 15 minutes

INGREDIENTS

1 lb stewing beef, diced
2 garlic cloves, minced
2 tbsp olive oil
2 shallots, chopped
4 ripe tomatoes, diced
16 Kalamata olives, chopped
½ cup black olives, chopped
½ tsp dried oregano
1 tsp dried basil
¼ cup red wine
½ cup marinara sauce
Salt and pepper to taste

DIRECTIONS

Warm olive oil over medium heat in a skillet. Sear the beef for 5 minutes. Add shallots and garlic and cook for 5 minutes.Transfer to your Slow Cooker. Stir in tomatoes, Kalamata olives, black olives, oregano, basil, red wine, and marinara sauce. Season with salt and pepper. Cover and cook for 6 hours on Low. Serve warm and enjoy!

159. Whisky Beans with Bacon

Serves: 6 | Total Time: 6 hours 15 minutes

INGREDIENTS

2 shallots, sliced
6 bacon slices, chopped
2 cans navy beans, drained
1 garlic clove, minced
1 cup salsa
½ cup vegetable broth
1 tbsp brown sugar
1 tbsp honey
½ tsp chili powder
1 tbsp apple cider vinegar
2 tbsp whisky
Salt and pepper to taste

DIRECTIONS

In a skillet over medium heat, cook bacon until crispy. Transfer to your Slow Cooker. Add navy beans, shallots, garlic, salsa, vegetable broth, brown sugar, honey, chili powder, vinegar, whisky, salt, and pepper. Cover and cook for 6 hours on Low. After cooking, mash some beans for a thicker texture. Serve warm and enjoy!

160. Tropical Meatballs

Serves: 6 | Total Time: 7 hours 30 minutes

INGREDIENTS

1 can pineapple chunks (keep the juices)
2 poblano peppers, minced
4 garlic cloves, minced
¼ cup honey
2 tbsp soy sauce
2 tbsp cornstarch
1 tbsp orange juice
2 lb ground pork
1 lb ground beef
1 tsp dried oregano
1 egg
¼ cup breadcrumbs
Salt and pepper to taste

DIRECTIONS

Combine pineapple chunks with juices, poblano peppers, honey, soy sauce, cornstarch, and orange juice in your Slow Cooker. Stir to blend the ingredients.

Mix ground pork, beef, garlic, dried oregano, egg, breadcrumbs, salt, and pepper in a bowl. Form small meatballs and place them into the Slow Cooker pot. Cover with the lid and cook for 7 hours on Low. When done, remove the lid and stir gently. Serve warm or chilled. Enjoy!

161. Turkey Meatball Feast

Serves: 4 | Total Time: 7 hours 30 minutes

INGREDIENTS

1 lb ground turkey
1 egg
½ cup breadcrumbs
1 onion, chopped
½ tsp ground cloves
1 thyme sprig
1 tbsp apricot preserves
½ cup BBQ sauce
½ tsp hot sauce
Salt and pepper to taste

DIRECTIONS

Mix apricot preserves, BBQ sauce, hot sauce, and thyme in your Slow Cooker. Combine ground turkey, egg, breadcrumbs, shallot, cloves, salt, and pepper in a bowl. Form small balls from the mixture. Place the meatballs into the Slow Cooker pot with the sauce. Cover with the lid and cook for 7 hours on Low. Serve warm and enjoy!

162. Cheesy Anchovy Dip with Pancetta

Serves: 6 | Total Time: 2 hours 15 minutes

INGREDIENTS

4 canned anchovies, drained and chopped
1 lb pancetta, diced
1 cup cream cheese
½ cup grated mozzarella cheese
1 tsp Worcestershire sauce
1 tsp yellow mustard
1 tsp hot sauce

DIRECTIONS

In a skillet over medium heat, cook pancetta for 5 minutes. Transfer to the Slow Cooker. Add in cream cheese, mozzarella cheese, Worcestershire sauce, mustard, anchovies, and hot sauce. Cover with the lid and cook for 2 hours on High. Serve warm or chilled and enjoy!

163. Chicken Fajita Taquitos

Serves: 6 | Total Time: 6 hours 30 minutes

INGREDIENTS

4 chicken breasts, cooked and diced
12 taco-sized flour tortillas
1 cup cream cheese
2 serrano peppers, minced
½ cup mixed bell pepper, minced
½ cup canned sweet corn
½ tsp cumin powder
4 garlic cloves, minced
2 cups grated Monterey Jack cheese

DIRECTIONS

In a bowl, combine cooked chicken, cream cheese, serrano peppers, garlic, cumin, mixed bell pepper, and Monterey Jack cheese. Lay flour tortillas onto a flat surface and fill each with the chicken mixture. Roll each tortilla into a tight roll and place them in your Slow Cooker. Cover with the lid and cook for 6 hours on Low. Enjoy!

164. Cheddar Mushroom Dip

Serves: 6 | Total Time: 4 hours 15 minutes

INGREDIENTS

1 can condensed cream of celery soup
1 lb cremini mushrooms, chopped
1 cup white wine
1 cup cream cheese
1 cup heavy cream
½ cup grated Cheddar cheese
1 tsp dried tarragon
½ tsp dried oregano
Salt and pepper to taste

DIRECTIONS

In your Slow Cooker, combine condensed cream of celery soup, cremini mushrooms, white wine, cream cheese, heavy cream, Cheddar cheese, tarragon, and oregano. Sprinkle with salt and pepper to taste. Cover with the lid and cook for 4 hours on Low. Remove the lid and serve warm or chilled. Enjoy!

165. Smoky Sausages in Buffalo Glaze

Serves: 6 | Total Time: 2 hours 15 minutes

INGREDIENTS

1 tsp ancho chile seasoning
3 lb small smoked sausages
1 cup Buffalo sauce
1 tbsp tomato paste
¼ cup apple cider vinegar
Salt and pepper to taste

DIRECTIONS

Mix sausages, Buffalo sauce, ancho chile seasoning, tomato paste, and apple cider vinegar in your Slow Cooker. Sprinkle with salt and pepper to taste. Cover with the lid and cook for 2 hours on High. Serve warm and enjoy!

166. Mexican Street Chilaquiles

Serves: 6 | Total Time: 8 hours 30 minutes

INGREDIENTS

2 cups grated cheddar cheese
2 lb flank steak
6 oz tortilla chips
2 tbsp olive oil
1 tsp smoked paprika
½ tsp chili powder
2 tbsp brown sugar
1 tsp cumin powder
1 tsp garlic powder
1 cup dark beer
1 cup green salsa
1 can sweet corn, drained
Salt to taste
Sour cream for serving
2 tbsp chopped cilantro

DIRECTIONS

In a bowl, combine salt, paprika, chili powder, brown sugar, cumin, and garlic powder. Rub the mixture over the flank steak until well coated.

Warm olive oil in a skillet over medium heat. Sear the steak for 4-5 minutes on all sides. Transfer the steak to the Slow Cooker and pour in the dark beer. Cover and cook for 6 hours on Low. When done, remove the lid, remove the meat, and cut it into thin slices. Clean the pot.

Place tortilla chips at the bottom of the Slow Cooker. Pour green salsa over the chips and top with steak slices, sweet corn, and cheddar cheese. Cover with the lid and cook for 2 hours on Low. Remove the lid and serve the chilaquiles topped with sour cream and cilantro. Enjoy!

167. Beefy Cheddar Corn Dip

Serves: 6 | Total Time: 2 hours 15 minutes

INGREDIENTS

1 lb ground beef
1 onion, chopped
2 cups grated mozzarella
1 can sweet corn, drained
1 can pinto beans, drained
½ cup beef stock
2 tbsp olive oil
1 cup diced tomatoes
½ cup black olives, chopped
1 tsp dried oregano
½ tsp chili powder
½ tsp cumin powder
¼ tsp garlic powder
Salt and pepper to taste
Tortilla chips for serving

DIRECTIONS

Warm olive oil in a skillet over medium heat. Add ground beef and cook for 5-7 minutes, stirring often, until browned. Place the cooked beef, onion, corn, pinto beans, beef stock, tomatoes, black olives, oregano, chili powder, cumin, garlic powder, and mozzarella in your Slow Cooker. Season with salt and pepper to taste. Cover with the lid and cook for 2 hours on High. Serve warm with tortilla chips. Enjoy!

168. Sour Caramelized Onion Spread

Serves: 6 | Total Time: 6 hours 15 minutes

INGREDIENTS

1 cup frozen cranberries
4 red onions, sliced
1 apple, peeled and diced
¼ cup balsamic vinegar
¼ cup fresh lemon juice
2 tbsp olive oil
2 tbsp honey
1 tsp lemon zest
1 bay leaf
1 thyme sprig
1 tsp salt

DIRECTIONS

Warm olive oil in a skillet over medium heat. Add onions and cook for 10 minutes until caramelized. Transfer caramelized onions, apples, cranberries, balsamic vinegar, orange juice, honey, orange zest, bay leaf, thyme, and salt to your Slow Cooker. Cover with the lid and cook for 6 hours on Low. Serve and enjoy!

169. Swiss-Style Onion Dip

Serves: 6 | Total Time: 4 hours 30 minutes

INGREDIENTS

1 cup chicken stock
4 sweet onions, sliced
2 tbsp butter
1 tbsp olive oil
1 tsp dried thyme
½ cup dry white wine
2 cups grated Gruyère cheese
1 tbsp cornstarch
Salt and pepper to taste

DIRECTIONS

In a skillet, melt butter and olive oil over medium heat. Caramelize onions until golden brown. Transfer caramelized onions to the Slow Cooker. Add stock, thyme, white wine, Gruyère cheese, and cornstarch. Season with salt and pepper. Cover and cook on Low for 4 hours. Remove the lid and serve warm with vegetable sticks.

170. Bourbon-Glazed Cocktail Sausages

Serves: 6 | Total Time: 4 hours 15 minutes

INGREDIENTS

½ cup peach preserves
2 lb tiny sausage links
¼ cup honey
2 tbsp Bourbon

DIRECTIONS

In your Slow Cooker, combine peach preserves, sausage links, honey, and Bourbon. Cover with the lid and cook for 4 hours on Low. When done, remove the lid and serve warm or chilled with cocktail skewers.

171. Cholula Crunch Mix

Serves: 6 | Total Time: 1 hour 45 minutes

INGREDIENTS

4 cups cereals
4 cups mixed crunchy cereals
½ cup melted butter
2 cups mixed nuts
1 cup mixed seeds
2 tbsp Worcestershire sauce
1 tsp Cholula sauce
Salt to taste
½ tsp smoked paprika

DIRECTIONS

In your Slow Cooker, combine cereals, crunchy cereals, melted butter, mixed nuts, mixed seeds, Worcestershire sauce, Cholula sauce, salt, and smoked paprika. Toss to combine all ingredients. Cover with the lid and cook for 1 1/2 hours on High. When done, remove the lid and let cool before serving.

172. Spooky Meatballs

Serves: 6 | Total Time: 7 hours 30 minutes

INGREDIENTS

2 chipotle peppers in adobo sauce, chopped
2 shallots, chopped
3 lb ground beef
2 garlic cloves, minced
2 cups BBQ sauce
¼ cup apricot sauce
Salt and pepper to taste

DIRECTIONS

Mix the BBQ sauce, apricot sauce, salt, and pepper in your Slow Cooker. Combine the ground beef, garlic, shallots, chipotle peppers, salt, and pepper in a bowl. Shape the mixture into meatballs. Place the meatballs into the Slow Cooker, submerging them in the sauce. Cook for 7 hours on Low. Serve and enjoy!

173. Fajita Turkey-Cheese Dip

Serves: 12 | Total Time: 4 hours 15 minutes

INGREDIENTS

1 tomato, diced
3 jalapeños, seeded and chopped
1 ½ cups shredded cooked turkey
1 tbsp cornstarch
4 oz grated Monterey Jack cheese
4 oz grated Colby cheese
1 (12-ounce) can evaporated milk
⅓ cup sour cream
2 diced green onins
1 tsp Fajita seasoning
½ cup green peas
1 cup cooked pinto beans, rinsed

DIRECTIONS

Combine tomato, jalapeños, cooked turkey, cornstarch, Monterey Jack cheese, Colby cheese, evaporated milk, sour cream, green onins, Fajita seasoning, green peas, and pinto beans in your Slow Cooker, gently mixing with a spatula. Cover with the lid and cook for 4 hours on Low.

When ready, remove the lid and stir the dip. Serve hot. Enjoy!

174. Bacon-Wrapped Chicken Wing Bites

Serves: 6 | Total Time: 3 hours 30 minutes

INGREDIENTS

2 lb chicken wings
Bacon slices as needed

DIRECTIONS

Place a chicken wing on each bacon slice and wrap them. Secure the bacon with toothpicks. Arrange the wrapped wings in your Slow Cooker. Cover with the lid and cook for 3 hours on High until the bacon is crispy and the chicken wings are cooked through. When done, remove the lid and serve warm. Enjoy!

175. Chipotle Chicken Drumsticks

Serves: 6 | Total Time: 4 hours 10 minutes

INGREDIENTS

2 lb chicken drumsticks
2 tsp garlic, minced
Black pepper to taste
¼ cup maple syrup
2 tbsp chipotle sauce
1 ¼ cups barbecue sauce

DIRECTIONS

Combine chipotle sauce, barbecue sauce, maple syrup, garlic, and black pepper in a bowl. Mix well. Place the chicken drumsticks in your Slow Cooker. Pour the sauce mixture over the drumsticks in the Slow Cooker and cook on Low for 4 hours. Serve and enjoy!

176. Beef and Bell Pepper Dip

Serves: 6 | Total Time: 6 hours 15 minutes

INGREDIENTS

1 cup cream cheese
4 beef meat, cooked and shredded
¼ cup all-purpose flour
2 roasted red bell peppers, diced
1 cup shredded cheddar cheese
Salt and pepper to taste

DIRECTIONS

Place cream cheese, bell peppers, salt, and pepper in your blender and pulse until smooth. Pour the blended mixture into your Slow Cooker. Add in cooked and shredded beef, flour, and cheddar cheese. Cover with the lid and cook for 6 hours on Low. When done, remove the lid and stir well. Serve warm or chilled.

177. Sweet BBQ Kielbasa

Serves: 6 | Total Time: 6 hours 15 minutes

INGREDIENTS

2 lb kielbasa sausages, sliced
1 cup BBQ sauce
½ cup honey
1 tsp horseradish sauce
Salt and black pepper to taste
¼ tsp nutmeg powder

DIRECTIONS

In your Slow Cooker, combine sliced kielbasa sausages, BBQ sauce, honey, horseradish sauce, black pepper, nutmeg powder, and salt to taste. Cover with the lid and cook for 6 hours on Low. Serve warm. Enjoy!

178. Savory Cheeseburger Dip

Serves: 6 | Total Time: 6 hours 15 minutes

INGREDIENTS

1 lb ground beef
1 lb ground pork
4 garlic cloves, chopped
1 tbsp olive oil
2 onions, chopped
½ cup tomato sauce
1 tbsp yellow mustard
2 tbsp pickle relish
2 cups grated Monterey Jack cheese

DIRECTIONS

Warm the olive oil in a skillet over medium heat. Add the ground beef and pork and cook for 5 minutes, breaking it apart with a spoon, until browned. Drain excess fat. Transfer it to your Slow Cooker. Add onions, garlic, tomato sauce, mustard, pickle relish, and Monterey Jack cheese. Mix well. Cook for 6 hours on Low. Enjoy!

179. Salami Dip

Serves: 6 | Total Time: 6 hours 15 minutes

INGREDIENTS

½ lb salami, diced
1 onion, chopped
1 lb mild Italian sausages, sliced
1 red bell pepper, diced
1 yellow bell pepper, sliced
2 garlic cloves, minced
2 cups marinara sauce
½ cup grated Parmesan cheese
1 cup shredded mozzarella cheese
½ tsp dried basil
½ tsp dried oregano

DIRECTIONS

In your Slow Cooker, combine salami, onion, Italian sausages, red bell pepper, yellow bell pepper, garlic, marinara sauce, Parmesan, mozzarella, basil, and oregano. Cover with the lid and cook on Low for 6 hours. Serve warm.

180. Favorite Meat Dip

Serves: 6 | Total Time: 6 hours 15 minutes

INGREDIENTS

2 tbsp olive oil
1 lb ground pork
2 garlic cloves, chopped
2 cups diced turkey ham
1 shallot, chopped
1 tsp Dijon mustard
1 cup tomato sauce
½ cup sweet chili sauce
Salt and pepper to taste

DIRECTIONS

Warm olive oil in a skillet over medium heat. Brown ground pork and garlic for 5 minutes. Transfer to the Slow Cooker. Add turkey ham, shallot, mustard, tomato sauce, and chili sauce. Season with salt and pepper. Cover and cook on Low for 6 hours. Serve and enjoy!

181. Chicken & Mozzarella Quesadillas

Serves: 6 | Total Time: 7 hours 30 minutes

INGREDIENTS

4 tomatoes, sliced
4 cooked chicken breasts, shredded
1 tsp dried basil
1 tsp dried oregano
1 cup cream cheese, softened
¼ tsp chili powder
6 large corn tortillas
2 cups shredded cheddar cheese
Salt and pepper to taste

DIRECTIONS

In a bowl, combine chicken, basil, oregano, cream cheese, chili powder, salt, and pepper. Layer half of the chicken mixture in the bottom of your Slow Cooker. Add a layer of sliced tomatoes on top of the chicken mixture.

Place three tortillas on top of the tomatoes. Sprinkle half of the shredded cheese over the tortillas. Repeat the layers with the remaining chicken mixture, sliced tomatoes, tortillas, and cheese. Cook for 7 hours on Low. When done, remove the lid and let it cool slightly before slicing into wedges. Enjoy!

182. Spicy Jalapeño-Tomato Sauce

Serves: 6 | Total Time: 3 hours

INGREDIENTS

2 small onions, chopped
4 ripe tomatoes, sliced
1 bay leaf
2 tbsp olive oil
½ tsp dried mint
1 jalapeno pepper, chopped
1 can pinto beans, drained
¼ cup vegetable broth
Salt and pepper to taste

DIRECTIONS

Preheat the oven to 350°F. Place tomato slices on a baking sheet and sprinkle with salt, pepper, mint, and olive oil. Bake for 35 minutes until caramelized. Transfer the caramelized tomatoes, onions, jalapeño, pinto beans, broth, and bay leaf to your Slow Cooker. Cook for 2 hours on High. Remove the bay leaf. Serve warm. Enjoy!

183. Mascarpone Sausage Dip

Serves: 6 | Total Time: 6 hours 15 minutes

INGREDIENTS

2 lb spicy pork sausages
1 cup mascarpone cheese
1 can diced tomatoes
2 poblano peppers, minced
1 tsp dried thyme
Salt and pepper to taste

DIRECTIONS

Combine sausages, mascarpone cheese, tomatoes, poblano peppers, thyme, salt, and pepper in your Slow Cooker. Stir to mix well. Cover with the lid and cook for 6 hours on Low. When done, stir the dip. Serve warm or chilled.

184. Beer-Beef Dip

Serves: 6 | Total Time: 3 hours 15 minutes

INGREDIENTS

1 lb grated cheddar
2 lb ground beef
½ cup cream cheese
½ cup beer
1 poblano pepper, chopped
2 tbsp fresh parsley, chopped

DIRECTIONS

Combine ground beef, grated cheddar, cream cheese, beer, and chopped poblano peppers in your Slow Cooker. Cover with the lid and cook for 3 hours on High. When done, remove the lid and stir. Garnish with fresh parsley.

185. Swiss Cheese and Bacon Dip

Serves: 6 | Total Time: 4 hours 15 minutes

INGREDIENTS

1 (14-oz) can condensed cream of mushroom soup
1 lb bacon, minced
1 cup cream cheese
1 (14-oz) can condensed onion soup
2 cups grated mozzarella cheese
½ tsp paprika

DIRECTIONS

Combine bacon, cream cheese, condensed onion soup, mushroom soup, grated mozzarella cheese, and paprika in your Slow Cooker. Cover with the lid and cook for 4 hours on Low. Serve and enjoy!

186. Strawberry-Marinated Mushrooms

Serves: 6 | Total Time: 8 hours 15 minutes

INGREDIENTS

2 lb mushrooms, trimmed
1 cup soy sauce
1 cup water
½ cup honey
¼ cup strawberry vinegar
½ tsp paprika

DIRECTIONS

Combine cleaned and trimmed mushrooms, soy sauce, water, honey, strawberry vinegar, and paprika in your Slow Cooker. Cover with the lid and cook for 8 hours on Low. Let cool before serving. Enjoy!

187. Bean and Beef Dip

Serves: 6 | Total Time: 4 hours 15 minutes

INGREDIENTS

1 can kidney beans, drained
2 lb ground beef
1 can diced tomatoes
2 banana peppers, minced
2 cups grated Monterey Jack cheese
Salt and pepper to taste

DIRECTIONS

Combine drained kidney beans, ground beef, tomatoes, banana peppers, and Monterey Jack cheese in your Slow Cooker. Sprinkle with salt and pepper to taste. Cover with the lid and cook for 4 hours on High. When done, remove the lid and serve warm. Enjoy!

188. Picante Chicken Wings

Serves: 6 | Total Time: 8 hours 15 minutes

INGREDIENTS

4 lb chicken wings
¼ cup butter, melted
1 cup buffalo wing sauce
1 tbsp Worcestershire sauce
1 tsp dried oregano
1 tsp dried basil
1 tsp onion powder
1 tsp garlic powder
½ tsp cumin powder
½ tsp cinnamon powder
1 tsp Tabasco sauce
Salt to taste

DIRECTIONS

Combine butter, chicken wings, buffalo wing sauce, Worcestershire sauce, oregano, basil, onion powder, garlic powder, cumin, cinnamon, tabasco sauce, and salt in your Slow Cooker.Toss until everything is well coated. Cover with the lid and cook for 8 hours on Low. When done, remove the lid and serve warm or chilled. Enjoy!

189. Tangy Glazed Meatballs

Serves: 6 | Total Time: 8 hours 15 minutes

INGREDIENTS

½ cup molasses
¼ cup soy sauce
2 tbsp lemon juice
½ cup beef stock
1 tbsp Worcestershire sauce
2 garlic cloves, minced
1 shallot, chopped
1 lb ground pork
1 lb ground beef
½ cup oat flour
½ tsp cumin powder
½ tsp smoked paprika
1 egg
Salt and pepper to taste

DIRECTIONS

In your Slow Cooker, mix molasses, soy sauce, lemon juice, beef stock, and Worcestershire sauce. Mix ground beef, pork, garlic, shallot, oat flour, cumin powder, smoked paprika, egg, salt, and pepper in a bowl. Form the mixture into small balls and place them in the Slow Cooker. Cover with the lid and cook for 8 hours on Low. When done, remove the lid and serve warm or chilled. Enjoy1

190. Orange-Glazed Lamb Meatballs

Serves: 6 | Total Time: 7 hours 15 minutes

INGREDIENTS

2 garlic cloves, minced
3 lb ground lamb
1 shallot, chopped
1 tbsp orange zest
¼ tsp five-spice powder
½ tsp cumin powder
¼ tsp chili powder
½ cup dried apricots, chopped
1 tsp dried mint
1 red chili, chopped
2 cups tomato sauce
1 orange, juiced
1 bay leaf
2 rosemary sprigs
Salt and pepper to taste

DIRECTIONS

Combine tomato sauce, orange juice, bay leaf, rosemary, and red chili in your Slow Cooker. Mix ground lamb, shallot, garlic, orange zest, five-spice powder, cumin, chili powder, apricots, mint, salt, and pepper in a bowl. Shape the mixture into small meatballs and place them into the pot. Cover and cook for 7 hours on Low. When done, remove the lid and serve warm or chilled. Enjoy!

191. Teriyaki Chicken Wings

Serves: 6 | Total Time: 7 hours 15 minutes

INGREDIENTS

4 lb chicken wings
2 tbsp butter
½ cup hoisin sauce
½ cup teriyaki sauce
1 tbsp five-spice powder
½ tsp red pepper flakes

DIRECTIONS

Mix melted butter, hoisin sauce, teriyaki sauce, five-spice powder, and red pepper flakes in your Slow Cooker. Add chicken wings and toss until everything is well coated. Cover with the lid and cook for 7 hours on Low. When done, remove the lid and serve warm or chilled. Enjoy!

CHICKEN RECIPES

192. Sweet BBQ Chicken

Serves: 4 | Total Time: 6 hours 10 minutes

INGREDIENTS

4 chicken breast halves
2 tbsp hot pepper sauce
½ tsp cayenne pepper
½ tsp chili powder
2 tbsp Worcestershire sauce
½ cup honey
¼ tsp garlic powder
2 tsp lemon juice
2 tbsp Dijon mustard
1 cup ketchup
2 tbsp basmati rice, cooked
2 tbsp chopped chervil

DIRECTIONS

Layer the chicken in your Slow Cooker. Combine the hot sauce, cayenne pepper, chili powder, Worcestershire sauce, honey, garlic powder, lemon juice, mustard and ketchup in a bowl, mixing well. Add the sauce mixture to the Slow Cooker, coating the chicken with it. Cover and cook on Low heat for 6 hours. Shred the chicken using two forks, then cook for an additional 30 minutes. Stir the dish well before serving on top of cooked rice. Garnish with chervil before serving. Enjoy!

193. Caribbean Spice Chicken

Serves: 4 | Total Time: 6 hours 15 minutes

INGREDIENTS

2 potatoes, sliced
1 tsp garlic powder
1 tsp onion powder
1 tsp brown sugar
Salt and black pepper to taste
½ tsp ground smoked paprika
½ tsp ground allspice
¼ tsp ground cayenne pepper
¼ tsp ground nutmeg
1 tsp ground cinnamon
8 chicken legs

DIRECTIONS

Place the potatoes in your Slow Cooker. In a small bowl, blend the garlic powder, onion powder, brown sugar, paprika, allspice, cayenne pepper, salt, pepper, nutmeg, and cinnamon. Rub the spice mixture onto the chicken legs. Arrange them on top of the potatoes in the Slow Cooker. Cover and cook on Low for 8 hours. Serve.

194. Flavored Whole Chicken with Quinoa

Serves: 4 | Total Time: 6 hours 20 minutes

INGREDIENTS

2 carrots, sliced
2 large onions, sliced
1 (3.5-lb) whole chicken
Salt and black pepper to taste
2 tbsp lemon juice
2 garlic cloves, minced
1 tsp ground cumin
¼ cup tomato paste
½ cup raisins, soaked
1 tsp ground cinnamon
2 cups vegetable broth
2 tbsp flour
2 cups cooked quinoa
2 tbsp chopped fresh parsley

DIRECTIONS

Spray the inside of your Slow Cooker with cooking oil. Add in the carrots and onions. Season the chicken with salt, pepper, and cumin and transfer it to the Slow Cooker. Top the chicken with soaked raisins.

In a small mixing bowl, whisk together broth, tomato paste, lemon juice, flour, cinnamon, and garlic until well combined. Pour the broth mixture over the chicken. Cover and cook for 6 hours on Low. Once ready, serve hot over cooked quinoa and sprinkle with chopped fresh parsley before serving. Enjoy!

195. Lemongrass Thai Chicken

Serves: 6 | Total Time: 8 hours 20 minutes

INGREDIENTS

3 chicken breasts, cut into strips
½ cup roasted cashews, chopped
1 red bell pepper, cut into strips
3 green onions, chopped
¼ cup lime juice
2/3 cup almond butter
1 tbsp lemongrass paste
2 tbsp cornstarch
Salt and black pepper to taste
½ tsp red pepper flakes
3 cloves garlic, minced
1 tbsp ground cumin
½ cup chicken broth
1 large onion, chopped
¼ cup basil leaves, chopped
2 cups cooked jasmine rice

DIRECTIONS

Combine chicken, cashews, bell pepper, green onions, salt, black pepper, red pepper flakes, garlic, cumin, chicken broth, onion and basil in your Slow Cooker. Cover with the lid and cook on Low for 8 hours.

In a mixing bowl, add almond butter, lime juice, lemongrass paste, and cornstarch and 1 cup of cooking liquid. Add the sauce to the slow cooker and mix in when it becomes thick. Cover and cook for an additional 30 minutes on High. Garnish with basil leaves, cashews, and green onions. Serve over cooked jasmine rice. Enjoy!

196. Savory Fig Balsamic Chicken Wings

Serves: 4 | Total Time: 4 hours 10 minutes

INGREDIENTS

5 tbsp fig balsamic vinegar
2 lb chicken wings
Salt and black pepper to taste
3 garlic cloves, minced
1 tbsp fresh lime juice
¼ cup chicken broth
1/3 cup fig preserves
1/3 cup soy sauce
2 tsp chili paste
1 tsp ground coriander
3 tbsp cornstarch
2 tbsp cilantro, chopped

DIRECTIONS

Sprinkle the chicken wings with salt and pepper. Place them in your Slow Cooker. In a small bowl, combine fig preserves, broth, vinegar, soy sauce, garlic, lime juice, ground coriander, and chili paste. Mix well and pour the mixture over the chicken wings. Toss to coat. Close the lid and cook on High for 4 hours.

Whisk the cornstarch with ¼ cup cold water until smooth. Add to the slow cooker and stir gently. Cook for an additional 15 minutes on High, allowing the sauce to thicken. Serve topped with chopped cilantro. Enjoy!

197. Mango Honey-Garlic Chicken

Serves: 6 | Total Time: 4 hours 20 minutes

INGREDIENTS

6 chicken thighs, boneless, skinless
1 (20 oz) can mango chunks, drained with juice reserved
3 tbsp vegetable oil
¼ cup water
3 tbsp soy sauce
2 tbsp cornstarch
1 tbsp ginger root, minced
2 cloves garlic, minced
3 tbsp ketchup
1 tbsp honey
2 tbsp chopped cilantro

DIRECTIONS

Heat vegetable oil in a pan over medium heat. Cook the chicken until no pink meat remains, about 10 minutes. In a mixing bowl, combine honey, ginger, ketchup, garlic, soy sauce, and mango juice. Mix well. Add the cooked chicken and the mixture to your Slow Cooker. Close the lid and cook on High for 4 hours.

In another bowl, mix cornstarch and water. Add this mixture to the slow cooker to thicken the sauce. Stir gently. Drizzle the sauce over the chicken and serve, topped with chopped cilantro and mango chunks. Enjoy!

198. Curried Chicken Tikka Masala

Serves: 4 | Total Time: 2 hours 30 minutes

INGREDIENTS

4 chicken thighs
2 shallots, chopped
4 garlic cloves, minced
2 cups cooked basmati rice
1 cup diced tomatoes
1 lime, juiced
1 cup coconut milk
½ cup chicken stock
2 tbsp olive oil
2 tbsp curry powder
2 tbsp tomato paste
2 tbsp chopped cilantro
½ tsp turmeric powder
Salt and black pepper to taste

DIRECTIONS

Heat olive oil in a pan over medium heat, sauté chicken for 2-3 minutes until golden on all sides. Transfer it to your Slow Cooker. Add shallots, garlic, curry powder, turmeric powder, tomato paste, tomatoes, lime juice, coconut milk, chicken stock, salt, and pepper. Mix well. Cover with the lid and cook for 2 hours on High. Serve over cooked basmati rice and garnish with chopped cilantro. Enjoy!

199. Citrus-Infused Chicken

Serves: 4 | Total Time: 8 hours 10 minutes

INGREDIENTS

2 tsp red pepper flakes
1 cup orange juice
4 chicken breast halves
1/3 cup maple syrup
Salt and black pepper to taste
1 red bell pepper, thinly sliced
2 tbsp chopped cilantro

DIRECTIONS

Put the chicken breasts in your greased Slow Cooker. In a mixing bowl, combine red pepper flakes, orange juice, maple syrup, salt, and pepper. Mix well. Pour the mixture over the chicken and top with sliced red bell pepper. Cover with the lid and cook on Low for 8 hours. Serve hot, sprinkled with cilantro. Enjoy!

200. Glazed Chicken with Potatoes

Serves: 4 | Total Time: 8 hours 10 minutes

INGREDIENTS

8 chicken thighs, skin removed
1 cup orange marmalade
½ cup chicken broth
4 potatoes, chopped
Salt and black pepper to taste
1 tbsp soy sauce
1 tsp grated ginger

DIRECTIONS

Place the potatoes in your Slow Cooker. Season them with salt, pepper, soy sauce, and grated ginger. Place the chicken thighs on top and season with additional salt and pepper. In a small mixing bowl, combine chicken broth and orange marmalade. Mix well. Pour the mixture over the chicken. Cook on Low for 8 hours. Serve and enjoy!

201. Cheddar Herb Chicken

Serves: 4 | Total Time: 6 hours 15 minutes

INGREDIENTS

½ cup chicken stock
1 ½ cups grated cheddar cheese
4 chicken breasts
½ tsp cumin powder
¼ tsp chili powder
1 tsp dried thyme
Salt and black pepper to taste
1 tbsp olive oil
2 tbsp chopped fresh parsley

DIRECTIONS

In a small bowl, combine cumin powder, chili powder, salt, and pepper. Rub the spice mixture over the chicken breasts, ensuring they are well coated. Heat olive oil in a pan over medium heat. Add the chicken and sear on both sides until golden brown. Transfer it to your Slow Cooker. Top with thyme and pour in the chicken stock. Scatter the grated cheddar cheese on top of the chicken. Cook for 6 hours on Low. Serve, garnished with parsley.

202. Curried Chicken with Broccoli

Serves: 6 | Total Time: 3 hours 15 minutes

INGREDIENTS

½ head broccoli, cut into florets
2 chicken breasts, cubed
1 can (15-oz) lentils, rinsed
1 onion, chopped
1 celery stalk, sliced
1 carrot, sliced
1 cup vegetable stock
½ cup coconut milk
2 tbsp olive oil
1 tsp curry powder
¼ tsp chili powder
Salt and black pepper to taste

DIRECTIONS

Heat olive oil in a pan over medium heat. Cook the chicken for 2-3 minutes until golden brown on all sides. Transfer it to your Slow Cooker. Add onion, celery, carrot, broccoli, lentils, stock, coconut milk, curry powder, chili powder, salt, and pepper. Cover with the lid and cook for 3 hours on High. Enjoy!

203. Chicken and Vegetable Delight

Serves: 6 | Total Time: 6 hours 30 minutes

INGREDIENTS

FOR CHICKEN

2 garlic cloves, chopped
2 chicken breasts, cubed
½ lb baby spinach leaves
1 shallot, chopped
1 leek, sliced
1 ½ cups green peas
1 tbsp cornstarch
1 cup vegetable stock
¼ cup white wine

FOR TOPPING

½ cup cold butter, cubed
1 cup whole wheat flour
½ cup buttermilk, chilled
Salt and black pepper to taste

DIRECTIONS

Place shallot, leek, garlic, chicken, green peas, spinach, cornstarch, vegetable stock, wine, salt, and pepper in your Slow Cooker. Combine flour, butter, buttermilk, salt, and pepper in your blender. Pulse until crumbly. Pour the mixture over the chicken mixture. Cover with the lid and cook for 6 hours on Low. Serve right away and enjoy!

204. Mozzarella-Topped Chicken Breasts

Serves: 4 | Total Time: 4 hours 15 minutes

INGREDIENTS

1 onion, chopped
4 garlic cloves, minced
4 chicken breasts
2 tbsp butter
1 tsp dried Italian herbs
1 can cream of chicken soup
1 cup shredded mozzarella cheese
Salt and black pepper to taste
Fresh basil leaves for garnish

DIRECTIONS

Season chicken breasts with Italian herbs, salt, and pepper. Melt butter in a pan over medium heat and cook the chicken until golden brown on all sides. Transfer the chicken to your Slow Cooker. Add onion, garlic, cream of chicken soup, mozzarella cheese, and ½ cup of water. Cook for 4 hours on Low. Serve, garnished with basil.

205. Chicken and Squash Barley Salad

Serves: 6 | Total Time: 6 hours 15 minutes

INGREDIENTS

2 cups butternut squash cubes
1 lb ground chicken
1 onion, chopped
2 garlic cloves, chopped
1 cup pearl barley
1 cup sweet corn
2 cups vegetable stock
2 tbsp olive oil
2 tbsp chopped parsley
Salt and black pepper to taste
Zest of 1 lemon
Lemon wedges for serving

DIRECTIONS

Heat olive oil in a pan over medium heat. Place the ground chicken and cook it for 2-3 minutes until golden on all sides. Transfer chicken to your Slow Cooker. Add chopped onion, garlic, pearl barley, sweet corn, butternut squash cubes, vegetable stock, salt, and pepper. Cover with the lid and cook for 6 hours on Low. Sprinkle the zest over the salad. Toss gently. Serve hot, garnished with parsley, and accompanied by lemon wedges. Enjoy!

206. Cheesy Cauliflower Chicken Gratin

Serves: 6 | Total Time: 6 hours 15 minutes

INGREDIENTS

1 can condensed cream of chicken soup
1 head cauliflower, cut into florets
2 chicken breasts, cubed
½ tsp garlic powder
1 tsp cayenne pepper
Salt and black pepper to taste
1 ½ cups grated Parmesan cheese
1/2 cup breadcrumbs
2 tbsp chopped fresh parsley

DIRECTIONS

In your Slow Cooker, mix together cauliflower, chicken, garlic powder, cayenne pepper, condensed cream of chicken soup, salt, and pepper. Top with grated Parmesan cheese. Cover with the lid and cook for 6 hours on Low. Just before serving, sprinkle breadcrumbs over. Cover and let it cook for an additional 15 minutes until the breadcrumbs are golden and crispy. Serve immediately, garnished with chopped fresh parsley. Enjoy!

207. Smoked Pulled Chicken

Serves: 6 | Total Time: 8 hours 15 minutes

INGREDIENTS

2 onions, sliced
4 chicken breasts
1 cup apple cider
1 cup BBQ sauce
1 tsp grated ginger
1 tbsp Worcestershire sauce
½ tsp smoked paprika
Salt and black pepper to taste

DIRECTIONS

In your Slow Cooker, combine onions, chicken breasts, grated ginger, apple cider, BBQ sauce, salt, pepper, Worcestershire sauce, and smoked paprika. Cover with the lid and cook for 8 hours on Low. When done, remove the lid and, using two forks, shred the chicken. Serve and enjoy!

208. Chicken and Edamame Pilaf

Serves: 6 | Total Time: 6 hours 30 minutes

INGREDIENTS

1 cup frozen edamame
1 cup spinach leaves
1 peeled sweet potato, cubed
2 chicken breasts, cubed
½ cup wild rice
½ cup quinoa

1 leek, sliced
2 garlic cloves, chopped
2 cups vegetable stock
½ tsp dried sage
½ tsp dried oregano
Salt and black pepper to taste

DIRECTIONS

In your Slow Cooker, combine chicken, rice, quinoa, leek, garlic, edamame, spinach, sweet potato, vegetable stock, sage, oregano, salt, and pepper. Cover with the lid and cook on Low for 6 hours. After 6 hours, remove the lid, stir in the parsley, and serve warm. Enjoy!

209. Rustic Chicken Casserole

Serves: 6 | Total Time: 7 hours 30 minutes

INGREDIENTS

2 peeled potatoes, cubed
1 lb chicken breasts, cubed
2 carrots, sliced
2 celery stalks, sliced
1 parsnip, sliced
2 cups vegetable stock
1 thyme sprig
1 rosemary sprig
Salt and black pepper to taste
1 cup frozen green peas
2 cloves garlic, minced

DIRECTIONS

In your Slow Cooker, combine chicken, carrots, celery, parsnip, potatoes, vegetable stock, thyme, rosemary, salt, pepper, frozen green peas, and minced garlic. Toss to combine. Cover with the lid and cook for 7 hours on Low, allowing the flavors to meld and the vegetables to become tender. Serve warm and enjoy!

210. Cajun Chicken and Shrimp Jambalaya

Serves: 6 | Total Time: 8 hours 15 minutes

INGREDIENTS

1 lb fresh cleaned shrimp, peeled
1 ½ lb chicken thighs, cubed
2 large onions, chopped
2 red bell peppers, diced
1 celery stalk, sliced
2 garlic cloves, chopped
1 cup diced tomato
1 ½ cups chicken stock
2 tbsp olive oil
½ tsp Cajun seasoning
Salt and black pepper to taste
1 cup cooked brown rice

DIRECTIONS

Place a skillet over medium heat and warm olive oil. Add chicken thighs and cook for 5 minutes until golden on all sides. Transfer the chicken to your Slow Cooker. Add in onions, bell peppers, celery, garlic, Cajun seasoning, tomato, chicken stock, salt, and pepper. Cover with the lid and cook for 6 hours on Low. After 6 hours, add in the shrimp and continue cooking for another 2 hours. Serve over cooked brown rice and enjoy!

211. Mushroom Chicken Pasta

Serves: 6 | Total Time: 6 hours 15 minutes

INGREDIENTS

3 chicken thighs, cubed
2 celery stalks, sliced
2 shallots, chopped
2 garlic cloves, chopped
1 cup sour cream
2 cups sliced mushrooms
1 cup chicken stock
2 tbsp butter
1 tsp dried thyme
Salt and black pepper to taste
16 oz cooked fettuccine pasta

DIRECTIONS

In a pan over medium heat, melt butter. Add chicken thighs and cook until golden brown on all sides. Transfer the chicken to your Slow Cooker. Add in celery, shallots, garlic, thyme, sour cream, mushrooms, chicken stock, salt, and pepper. Cover with the lid and cook for 6 hours on Low. Serve over cooked fettuccine pasta and enjoy!

212. Spiced Yogurt Chicken

Serves: 6 | Total Time: 8 hours 15 minutes

INGREDIENTS

1 cup chicken broth
6 chicken thighs
½ cup plain yogurt
1 tbsp grated ginger
1 tsp curry powder
1 tsp garlic powder
½ tsp ground coriander
½ tsp ground turmeric
¼ tsp cayenne pepper
Salt and black pepper to taste
2 cups cooked basmati rice

DIRECTIONS

Season chicken thighs with ginger, curry powder, garlic powder, ground coriander, turmeric, cayenne pepper, salt, and pepper. Ensure the spices coat the chicken evenly. Place it into your Slow Cooker and pour in plain yogurt and chicken broth. Cover with the lid and cook for 8 hours on Low. Serve over basmati rice and enjoy!

213. Chicken with Asian Greens

Serves: 4 | Total Time: 6 hours 30 minutes

INGREDIENTS

1 onion, chopped
4 chicken thighs, boneless and skinless
1 head bok choy, shredded
4 garlic cloves, minced
2 tbsp soy sauce
1 tbsp honey
1 ½ tsp paprika
1 cup chicken stock

DIRECTIONS

In your Slow Cooker, combine chicken thighs, garlic, onion, soy sauce, honey, paprika, and chicken stock. Toss to coat the chicken evenly. Cover with the lid and cook for 4 hours on Low. After 4 hours, add in the shredded bok choy and continue cooking for another 2 hours, ensuring the bok choy becomes tender but still slightly crisp. Serve over steamed rice or noodles and enjoy!

214. Mushroom Chicken Pot Pie Casserole

Serves: 6 | Total Time: 6 hours 15 minutes

INGREDIENTS

2 chicken thighs, boneless and skinless, cubed
4 cups sliced cremini mushrooms
4 carrots, sliced
1 large onion, chopped
1 cup frozen peas
1 cup chicken broth
½ tsp dried thyme
1 sheet puff pastry
Salt and black pepper to taste

DIRECTIONS

In your Slow Cooker, combine sliced cremini mushrooms, cubed chicken thighs, carrots, chopped onion, frozen peas, dried thyme, chicken broth, salt, and pepper. Mix well. Top the mixture with a sheet of puff pastry. Cover with the lid and cook for 6 hours on Low. Serve hot and enjoy!

215. Sweet and Tangy Balsamic Glazed Chicken

Serves: 4 | Total Time: 6 hours 15 minutes

INGREDIENTS

½ cup chicken broth
4 chicken thighs
2 tbsp honey
1 tsp cumin powder
½ tsp smoked paprika
½ tsp garlic powder
2 tbsp balsamic vinegar
1 tbsp soy sauce

DIRECTIONS

Whisk together honey, cumin powder, smoked paprika, garlic powder, balsamic vinegar, and soy sauce in a bowl to create the glaze. Rub the chicken thighs with the glaze mixture. Coat them evenly and gently lift the skin to spread some under it. Place it into your Slow Cooker and pour in chicken broth. Cover with the lid and cook for 6 hours on Low. Serve immediately and enjoy!

216. Herb-Infused Garlic Butter Chicken

Serves: 6 | Total Time: 8 hours 15 minutes

INGREDIENTS

1 whole chicken
6 garlic cloves, minced
¼ cup butter, softened
½ cup chicken broth
2 tbsp chopped parsley
1 tsp dried thyme
Salt and black pepper to taste

DIRECTIONS

Blend softened butter, minced garlic, parsley, thyme, salt, and pepper in a bowl. Place the chicken on a cutting board and gently lift the skin of the breast and thighs. Fill the pockets between the skin and meat with the herb-infused butter mixture, spreading it evenly. Transfer it to your Slow Cooker and pour chicken broth around it. Cover and cook for 8 hours on Low. Serve warm and enjoy!

217. Infused Chicken Medley

Serves: 4 | Total Time: 6 hours 15 minutes

INGREDIENTS

4 chicken thighs, boneless and skinless
2 carrots, sliced
2 oranges, zest and juice
1 fennel bulb, sliced
1 onion, sliced
1 bay leaf
1 ½ cups chicken broth
Salt and black pepper to taste

DIRECTIONS

In your Slow Cooker, combine sliced carrots, orange zest and juice, chicken thighs, sliced fennel, sliced onion, bay leaf, chicken broth, salt, and pepper. Mix well to ensure the flavors meld. Cover with the lid and cook for 6 hours on Low. When done, remove the lid and serve warm. Enjoy!

218. Pancetta Chicken Chili

Serves: 8 | Total Time: 8 hours 15 minutes

INGREDIENTS

4 pancetta slices, chopped
2 lb chicken breasts, cubed
1 can (15 oz) white beans
1 can (15 oz) kidney beans
1 can (15 oz) sweet corn
2 celery stalks, sliced
2 large red onions, chopped
1 cup tomato sauce
2 cups red salsa
2 tbsp olive oil
1 tsp chili powder
1 tsp cumin powder
1 tsp garlic powder
1 ½ cups chicken stock
Salt and black pepper to taste
2 tbsp grated cheddar cheese

DIRECTIONS

In a pan over medium heat, warm olive oil. Add chopped pancetta and cook until crispy. Add in chicken and cook for 2-3 minutes until golden brown on all sides. Transfer it to your Slow Cooker. Add in red salsa, white beans, kidney beans, sweet corn, celery, onions, tomato sauce, chili powder, cumin powder, garlic powder, chicken stock, salt, and pepper. Cover and cook for 8 hours on Low. Serve hot, topped with grated cheddar cheese. Enjoy!

219. Asian-Inspired Sweet and Spicy Chicken

Serves: 6 | Total Time: 3 hours 15 minutes

INGREDIENTS

2 shallots, finely chopped
6 chicken thighs
2 garlic cloves, minced
¼ cup rice vinegar
¼ cup soy sauce
1 bay leaf
2 tbsp honey
½ tsp crushed red pepper flakes
Salt and black pepper to taste
2 cups cooked jasmine rice

DIRECTIONS

In your Slow Cooker, combine finely chopped shallots, minced garlic, chicken thighs, rice vinegar, soy sauce, bay leaf, honey, crushed red pepper flakes, salt, and pepper. Stir well to coat the chicken evenly. Cover with the lid and cook for 3 hours on High. Once done, remove the lid and serve over cooked jasmine rice. Enjoy!

220. Smoky BBQ Chicken

Serves: 6 | Total Time: 8 hours 15 minutes

INGREDIENTS

3 chicken thighs, boneless and skinless, halved
1 cup BBQ sauce
1 tsp mustard seeds
2 tbsp lemon juice
½ tsp garlic powder
2 tbsp maple syrup
½ tsp smoked paprika
1 tsp soy sauce
½ cup chicken stock
Salt and black pepper to taste

DIRECTIONS

Place chicken thighs, BBQ sauce, mustard seeds, lemon juice, garlic powder, maple syrup, smoked paprika, soy sauce, chicken stock, salt, and pepper in your Slow Cooker. Stir to coat the chicken evenly. Cover with the lid and cook for 8 hours on Low. Serve over rice, mashed potatoes, or your favorite side dish and enjoy!

221. Basic Cheesy Chicken

Serves: 2 | Total Time: 2 hours 15 minutes

INGREDIENTS

1 cup grated sharp cheddar cheese
2 chicken breasts
1 cup chicken broth
¼ tsp garlic powder
Salt and black pepper to taste

DIRECTIONS

In your Slow Cooker, combine grated sharp cheddar cheese, chicken breasts, chicken broth, garlic powder, salt, and pepper. Stir well to ensure the chicken is coated evenly. Cover with the lid and cook for 2 hours on High.

222. Swiss Chicken Supreme

Serves: 4 | Total Time: 3 hours 15 minutes

INGREDIENTS

1 can cream of mushroom soup
1 shallot, finely chopped
4 boneless chicken thighs
1 celery stalk, sliced
1 cup grated Gruyère cheese
Salt and black pepper to taste

DIRECTIONS

Season chicken thighs with salt and pepper. Place them in your Slow Cooker along with chopped shallot, celery, mushroom soup, ½ cup of water, and Gruyère cheese. Cover with the lid and cook for 3 hours on High, allowing the flavors to meld and the chicken to become tender. Serve warm and enjoy!

223. Blue Cheese Oregano Chicken

Serves: 4 | Total Time: 2 hours 15 minutes

INGREDIENTS

½ cup crumbled blue cheese
4 chicken thighs
1 tsp dried oregano
½ cup chicken stock
Salt and black pepper to taste

DIRECTIONS

Season chicken thighs with dried oregano, salt, and pepper. Place seasoned chicken and crumbled blue cheese in your Slow Cooker. Pour in chicken stock. Cover and cook on High for 2 hours. Serve warm and enjoy!

224. Lemon Herb Infused Chicken Thighs

Serves: 6 | Total Time: 6 hours 15 minutes

INGREDIENTS

6 chicken thighs
1 lemon, thinly sliced
6 garlic cloves, minced
½ cup chicken broth
2 tbsp butter
1 thyme sprig
1 rosemary sprig
Salt and black pepper to taste

DIRECTIONS

Season chicken thighs with salt and pepper and place them into your Slow Cooker. Arrange lemon slices and minced garlic on top of the chicken. Drizzle with butter and add thyme and rosemary sprigs. Pour chicken broth around the chicken. Cover and cook for 6 hours on Low. Serve warm and enjoy!

225. Sesame Hoisin Chicken

Serves: 6 | Total Time: 3 hours 15 minutes

INGREDIENTS

6 chicken thighs
2 tbsp soy sauce
1 tbsp honey
2 tbsp fresh lemon juice
2 tbsp hoisin sauce
1 tbsp sesame oil
1 tsp grated ginger
1 tbsp cornstarch
2 tbsp water
1 tbsp sesame seeds

DIRECTIONS

Place sesame oil, chicken thighs, soy sauce, honey, lemon juice, hoisin sauce, grated ginger, cornstarch, and water in your Slow Cooker. Stir well to ensure the chicken is coated evenly. Cover with the lid and cook for 3 hours on High. Once done, remove the lid and scatter with sesame seeds. Serve with your desired side dish and enjoy!

226. Pineapple-Ginger Chicken Drumsticks

Serves: 4 | Total Time: 5 hours 15 minutes

INGREDIENTS

2 green onions, chopped
2 lb chicken drumsticks
¼ cup chicken broth
1 tsp grated ginger
1 cup unsweetened pineapple juice
2 tbsp soy sauce
2 tbsp honey
¼ tsp red pepper flakes
2 cups cooked jasmine rice

DIRECTIONS

In your Slow Cooker, combine finely chopped green onions, chicken drumsticks, chicken broth, grated ginger, pineapple juice, soy sauce, honey, and red pepper flakes. Toss to coat the chicken evenly. Cover with the lid and cook for 5 hours on Low. Once done, remove the lid and serve over cooked jasmine rice. Enjoy!

227. Creole Chicken Stew

Serves: 6 | Total Time: 8 hours 15 minutes

INGREDIENTS

4 chicken breasts, cubed
1 can diced fire-roasted tomatoes
1 celery stalk, sliced
2 large onions, chopped
4 garlic cloves, chopped
1 jalapeno pepper, chopped
½ cup chicken stock
2 tbsp Cajun seasoning
Salt and black pepper to taste

DIRECTIONS

Place chicken, Cajun seasoning, fire-roasted tomatoes, celery, onions, garlic, jalapeño peppers, chicken stock, salt, and pepper in your Slow Cooker. Cover with the lid and cook for 8 hours on Low. Serve and enjoy!

228. Coconut Spice Chicken

Serves: 6 | Total Time: 6 hours 45 minutes

INGREDIENTS

6 chicken thighs
1 large onion, chopped
4 garlic cloves, chopped
2 tbsp butter
1 tsp curry powder
1 tsp garam masala
½ tsp ground coriander
¼ tsp chili flakes
1 ½ cups coconut milk
Salt and black pepper to taste
½ cup Greek yogurt

DIRECTIONS

In a pan over medium heat, melt butter. Brown chicken thighs on all sides until golden brown. Transfer the chicken to your Slow Cooker. Add in onion, garlic, curry powder, garam masala, coriander, chili flakes, coconut milk, salt, and pepper. Cover with the lid and cook for 6 hours on Low. Serve with Greek yogurt and enjoy!

229. Chicken Cordon Bleu

Serves: 4 | Total Time: 6 hours 15 minutes

INGREDIENTS

4 slices Swiss cheese
4 chicken breasts
4 thick ham slices
1 tsp dried thyme
½ cup chicken broth
Salt and black pepper to taste

DIRECTIONS

Season chicken breasts with thyme, salt, and pepper. Place them in your Slow Cooker. Top each chicken breast with a slice of ham and Swiss cheese. Pour chicken broth over the chicken. Cook for 6 hours on Low.

230. Kidney & Chicken Chili

Serves: 6 | Total Time: 6 hours 15 minutes

INGREDIENTS

2 ripe tomatoes, diced
1 can (15-oz) kidney beans
2 yellow bell peppers, sliced
6 chicken thighs
1 large fennel bulb, sliced
1 large onion, sliced
2 garlic cloves, chopped
1 cup chicken stock
1 rosemary sprig
Salt and black pepper to taste

DIRECTIONS

Combine chicken, fennel, onion, garlic, tomatoes, kidney beans, yellow bell peppers, rosemary, chicken stock, salt, and pepper in your Slow Cooker. Cover and cook on Low for 6 hours. Serve hot and enjoy!

231. Buffalo Chicken Drumsticks

Serves: 6 | Total Time: 7 hours 15 minutes

INGREDIENTS

2 cups hot buffalo sauce
3 lb chicken drumsticks
2 tbsp tomato paste
1 tbsp cider vinegar
1 tsp Worcestershire sauce
1 cup cream cheese
Salt and black pepper to taste

DIRECTIONS

In your Slow Cooker, toss chicken drumsticks with hot buffalo sauce, tomato paste, cider vinegar, Worcestershire sauce, cream cheese, salt, and pepper. Cover and cook on Low for 7 hours. Serve immediately and enjoy!

232. Tropical Mango Chipotle Chicken

Serves: 6 | Total Time: 2 hours 45 minutes

INGREDIENTS

2 chicken breasts, cut into thin strips
1 large onion, sliced
4 garlic cloves, chopped
1 mango, peeled and cubed
1 chipotle pepper, chopped
1 can pineapple chunks, drained
1 cup chicken stock
2 tbsp olive oil
½ tsp cumin powder
¼ tsp grated ginger
Salt and black pepper to taste

DIRECTIONS

Heat olive oil in a pan over medium heat. Sear the chicken for 2-3 minutes until golden brown, then transfer it to your Slow Cooker. Add in onion, garlic, mango, chipotle pepper, pineapple chunks, cumin, ginger, chicken stock, salt, and pepper. Cover with the lid and cook for 2 ½ hours on High. Serve warm and enjoy!

233. Black Bean and Chicken Casserole

Serves: 6 | Total Time: 6 hours 15 minutes

INGREDIENTS

3 chicken breasts, cubed
2 cans (15-oz) black beans
2 celery stalks, sliced
2 carrots, sliced
1 large onion, chopped
2 garlic cloves, chopped
2 tbsp olive oil
¼ cup dry white wine
1 cup chicken stock
Salt and black pepper to taste

DIRECTIONS

Heat olive oil in a pan over medium heat. Sear the chicken for 2-3 minutes until golden brown, then transfer it to your Slow Cooker. Add in black beans, celery, carrots, onion, garlic, white wine, chicken stock, salt, and pepper. Cover with the lid and cook for 6 hours on Low. Remove the lid and serve warm. Enjoy!

234. Maple Glazed Chicken Wings

Serves: 4 | Total Time: 3 hours 15 minutes

INGREDIENTS

1 ½ tsp smoked paprika
2 lb chicken wings
½ tsp chili flakes
1 tbsp maple syrup
½ cup chicken stock
Salt and black pepper to taste

DIRECTIONS

Combine chicken wings, smoked paprika, chili flakes, maple syrup, salt, and pepper until well coated in your Slow Cooker. Pour in chicken stock. Cover and cook for 3 hours on High. Serve warm and enjoy!

235. Sriracha Chicken Thighs

Serves: 6 | Total Time: 8 hours 15 minutes

INGREDIENTS

6 chicken thighs
¼ cup Sriracha sauce
½ cup marinara sauce
½ cup vegetable stock
2 tbsp butter
½ tsp garlic powder
½ tsp cumin powder
Salt and black pepper to taste

DIRECTIONS

In your Slow Cooker, combine chicken, Sriracha sauce, butter, garlic powder, marinara sauce, vegetable stock, cumin, salt, and pepper. Toss the ingredients to combine. Cover with the lid and cook on Low for 8 hours. Serve immediately and enjoy!

236. Creamy Peanut Butter Chicken

Serves: 4 | Total Time: 2 hours 15 minutes

INGREDIENTS

¼ cup creamy peanut butter
2 chicken breasts, cut into thin strips
2 tbsp soy sauce
1 tbsp Sriracha sauce
1 tbsp lime juice
1 tsp honey

DIRECTIONS

In your Slow Cooker, combine chicken, soy sauce, Sriracha sauce, creamy peanut butter, lime juice, and honey. Mix the ingredients thoroughly. Cover with the lid and cook for 2 hours on High. Serve warm and enjoy!

237. Sticky Chicken Drumsticks

Serves: 6 | Total Time: 3 hours 15 minutes

INGREDIENTS

2 lb chicken drumsticks
2 garlic cloves, chopped
1 orange, juiced
2 tbsp butter
1 thyme sprig
1 cup chicken broth
Salt and black pepper to taste

DIRECTIONS

Mix chicken, butter, orange juice, garlic, thyme, chicken broth, salt, and pepper in your Slow Cooker. Cover with the lid and cook for 3 hours on High. Remove the lid and serve warm. Enjoy!

238. Paprika Chicken Drumsticks

Serves: 6 | Total Time: 6 hours 15 minutes

INGREDIENTS

1 lb snap peas
6 chicken drumsticks
¼ cup vegetable stock
3 tbsp honey
½ tsp cumin powder
½ tsp smoked paprika
½ tsp fennel seeds
2 tbsp hoisin sauce

DIRECTIONS

Whisk together honey, cumin powder, smoked paprika, fennel seeds, and hoisin sauce in a bowl until the chicken is well coated. Place snap peas and vegetable stock in your Slow Cooker and stir to combine. Top with the chicken mixture. Cover with the lid and cook for 6 hours on Low. Remove the lid and serve warm. Enjoy!

239. Bean Chicken Chili with Corn

Serves: 6 | Total Time: 8 hours 15 minutes

INGREDIENTS

1 can (15 oz) pinto beans
1 can (10 oz) sweet corn
3 chicken breasts, cubed
1 can (15 oz) diced tomatoes
1 cup green salsa
1 tsp taco seasoning
½ tsp chili powder
½ cup cream cheese
Salt and black pepper to taste

DIRECTIONS

In your Slow Cooker, combine chicken, tomatoes, green salsa, pinto beans, corn, taco seasoning, chili powder, 1 cup of water, cream cheese, salt, and pepper. Mix the ingredients thoroughly. Cover with the lid and cook for 8 hours on Low. Serve immediately and enjoy!

240. Mediterranean Chicken Farro

Serves: 6 | Total Time: 6 hours 30 minutes

INGREDIENTS

2 ripe tomatoes, diced
1 cup farro, rinsed
2 chicken breasts, cubed
1 celery stalk, diced
¼ cup pitted green olives
2 cups chicken stock
1 tsp dried oregano
½ tsp dried basil
½ tsp dried parsley
Salt and black pepper to taste
Feta cheese for serving

DIRECTIONS

In your Slow Cooker, combine farro, chicken, celery, tomatoes, green olives, dried oregano, dried basil, dried parsley, chicken stock, salt, and pepper. Toss the ingredients to combine. Cover with the lid and cook for 6 hours on Low. Serve scattered with feta cheese. Enjoy!

241. Shredded Chicken Fajitas

Serves: 6 | Total Time: 6 hours 15 minutes

INGREDIENTS

3 chicken breasts, halved
1 cup chicken stock
1 tbsp taco seasoning
½ tsp fresh coriander
¼ tsp chili powder
Taco shells for serving

DIRECTIONS

In your Slow Cooker, stir together chicken, taco seasoning, chicken stock, coriander, and chili powder. Cook for 6 hours on Low. After cooking, shred the chicken finely using two forks. Serve the chicken in taco shells. Enjoy!

242. Chicken Cacciatore

Serves: 4 | Total Time: 8 hours 30 minutes

INGREDIENTS

4 bone-in, skin-on chicken thighs
1 cup tomato sauce
1 bell pepper, sliced
1 onion, diced
2 cloves garlic, minced
1 tsp dried oregano
½ tsp dried thyme
Salt and pepper to taste
½ lb cooked spaghetti

DIRECTIONS

Place chicken thighs, tomato sauce, 1 cup of water, bell pepper, onion, garlic, oregano, thyme, salt, and pepper in your Slow Cooker. Cook for 8 hours on Low. Serve the chicken cacciatore over cooked pasta. Enjoy!

BEEF RECIPES

243. Spiced Beef Brisket

Serves: 6 | Total Time: 6 hours 15 minutes

INGREDIENTS

2 lb beef brisket
2 tbsp honey
1 tsp cumin powder
1 tsp smoked paprika
1 tsp chili powder
1 tsp celery seeds
1 tsp salt
¼ cup apple cider vinegar
½ cup beef stock
1 cup BBQ sauce
1 tbsp Worcestershire sauce
2 tbsp soy sauce

DIRECTIONS

Combine honey, cumin powder, smoked paprika, chili powder, celery seeds, and salt in a bowl. Rub the spice mixture over the beef brisket, massaging until well coated. In your Slow Cooker, mix apple cider vinegar, stock, BBQ sauce, Worcestershire sauce, and soy sauce. Place the seasoned beef brisket in the Slow Cooker. Cover with the lid and cook for 6 hours on Low. Cut the brisket into slices before serving. Enjoy!

244. Beef Enchilada Casserole

Serves: 6 | Total Time: 6 hours 15 minutes

INGREDIENTS

1 lb ground beef
1 shallot, finely chopped
4 garlic cloves, minced
1 leek, thinly sliced
2 cups sliced mushrooms
2 cups enchilada sauce
6 corn tortillas, shredded
2 tbsp olive oil
2 cups grated Mexican blend cheese

DIRECTIONS

In a pan, warm olive oil over medium heat and sear ground beef for 2-3 minutes until browned. Add in shallot and garlic and sauté until fragrant. Transfer the mixture to your Slow Cooker. Add in leek, mushrooms, enchilada sauce, and shredded corn tortillas. Top the mixture with grated Mexican blend cheese. Cover with the lid and cook for 6 hours on Low. Serve warm and enjoy!

245. Dilly Beef Stuffed Peppers

Serves: 6 | Total Time: 6 hours 30 minutes

INGREDIENTS

1 lb ground beef
2 onions, finely chopped
2 garlic cloves, minced
6 red bell peppers
1 ½ cups beef broth
1 lime, juiced
1 egg
1 cup brown rice
2 tbsp chopped fresh parsley
1 tbsp chopped fresh dill
Salt and pepper to taste

DIRECTIONS

Combine ground beef, onions, garlic, egg, brown rice, parsley, dill, salt, and pepper in a bowl. Slice the tops of the red bell peppers and remove the seeds and membranes. Fill the peppers with the beef mixture. Place the stuffed peppers into your Slow Cooker.

In a separate bowl, mix beef broth and lime juice. Pour the mixture over the stuffed peppers in the Slow Cooker. Cover with the lid and cook for 6 hours on Low. When done, remove the lid and serve warm. Enjoy!

246. Chuck Roast with Vegetables

Serves: 4 | Total Time: 8 hours 10 minutes

INGREDIENTS

2 lb chuck roast, fat trimmed
1 onion, cut into 8 wedges
1 parsnip, sliced
2 carrots, sliced
2 sweet potatoes, quartered
1 tsp minced rosemary
1 cup beef broth
Salt and pepper to taste

DIRECTIONS

Season the chuck roast with salt and pepper. Place it in your Slow Cooker. Arrange the onion, parsnip, carrots, and sweet potatoes around the sides and on top of the meat. Sprinkle with rosemary then pour in the beef broth. Cover and cook for 8 hours on Low until the meat is tender and easily shreds apart. Serve and enjoy!

247. Beef Pot Roast with Herbs

Serves: 6 | Total Time: 7 hours 15 minutes

INGREDIENTS

1 ½ lb baby potatoes, halved
1 ½ lb beef chuck
2 large onions, thinly sliced
6 shallots, peeled
1 cup beef broth
½ cup dry white wine
1 thyme sprig
1 rosemary sprig
Salt and pepper to taste

DIRECTIONS

In your Slow Cooker, combine beef chuck, onions, shallots, baby potatoes, beef broth, white wine, thyme, rosemary, salt, and pepper. Cover with the lid and cook for 7 hours on Low. Serve warm. Enjoy!

248. Beef Sandwiches with Bacon & Onions

Serves: 6 | Total Time: 9 hours 15 minutes

INGREDIENTS

3 bacon slices, chopped
2 lb beef chuck roast
2 onions, thinly sliced
1 tsp onion powder
½ cup white wine
1 thyme sprig
Salt and pepper to taste

DIRECTIONS

In your Slow Cooker, combine beef chuck roast, onions, bacon, onion powder, white wine, thyme sprig, salt, and pepper. Cover with the lid and cook for 9 hours on Low. After cooking, use two forks to shred the beef finely. Serve on your favorite sandwich buns. Enjoy!

249. Beef Roast with Shiitake Mushrooms

Serves: 6 | Total Time: 7 hours 15 minutes

INGREDIENTS

½ lb shiitake mushrooms
½ lb baby carrots
2 lb beef chuck roast
¼ cup soy sauce
1 tbsp rice vinegar
1 ½ cups beef broth
1 rosemary sprig
Salt and pepper to taste

DIRECTIONS

In your Slow Cooker, toss beef chuck roast, shiitake mushrooms, baby carrots, soy sauce, rice vinegar, beef broth, rosemary sprig, salt, and pepper. Cover with the lid and cook for 7 hours on Low. Serve warm or chilled. Enjoy!

250. Italian Style Braised Beef

Serves: 6 | Total Time: 8 hours 15 minutes

INGREDIENTS

½ cup tomato juice
2 lb beef chuck roast
1 lemon, juiced
¼ cup red wine
1 rosemary sprig
1 tbsp maple syrup
1 tsp Italian seasoning
Salt and pepper to taste

DIRECTIONS

In your Slow Cooker, mix beef chuck roast, lemon juice, red wine, maple syrup, Italian seasoning, tomato juice, rosemary sprig, salt, and pepper. Cover with the lid and cook for 8 hours on Low, allowing the flavors to meld together and the beef to become tender. After cooking, use two forks to shred the beef finely. Serve and enjoy!

251. BBQ Beef Sirloin

Serves: 6 | Total Time: 6 hours 15 minutes

INGREDIENTS

2 lb beef sirloin roast
6 bacon slices, chopped
2 onions, thinly sliced
4 garlic cloves, minced
1 can (15 oz) kidney beans, rinsed
1 cup BBQ sauce
1 tsp chili powder
Salt and pepper to taste
Coleslaw for serving

DIRECTIONS

In your Slow Cooker, combine beef sirloin roast, bacon, onions, garlic, kidney beans, BBQ sauce, chili powder, water, salt, and pepper. Cover with the lid and cook for 6 hours on Low, allowing the flavors to meld together and the beef to become tender. When done, remove the lid and serve topped with coleslaw. Enjoy!

252. Hearty Beef Goulash

Serves: 6 | Total Time: 7 hours 15 minutes

INGREDIENTS

2 lb potatoes, cubed
1 ½ lb beef stew meat, cubed
2 red bell peppers, thinly sliced
1 carrot, thinly sliced
2 garlic cloves, minced
1 red onion, thinly sliced
1 can fire-roasted tomatoes
2 bay leaves
1 cup tomato sauce
1 cup beef broth
2 tbsp tomato paste
2 tbsp olive oil
1 tsp smoked paprika
1 tsp ground cumin
Salt and pepper to taste

DIRECTIONS

In a pan, warm olive oil over medium heat and sear beef stew for 2-3 minutes until browned, stirring often. Transfer it to your Slow Cooker. Add in bell peppers, carrot, garlic, red onion, fire-roasted tomatoes, tomato paste, potatoes, paprika, ground cumin, bay leaves, tomato sauce, beef broth, salt, and pepper. Cover with the lid and cook for 7 hours on Low. Serve and enjoy!

253. Beef Sirloin with Bell Peppers

Serves: 4 | Total Time: 6 hours 15 minutes

INGREDIENTS

2 lb beef sirloin, thinly sliced
4 garlic cloves, minced
2 shallots, thinly sliced
2 red bell peppers, thinly sliced
2 yellow bell peppers, thinly sliced
1 tbsp apple cider vinegar
1 tbsp soy sauce
2 cups beef broth
Salt and pepper to taste

DIRECTIONS

In your Slow Cooker, toss beef sirloin, garlic, shallots, bell peppers, apple cider vinegar, soy sauce, beef broth, salt, and pepper. Cover with the lid and cook for 6 hours on Low, allowing the flavors to meld together and the sirloin to become tender. When done, remove the lid and serve immediately. Enjoy!

254. Red Wine Chili con Carne

Serves: 6 | Total Time: 7 hours 15 minutes

INGREDIENTS

4 garlic cloves, minced
2 cans (15-oz) white beans, rinsed
2 lb ground beef
1 large onion, chopped
1 can fire-roasted tomatoes
2 leek stalks, sliced
2 carrots, sliced
2 tbsp olive oil
1 tsp red chili flakes
1 tsp cumin powder
¼ cup red wine
1 cup beef broth
Salt and pepper to taste
Sour cream for serving

DIRECTIONS

Heat the olive oil in a pan over medium heat and sauté garlic and onion until translucent, about 2-3 minutes. Add in ground beef and cook, breaking it apart with a spoon, until browned. Transfer the mixture to your Slow Cooker. Add in white beans, fire-roasted tomatoes, leek, carrots, red chili flakes, cumin powder, red wine, beef broth, salt, and pepper. Cover with the lid and cook for 7 hours on Low. Serve topped with sour cream. Enjoy!

255. Sweet Potato Shepherd's Pie

Serves: 6 | Total Time: 6 hours 45 minutes

INGREDIENTS

2 lb sweet potatoes, cubed
1 lb ground beef
1 onion, finely chopped
2 carrots, grated
2 celery stalks, chopped
4 garlic cloves, minced
1 cup diced tomatoes
½ cup grated cheddar cheese
2 tbsp olive oil
½ tsp chili powder
Salt and pepper to taste

DIRECTIONS

Put the sweet potatoes in a steamer and cook for 15 minutes until softened. Transfer to a bowl and mash them. Season with salt and pepper to taste. Set aside.

In a pan, warm olive oil over medium heat and sear ground beef for 2-3 minutes, stirring often. Transfer it to your Slow Cooker. Add in onion, carrots, celery, garlic, tomatoes, chili powder, water salt, and pepper. Top the mixture with the mashed sweet potatoes and top with grated cheddar cheese. Cover and cook for 6 hours on Low. Serve.

256. Authentic Beef Stroganoff

Serves: 6 | Total Time: 6 hours 15 minutes

INGREDIENTS

1 large onion, finely chopped
4 garlic cloves, minced
2 lb beef sirloin steak, cubed
1 cup light cream cheese
1 tbsp Worcestershire sauce
½ cup beef broth
Salt and pepper to taste
Whole wheat pasta or egg noodles for serving

DIRECTIONS

In your Slow Cooker, combine beef sirloin, onion, garlic, cream cheese, Worcestershire sauce, beef broth, salt, and pepper. Cover with the lid and cook for 6 hours on Low, allowing the flavors to meld together and the beef to become tender. When done, serve over whole wheat pasta or egg noodles. Enjoy!

257. Beef & Rice Stuffed Cabbage Rolls

Serves: 6 | Total Time: 6 hours 30 minutes

INGREDIENTS

2 onions, finely chopped
2 garlic cloves, minced
16 green cabbage leaves
1 ½ lb ground beef
½ cup white rice
1 ½ cups beef broth
2 lime, juiced
2 tbsp chopped parsley
1 egg
1 tbsp all-purpose flour
Salt and pepper to taste

DIRECTIONS

Blanch cabbage leaves in a pot with boiling water for 2 minutes until slightly softened. Strain and let cool aside. In a bowl, combine ground beef, rice, onions, garlic, parsley, egg, flour, salt, and pepper. Lay cabbage leaves on a flat surface. Spoon the beef mixture onto each leaf and wrap them, pulling the ends inside to form rolls. Place the cabbage rolls in your Slow Cooker and pour in beef broth and lime juice. Cook for 6 hours on Low. Serve.

258. Saucy Sirloin

Serves: 6 | Total Time: 8 hours 15 minutes

INGREDIENTS

8 baby potatoes, halved
2 lb beef sirloin steak, cubed
½ lb baby carrots
1 cup green salsa
1 cup beef broth
Salt and pepper to taste

DIRECTIONS

In your Slow Cooker, toss cubed beef sirloin steak, halved baby potatoes, baby carrots, green salsa, beef broth, salt, and pepper. Cover with the lid and cook for 8 hours on Low, allowing the flavors to meld together and the beef to become tender. Serve warm with potatoes and carrots. Enjoy!

259. Roasted Beef Casserole with Mushrooms

Serves: 6 | Total Time: 6 hours 30 minutes

INGREDIENTS

2 carrots, diced
2 lb beef stew meat, cubed
1 celery stalk, diced
1 can fire-roasted tomatoes
1 lb button mushrooms, sliced
2 bay leaves
1 red chili, chopped
1 cup beef broth
1 tbsp all-purpose flour
2 tbsp olive oil
Salt and pepper to taste

DIRECTIONS

Rub the beef with salt, pepper, and flour, ensuring it's well coated. Warm the olive oil in a pan over medium heat and sear beef for 2-3 minutes until golden brown on all sides. Transfer it to your Slow Cooker. Add in carrots, celery, fire-roasted tomatoes, mushrooms, broth, bay leaves, red chili, salt, and pepper. Cook for 6 hours on Low. When done, remove the lid and serve warm. Enjoy!

260. Beef Roast with Caramelized Onions

Serves: 6 | Total Time: 8 hours 30 minutes

INGREDIENTS

1 rutabaga, cubed
1 sweet potato, cubed
4 lb beef roast
1 onion, sliced
2 carrots, sliced
1 cup beef stock
3 tbsp olive oil
½ cup water
Salt and pepper to taste

DIRECTIONS

In a pan, warm olive oil over medium heat and sauté onion for 10 minutes until caramelized. Transfer it to your Slow Cooker. Add in beef roast, carrots, rutabaga, sweet potato, beef stock, water, salt, and pepper. Cover with the lid and cook for 8 hours on Low, allowing the flavors to meld together and the beef to become tender. Serve with caramelized onions and tender root vegetables. Enjoy!

261. Savory Beef Meatloaf

Serves: 6 | Total Time: 8 hours 10 minutes

INGREDIENTS

2 lb ground beef
1 sweet potato, shredded
1 onion, chopped
2 garlic cloves, minced
2 tbsp parsley, minced
1 tsp thyme, minced
½ cup ketchup
2 tbsp BBQ sauce
2 eggs
Salt and pepper to taste
1 tsp olive oil

DIRECTIONS

Combine ground beef, sweet potato, onion, garlic, parsley, thyme, ketchup, BBQ sauce, eggs, salt, and pepper in your Slow Cooker. Mix thoroughly using your hands. Grease your Slow Cooker with olive oil. Transfer the meat mixture to the cooker and shape it into a loaf. Pour in 2 cups of water. Cover and cook for 8 hours on Low. Allow the meatloaf to rest for 10 minutes before slicing and serving. Enjoy!

262. Beef Ragout with a Twist

Serves: 4 | Total Time: 8 hours 10 minutes

INGREDIENTS

4 (8-oz) pieces beef chuck roast
1 yellow onion, finely chopped
1 tsp minced fresh rosemary
1 garlic clove, minced
1 small carrot, diced
1 bay leaf
2 plum tomatoes, diced
2 cups beef broth
1 cup dry red wine
1 tbsp red wine vinegar
1 tsp tomato paste
Salt to taste

DIRECTIONS

Combine beef chuck roast, onion, rosemary, garlic, carrot, bay leaf, plum tomatoes, beef broth, red wine, red wine vinegar, and tomato paste in your Slow Cooker. Cover and cook on Low for 8 hours until the meat is tender. Remove the chuck roast, shred it with a fork, and return it to the pot. Stir well to enhance the flavors. Season with salt to taste. Serve over mashed potatoes and enjoy!

263. Meat-Mushroom Bolognese

Serves: 6 | Total Time: 8 hours 15 minutes

INGREDIENTS

6 garlic cloves, minced
2 onions, chopped
2 lb ground beef
1 lb cremini mushrooms, chopped
1 can fire-roasted tomatoes
3 tbsp olive oil
1 tsp chili powder
2 tbsp tomato paste
1 tsp dried basil
1 tbsp balsamic vinegar
1 cup beef broth
Salt and pepper to taste

DIRECTIONS

In a pan, warm olive oil over medium heat and sear ground beef for 2-3 minutes until golden on all sides. Transfer to your Slow Cooker. Add in garlic, onions, cremini mushrooms, fire-roasted tomatoes, chili powder, tomato paste, basil, and balsamic vinegar. Season with salt and pepper to taste. Cover with the lid and cook for 8 hours on Low, allowing the flavors to meld together. Serve over your favorite pasta and enjoy!

264. Strong Beef Roast

Serves: 6 | Total Time: 6 hours 30 minutes

INGREDIENTS

4 potatoes, halved
2 carrots, sliced
1 onion, quartered
2 lb beef stew meat, cubed
2 cups sliced mushrooms
2 cups snap peas, trimmed
1 celery stalk, sliced
1 cup beef broth
¼ cup prepared horseradish
1 cup water
Salt and pepper to taste

DIRECTIONS

In your Slow Cooker, toss beef stew, potatoes, carrots, onion, mushrooms, snap peas, celery, beef broth, water, salt, and pepper. Cover with the lid and cook for 6 hours on Low, allowing the flavors to meld together and the beef to become tender. When done, serve warm, accompanied by prepared horseradish. Enjoy!

265. Beef Sloppy Joes

Serves: 6 | Total Time: 7 hours 15 minutes

INGREDIENTS

1 onion, finely chopped
2 lb lean ground beef
¼ cup hot ketchup
½ cup tomato juice
1 tbsp Worcestershire sauce
Salt and pepper to taste

DIRECTIONS

In your Slow Cooker, combine ground beef, onion, Worcestershire sauce, hot ketchup, tomato juice, ½ cup of water, salt, and pepper. Cover with the lid and cook for 7 hours on Low, allowing the flavors to meld together and the beef to absorb the sauce. When done, spoon the mixture onto whole wheat or whole grain bread buns.

266. Black Bean Beef Casserole

Serves: 6 | Total Time: 7 hours 30 minutes

INGREDIENTS

2 carrots, diced
2 red bell peppers, diced
2 lb beef stew meat, cubed
2 red onions, chopped
2 garlic cloves, chopped
1 can (15 oz) black beans, rinsed
4 cups vegetable stock
1 leek, sliced
1 ½ cups red salsa
1 bay leaf
2 tbsp olive oil
1 tsp cumin seeds
1 tsp chili powder
Salt and pepper to taste

DIRECTIONS

In a pan, warm olive oil over medium heat. Add beef stew meat and cook for 2-3 minutes until golden on all sides. Transfer to your Slow Cooker. Add in red onions, garlic cloves, carrots, red bell peppers, leek, red salsa, bay leaf, cumin seeds, chili powder, black beans, stock, salt, and pepper. Cook for 7 hours on Low. Serve and enjoy!

267. Spicy Beef Casserole with Zucchini

Serves: 6 | Total Time: 2 hours 45 minutes

INGREDIENTS

2 garlic cloves, minced
3 zucchinis, thinly sliced
1 lb beef stew meat, cubed
1 leek, thinly sliced
1 can fire-roasted tomatoes
½ cup beef broth
2 bay leaves
2 tbsp olive oil
½ tsp paprika
¼ tsp ground cumin
Salt and pepper to taste

DIRECTIONS

In a pan, warm olive oil over medium heat. Add cubed beef stew meat and cook for 2-3 minutes until browned, stirring often. Transfer it to your Slow Cooker. Add in leek, garlic, zucchinis, fire-roasted tomatoes, beef broth, bay leaves, paprika, ground cumin, salt, and pepper. Cover with the lid and cook for 2 1/2 hours on High. When done, remove the bay leaves and serve immediately. Enjoy!

268. Picante Beef Roast with Fire-Roasted Corn

Serves: 6 | Total Time: 8 hours 15 minutes

INGREDIENTS

2 chipotle peppers in adobo sauce, chopped
1 can fire-roasted corn
2 lb beef chuck roast
1 tsp chili powder
½ tsp cayenne pepper
½ tsp cumin powder
½ tsp garlic powder
1 can fire-roasted tomatoes
1 cup beef broth
Salt and pepper to taste

DIRECTIONS

In your Slow Cooker, combine beef chuck roast, chipotle peppers, chili powder, cayenne pepper, cumin powder, fire-roasted tomatoes, fire-roasted corn, garlic powder, beef broth, salt, and pepper. Cover with the lid and cook for 8 hours on Low, allowing the flavors to meld together and the beef to become tender. When done, remove the lid and serve immediately. Enjoy!

269. Pepperoncini Beef Casserole

Serves: 8 | Total Time: 7 hours 15 minutes

INGREDIENTS

4 red bell peppers, sliced
2 lb beef stew meat, cubed
6 garlic cloves, minced
1 large onion, finely chopped
1 leek stalk, diced
2 tbsp olive oil
1 jar pepperoncini
1 can fire-roasted tomatoes
1 bay leaf
Salt and pepper to taste

DIRECTIONS

Heat olive oil in a pan over medium heat and sear beef for 2-3 minutes until golden brown on all sides. Transfer it to your Slow Cooker. Add in garlic, onion, leek, bell peppers, pepperoncini, fire-roasted tomatoes, bay leaf, salt, and pepper. Cover with the lid and cook for 7 hours on Low, allowing the flavors to meld together and the beef to become tender. When done, remove the lid and serve warm. Enjoy!

270. Rustic Ranch-Style Sirloin

Serves: 6 | Total Time: 8 hours 15 minutes

INGREDIENTS

2 sweet potatoes, cubed
1 celery stalk, sliced
2 lb beef stew meat, cubed
½ lb baby carrots
1 large onion, chopped
4 garlic cloves, minced
1 thyme sprig
1 cup dark beer
½ cup beef broth
Salt and pepper to taste

DIRECTIONS

In your Slow Cooker, combine beef, sweet potatoes, celery, baby carrots, onion, garlic, thyme sprig, dark beer, beef broth, salt, and pepper. Cover with the lid and cook for 8 hours on Low, allowing the flavors to meld together and the stew meat to become tender. When done, serve hot. Enjoy!

271. Corned Beef and Sauerkraut

Serves: 6 | Total Time: 8 hours 15 minutes

INGREDIENTS

1 lb sauerkraut, shredded
3 lb corned beef brisket
4 large carrots, sliced
1 large onion, sliced
½ tsp caraway seeds
Salt and pepper to taste

DIRECTIONS

In your Slow Cooker, mix sauerkraut, beef brisket, carrots, onion, caraway seeds, 1 cup of water, salt, and pepper. Cover with the lid and cook for 8 hours on Low, allowing the flavors to meld together and the corned beef to become tender. When done, serve warm. Enjoy!

272. Barbecue Short Ribs

Serves: 6 | Total Time: 9 hours 15 minutes

INGREDIENTS

1 cup Buffalo sauce
1 red onion, thinly sliced
2 lb beef short ribs
2 tsp balsamic vinegar
1 tbsp honey
1 tbsp hot sauce
1 tbsp apricot preserves
1 tbsp Worcestershire sauce
1 tsp Dijon mustard
1 tsp garlic powder
1 tsp cumin powder
Salt and pepper to taste

DIRECTIONS

In your Slow Cooker, mix Buffalo sauce, red onion, balsamic vinegar, honey, hot sauce, apricot preserves, Worcestershire sauce, Dijon mustard, garlic powder, cumin powder, salt, and pepper. Add in beef short ribs and toss until well coated with the sauce mixture. Cover with the lid and cook for 9 hours on Low. Enjoy!

273. Peppery Rump Roast

Serves: 6 | Total Time: 10 hours 15 minutes

INGREDIENTS

1 tsp smoked paprika
1 tsp chili powder
2 lb rump roast
1 tsp garlic powder
1 tsp crushed red pepper flakes
Salt and pepper to taste

DIRECTIONS

Mix smoked paprika, chili powder, garlic powder, and crushed red pepper flakes in a bowl. Rub the spice blend onto the rump roast, ensuring it's well coated. Place the seasoned meat in your Slow Cooker. Add mustard seeds, 1 cup of water, salt, and pepper. Cook for 10 hours on Low. After cooking, slice the rump roast and serve hot.

274. Marinara Flank Steaks

Serves: 4 | Total Time: 5 hours 15 minutes

INGREDIENTS

2 cups marinara sauce
4 flank steaks
1 cup shredded cheddar cheese
1 tbsp balsamic vinegar
1 tsp dried Italian herbs
Salt and pepper to taste

DIRECTIONS

Place flank steaks in the Slow Cooker. Pour marinara sauce and balsamic vinegar over the steaks. Sprinkle with dried Italian herbs, salt, and pepper. Scatter shredded cheddar cheese on top. Cover with the lid and cook for 5 hours on Low, allowing the flavors to meld and the steaks to tenderize. Once cooked, serve warm. Enjoy!

275. Sirloin Casserole with Zesty Slaw

Serves: 6 | Total Time: 6 hours 30 minutes

INGREDIENTS

1 lb beef sirloin, cut into thin strips
1 small head red cabbage, shredded
2 ripe tomatoes, diced
1 cup white rice
1 onion, chopped
1 carrot, grated
1 cup beef stock
2 tbsp olive oil
2 tbsp tomato paste
½ tsp cumin seeds
½ tsp chili powder
Salt and pepper to taste

DIRECTIONS

Heat olive oil in a pan over medium heat. Cook beef for 2-3 minutes until golden, then transfer it to your Slow Cooker. Add cabbage, onion, carrot, tomatoes, rice, beef stock, ¼ cup of water, tomato paste, cumin seeds, chili powder, salt, and pepper. Cover and cook on Low for 6 hours. Serve warm with a side of zesty coleslaw. Enjoy!

276. Buffalo Ground Beef

Serves: 6 | Total Time: 7 hours 15 minutes

INGREDIENTS

1 large bell pepper, chopped
4 garlic cloves, chopped
2 celery stalks, chopped
2 lb ground beef
1 ½ cups Buffalo sauce
½ cup beef broth
1 tbsp apple cider vinegar
1 tsp Dijon mustard
1 tbsp agave syrup
Salt and pepper to taste

DIRECTIONS

Combine ground beef, bell pepper, garlic, celery, apple cider vinegar, mustard, agave syrup, Buffalo sauce, beef broth, salt, and pepper in your Slow Cooker. Cover and cook on Low for 7 hours. Serve warm and enjoy!

277. Sirloin & Okra Casserole

Serves: 6 | Total Time: 6 hours 15 minutes

INGREDIENTS

1 ½ lb sirloin steak, cut into strips
2 large sweet potatoes, cubed
1 can (15 oz) diced tomatoes
1 large onion, chopped
4 garlic cloves, minced
12 oz frozen okra, chopped
1 cup beef stock
1 thyme sprig
Salt and pepper to taste

DIRECTIONS

Combine beef, onion, garlic, tomatoes, okra, sweet potatoes, beef stock, thyme, salt, and pepper in your Slow Cooker. Cover and cook on Low for 6 hours. Just before serving, sprinkle with chopped parsley. Serve and enjoy!

278. Beef Barbacoa

Serves: 6 | Total Time: 6 hours 30 minutes

INGREDIENTS

2 yellow onions, sliced
4 garlic cloves, minced
2 lb beef chuck roast
3 tbsp red wine vinegar
1 ½ cups tomato sauce
Salt and pepper to taste

DIRECTIONS

Combine chuck roast, onions, garlic, wine vinegar, tomato sauce, salt, and pepper in your Slow Cooker. Cover and cook on Low for 6 hours. Serve hot and enjoy!

279. Tomato Beef Roast

Serves: 6 | Total Time: 5 hours 15 minutes

INGREDIENTS

1 shallot, finely chopped
4 garlic cloves, minced
4 heirloom tomatoes, cubed
2 lb beef stew meat, cubed
1 cup beef broth
2 tbsp olive oil
½ tsp ground cumin
½ tsp dried oregano
Salt and pepper to taste

DIRECTIONS

In a pan over medium heat, warm the olive oil and sear beef for 5 minutes until golden brown on all sides. Transfer the browned beef, shallot, garlic, heirloom tomatoes, beef broth, ground cumin, oregano, salt, and pepper to your Slow Cooker. Cover with the lid and cook for 5 hours on Low, allowing the flavors to meld together and the beef to become tender. When done, serve warm. Enjoy!

280. Mustardy Beef Roast

Serves: 6 | Total Time: 10 hours 15 minutes

INGREDIENTS

1 cup apple juice
2 lb beef chuck roast
2 tbsp all-purpose flour
2 tbsp mustard seeds
1 tsp prepared horseradish
Salt and pepper to taste

DIRECTIONS

Rub beef chuck roast with salt, pepper, and flour, ensuring it's well coated. Place it in your Slow Cooker. Add mustard seeds, prepared horseradish, apple juice, ½ cup of water, salt, and pepper. Stir to combine. Cook for 10 hours on Low. When done, remove the lid and serve immediately. Enjoy!

281. Spicy Beef Curry

Serves: 6 | Total Time: 7 hours 15 minutes

INGREDIENTS

1 cup diced tomatoes
1 cup sweet corn
2 lb beef stew meat, cubed
2 garlic cloves, minced
1 large onion, chopped
1 jalapeño pepper, chopped
1 cup beef broth
2 tbsp olive oil
1 tsp grated ginger
1 tbsp curry powder
1 bay leaf
1 lemongrass stalk, crushed
Salt and pepper to taste
2 tbsp chopped cilantro

DIRECTIONS

In a pan over medium heat, warm the olive oil and sear beef for 5 minutes until golden brown on all sides. Transfer it to your Slow Cooker. Add in garlic, onion, jalapeño pepper, ginger, curry powder, tomatoes, sweet corn, beef broth, bay leaf, lemongrass, salt, and pepper. Cover with the lid and cook for 7 hours on Low, allowing the flavors to meld together and the beef to become tender. Garnish with chopped cilantro. Enjoy!

282. Three-Bean Beef Chili with Bacon & Cheddar

Serves: 6 | Total Time: 6 hours 15 minutes

INGREDIENTS

2 carrots, diced
1 celery stalk, diced
4 garlic cloves, chopped
1 lb ground beef
4 pancetta slices, chopped
1 can (15 oz) black beans
1 can (15 oz) cannellini beans
1 can (15 oz) kidney beans
1 ½ cups grated cheddar

2 tbsp olive oil
1 tbsp molasses
¼ tsp cayenne pepper
1 cup beef stock
¼ cup tomato sauce
Salt and pepper to taste

DIRECTIONS

In a pan, heat olive oil over medium heat. Add ground beef and pancetta and cook for 5 minutes, stirring often. Transfer to Slow Cooker. Add in beans, beans, beans, carrots, celery, garlic, molasses, cayenne pepper, stock, tomato sauce, salt, and pepper. Sprinkle with cheddar cheese. Cover and cook on Low for 6 hours. Enjoy!

283. Wine-Glazed Chuck Roast with Onions

Serves: 6 | Total Time: 7 hours 15 minutes

INGREDIENTS

2 yellow onions, sliced
2 lb beef chuck roast
1 cup dark beer
1 thyme sprig
1 tsp ground coriander
1 tsp cumin powder
Salt and pepper to taste

DIRECTIONS

Season the chuck roast with ground coriander, cumin, salt, and pepper, ensuring an even coating. Place the seasoned chuck roast in the Slow Cooker. Add onions, dark beer, and thyme sprig. Cover with the lid and cook for 7 hours on Low, allowing the flavors to meld and the beef to become tender. After cooking, slice the beef and serve it with the glazed red onions. Enjoy!

284. Sunday Night Cheeseburger Casserole

Serves: 6 | Total Time: 7 hours 30 minutes

INGREDIENTS

1 can condensed cream of mushroom soup
1 ½ lb beef sirloin, cut into strips
1 cup processed meat, shredded
2 potatoes, sliced
1 celery stalk, sliced
2 onions, sliced
1 cup sliced mushrooms
1 cup grated mozzarella cheese
Salt and pepper to taste

DIRECTIONS

In your Slow Cooker, combine beef sirloin, potatoes, celery, onions, mushrooms, condensed cream of mushroom soup, salt, and pepper. Scatter the shredded processed meat on the mixture, followed by grated mozzarella cheese. Cover with the lid and cook for 7 hours on Low, allowing the flavors to meld and the casserole to become tender and cheesy. Once cooked, serve warm. Enjoy!

285. Coffee-Infused Flank Steak

Serves: 6 | Total Time: 4 hours 15 minutes

INGREDIENTS

4 garlic cloves, minced
2 lb flank steak
1 cup strong brewed coffee
½ cup beef stock
2 tbsp olive oil
1 bay leaf
Salt and pepper to taste

DIRECTIONS

In your Slow Cooker, combine garlic, olive oil, strong brewed coffee, beef stock, bay leaf, salt, and pepper. Add the flank steak to the mixture. Cover with the lid and cook for 4 hours on High, allowing the flavors to meld and the sirloin to absorb the coffee-infused richness. Once cooked, slice the flank steak and serve it with the flavorful coffee-infused sauce. Enjoy!

286. Winter Beef Casserole

Serves: 6 | Total Time: 8 hours 30 minutes

INGREDIENTS

2 carrots, sliced
2 cups butternut squash, cubed
1 celery root, cubed
2 lb beef sirloin roast, cubed
3 garlic cloves, chopped
4 potatoes, cubed
1 turnip, peeled and cubed
1 bay leaf
1 lime, juiced
1 tsp Worcestershire sauce
1 cup beef broth
Salt and pepper to taste

DIRECTIONS

In your Slow Cooker, combine beef sirloin, carrots, butternut squash, celery root, garlic, potatoes, turnip, bay leaf, lime juice, Worcestershire sauce, beef broth, salt, and pepper. Cover with the lid and cook for 8 hours on Low, allowing the flavors to meld and the vegetables to become tender. After cooking, serve warm. Enjoy!

287. Traditional Bolognese Pasta

Serves: 6 | Total Time: 6 hours 15 minutes

INGREDIENTS

1 can (15 oz) crushed tomatoes
2 lb ground beef
1 carrot, grated
1 celery stalk, chopped
4 garlic cloves, minced
2 tbsp olive oil
2 tbsp marinara sauce
½ tsp dried oregano
½ tsp dried basil
¼ cup red wine
½ cup beef broth
Salt and pepper to taste
2 tbsp grated mozzarella cheese
16 oz cooked pasta

DIRECTIONS

In a pan over medium heat, warm the olive oil. Add the ground beef and cook for 2-3 minutes, stirring often until browned. Transfer it to the Slow Cooker. Add in carrot, celery, garlic, tomatoes, marinara sauce, dried oregano, basil, red wine, beef broth, salt, and pepper. Stir to combine. Cover and cook for 6 hours on Low, allowing the flavors to meld and the sauce to thicken. Serve over cooked pasta. Enjoy!

288. Southern Sirloin

Serves: 6 | Total Time: 8 hours 15 minutes

INGREDIENTS

1 chipotle pepper, chopped
1 green chile pepper, chopped
2 lb beef sirloin roast
1 shallot, chopped
1 cup Buffalo sauce
1 tbsp maple syrup
½ tsp garlic powder
½ tsp chili powder
Salt and pepper to taste

DIRECTIONS

In your Slow Cooker, stir chipotle pepper, red bell pepper, shallot, Buffalo sauce, maple syrup, garlic powder, chili powder, salt, and pepper. Add beef sirloin and toss until well coated. Cover and cook on Low for 8 hours. Serve.

289. Juicy & Savory Beef Steaks

Serves: 4 | Total Time: 8 hours 15 minutes

INGREDIENTS

2 yellow bell peppers, sliced
1 red onion, sliced
1 can (15 oz) diced tomatoes
4 beef steaks
2 tbsp olive oil
2 tbsp all-purpose flour
1 cup beef broth
Salt and pepper to taste

DIRECTIONS

Rub beef steaks with salt, pepper, and flour. Warm olive oil in a pan over medium heat. Cook beef for 5 minutes until golden on all sides. Transfer to your Slow Cooker. Add yellow bell peppers, red onion, beef broth, and tomatoes. Cover and cook on Low for 8 hours. Serve and enjoy!

290. Easy Beef Fajitas

Serves: 6 | Total Time: 6 hours 30 minutes

INGREDIENTS

2 onions, chopped
3 garlic cloves, minced
4 potatoes, cubed
2 lb beef chuck roast, cubed
1 red bell pepper, diced
1 green bell pepper, diced
¼ tsp red chili flakes
½ tsp cumin powder
1 ½ cups beef stock
1 cup tomato sauce
Salt and pepper to taste

DIRECTIONS

In your Slow Cooker, combine beef chuck roast, red bell peppers, onions, garlic, potatoes, red chili flakes, cumin, beef stock, tomato sauce, salt, and pepper. Cover and cook on Low for 6 hours. Serve over rice or enjoy it wrapped in tortillas or burritos. Enjoy!

291. Beef Chili

Serves: 6 | Total Time: 8 hours 15 minutes

INGREDIENTS

2 red onions, chopped
4 garlic cloves, chopped
1 lb dried kidney beans
1 can fire-roasted tomatoes
2 lb beef meat, cubed
2 cups vegetable broth
2 serrano peppers, chopped
1 tsp dried oregano
1 tsp dried basil
1 tsp cumin powder
1 tsp chili powder
Salt and pepper to taste

DIRECTIONS

Stir onions, garlic, beans, tomatoes, broth, serrano peppers, oregano, basil, cumin, chili powder, beef meat, salt, and pepper in your Slow Cooker. Cover with the lid and cook for 8 hours on Low. Serve warm and enjoy!

292. Autumn Beef Medley

Serves: 4 | Total Time: 6 hours 15 minutes

INGREDIENTS

1 lb beef stew meat, cubed
2 baby carrots, chopped
2 cups butternut squash, diced
1 onion, chopped
2 cloves garlic, minced
1 cup mushrooms, sliced
1 cup beef broth
½ cup red wine
2 tbsp tomato paste
1 tsp dried thyme
1 tsp dried rosemary
1 tsp paprika
Salt and black pepper to taste
2 tbsp olive oil

DIRECTIONS

Season the beef with salt and pepper. Warm olive oil in a skillet over medium heat, brown the beef and then transfer it to your Slow Cooker. Sauté onions, garlic, mushrooms, carrots, and butternut squash in the same skillet. Add sautéed veggies to your Slow Cooker.

Whisk together broth, wine, tomato paste, and spices. Pour over beef and veggies. Cook on low for 6-8 hours. Serve and enjoy!

PORK RECIPES

293. Sticky Sweet BBQ Pork Ribs

Serves: 8 | Total Time: 8 hours 15 minutes

INGREDIENTS

5 lb pork baby back ribs
1 cup BBQ sauce
1 cup apple juice
2 tbsp olive oil
4 tbsp honey
1 tbsp molasses
1 tsp chili powder
1 tsp dried thyme
Salt to taste

DIRECTIONS

Combine honey, molasses, olive oil, chili powder, thyme, and salt in a bowl. Rub ribs with the mixture until well-coated. Transfer them to your Slow Cooker. Pour in BBQ sauce and apple juice. Cook for 8 hours on Low. Serve.

294. Caramelized Onion-Infused Pork Tenderloin

Serves: 6 | Total Time: 8 hours 15 minutes

INGREDIENTS

3 large yellow onions, sliced
2 lb pork tenderloin
6 pancetta slices
1 thyme sprig
½ cup white wine
½ cup vegetable broth
2 tbsp olive oil
Salt and pepper to taste

DIRECTIONS

Heat the olive oil in a pan over medium heat and sauté onions for 10 minutes until softened and caramelized. Transfer them to your Slow Cooker. Add the pork, pancetta, thyme, wine, vegetable broth, salt, and pepper. Cover and cook for 8 hours on Low. Serve warm and enjoy!

295. Glazed Pork Ham with Fennel

Serves: 8 | Total Time: 6 hours 15 minutes

INGREDIENTS

2 fennel bulbs, sliced
1 grapefruit, zested and juiced
1 (4-lb) pork ham
½ cup white wine
1 cup chicken broth
2 bay leaves
1 thyme sprig
Salt and pepper to taste

DIRECTIONS

Combine fennel, grapefruit zest, juice, white wine, chicken broth, bay leaves, thyme, salt, and pepper in your Slow Cooker. Top with the pork ham. Cover with the lid and cook for 6 hours on Low. Serve immediately and enjoy!

296. Citrus-Marinated Cuban Pork Tacos

Serves: 4 | Total Time: 8 hours 20 minutes

INGREDIENTS

1 tbsp olive oil
1 lb pork shoulder, cut into chunks
1 orange, zested and juiced
1 lime, zested and juiced
2 garlic cloves, minced
½ tsp smoked paprika
1 tsp ground cumin
1 tsp ground coriander
Salt and pepper to taste
1 yellow onion, thinly sliced
1 red bell pepper, sliced
1 green bell pepper, sliced
1 cup vegetable broth
8 corn tortillas, warm
2 tbsp fresh cilantro, chopped

DIRECTIONS

Coat your slow cooker with olive oil and introduce the pork. In a small bowl, whisk together the orange zest, orange juice, lime zest, lime juice, garlic, smoked paprika, cumin, coriander, broth, salt, and pepper. Pour over the pork. Place the onion and bell peppers around and on top of the pork.

Cover and cook for 8 hours on Low until the meat is tender and cooked through. When ready, remove the pork to a plate and let it rest for 10 minutes. Shred it with a fork. Add the shredded meat back to the slow cooker and toss it with the vegetables and juices. Divide the meat mixture among the tortillas and top with cilantro. Serve.

297. Smoky Chipotle Pork Chili

Serves: 6 | Total Time: 8 hours 30 minutes

INGREDIENTS

2 cans (15-oz) navy beans
1 can fire-roasted tomatoes
2 lb pork shoulder, cubed
2 shallots, chopped
4 garlic cloves, chopped
3 chipotle peppers, chopped
1 cup tomato sauce
1 cup chicken stock
2 tbsp olive oil
1 tsp smoked paprika
½ tsp ground coriander
2 tbsp tomato paste
2 bay leaves
Salt and pepper to taste
1 lemon, juiced

DIRECTIONS

In a pan over medium heat, warm olive oil. Add pork and cook until golden on all sides. Transfer to the Slow Cooker. Add in shallots, garlic, chipotle peppers, navy beans, fire-roasted tomatoes, smoked paprika, coriander, tomato sauce, chicken stock, tomato paste, bay leaves, salt, and pepper. Cover and cook for 8 hours on Low. Sprinkle with lemon juice before serving. Enjoy!

298. Pork Chops with Caramelized Apples & Onions

Serves: 4 | Total Time: 8 hours 10 minutes

INGREDIENTS

2 apples, cored, peeled, and cut into 8 wedges
1 tbsp butter, melted
1 large onion, cut into rings
¼ tsp ground nutmeg
¼ cup apple juice
4 pork chops
Salt and pepper to taste

DIRECTIONS

Brush your Slow Cooker with butter. Add the apples, onion, and nutmeg; stir to combine. Pour in the apple juice. Sprinkle the pork with salt and pepper. Arrange the chops on top and cover. Cook for 8 hours on Low until the apples and onions are caramelized and the pork is tender and cooked through. Serve and enjoy!

299. Balsamic Pork with Savory Potatoes

Serves: 4 | Total Time: 8 hours 10 minutes

INGREDIENTS

1 tbsp olive oil
1 red onion, sliced
4 sweet potatoes, sliced
2 garlic cloves, minced
1 lb pork loin, trimmed
Salt and pepper to taste
½ cup balsamic vinegar
1 cup vegetable broth

DIRECTIONS

Coat the inside of your slow cooker with olive oil. Add the onion, sweet potatoes, and garlic and stir to combine. Season the pork loin with salt and pepper. Place the loin on top of the vegetables. Pour the balsamic vinegar and vegetable broth over the meat. Cook for 8 hours on Low. Serve and enjoy!

300. Rosemary Pork Chops with Tender Potatoes

Serves: 4 | Total Time: 8 hours 10 minutes

INGREDIENTS

4 sweet potatoes, diced
1 tbsp chopped rosemary
2 garlic cloves, minced
1 cup vegetable broth
4 pork chops
Salt and pepper to taste

DIRECTIONS

Add sweet potatoes, garlic, and vegetable broth to your slow cooker, then gently mix them together. Season the pork chops with salt and pepper and arrange them on top of the sweet potatoes. Cover and cook for 8 hours on Low until the sweet potatoes are completely soft and the pork is cooked through. Sprinkle with rosemary. Serve and enjoy!

301. Spiced Pork Tenderloin in Rich Red Salsa

Serves: 6 | Total Time: 8 hours 15 minutes

INGREDIENTS

2 yellow onions, sliced
2 lb pork tenderloin
1 tsp cumin powder
1 tsp ground coriander
1 tsp chili powder
2 tbsp agave syrup
2 cups red salsa
¼ cup red wine
Salt and pepper to taste

DIRECTIONS

Blend cumin, coriander seeds, chili powder, agave syrup, salt, and pepper in a bowl. Rub the pork tenderloin with the spice mixture until well-coated. In your Slow Cooker, Stir red salsa, onions, and wine and top with the seasoned pork. Cover and cook for 8 hours on Low. Serve and enjoy!

302. Salsa Verde Pork Shoulder

Serves: 8 | Total Time: 7 hours 15 minutes

INGREDIENTS

2 lb tomatillos, chopped
2 lb pork shoulder, cubed
1 large onion, chopped
4 garlic cloves, minced
2 green chilis, chopped
1 ½ cups vegetable broth
2 tbsp olive oil
1 tsp dried oregano
1 tsp cumin powder
½ tsp ground coriander
¼ tsp chili powder
1 bunch cilantro, chopped
Salt and pepper to taste

DIRECTIONS

Heat olive oil in a pan over medium heat and sear pork for 2-3 minutes until golden on all sides. Transfer it to your Slow Cooker. Add tomatillos, onion, garlic, oregano, cumin, coriander, chili powder, cilantro, green chilis, vegetable broth, salt, and pepper. Cover with the lid and cook for 7 hours on Low. Serve warm and enjoy!

303. Golden Bourbon Glazed Pork Chops

Serves: 6 | Total Time: 8 hours 15 minutes

INGREDIENTS

4 Golden apples, cored and sliced
6 pork loin chops
½ cup unsweetened applesauce
¼ cup bourbon
½ cup chicken broth
1 thyme sprig
1 rosemary sprig
Salt and pepper to taste

DIRECTIONS

Season pork chops with salt and pepper. Stir apples, applesauce, bourbon, chicken broth, thyme, and rosemary in your Slow Cooker and top with pork chops. Cover with the lid and cook for 8 hours on Low. Remove the lid and drizzle the sauce over the chops to serve. Enjoy!

304. Spicy Marinara Pork Roast

Serves: 4 | Total Time: 3 hours 15 minutes

INGREDIENTS

2 tbsp marinara sauce
2 lb pork roast, cubed
½ cup tomato sauce
½ cup chicken stock
2 tbsp olive oil
¼ tsp paprika
Salt and pepper to taste

DIRECTIONS

In the Slow Cooker, combine olive oil, pork roast, marinara sauce, chicken stock, tomato paste, paprika, salt, and pepper. Cover and cook for 3 hours on High. Serve and enjoy!

305. Greek Pork Chops

Serves: 6 | Total Time: 6 hours 15 minutes

INGREDIENTS

2 green onions, chopped
6 pork chops, bone-in
1 cup Greek yogurt
½ cup chicken broth
2 tbsp chopped parsley
Salt and pepper to taste

DIRECTIONS

In your Slow Cooker, mix pork chops, Greek yogurt, chicken broth, green onions, parsley, salt, and pepper. Cover and cook for 6 hours on Low. Drizzle with the creamy sauce before serving. Enjoy!

306. Flavorful Pulled Pork in Spicy Red Sauce

Serves: 6 | Total Time: 7 hours 15 minutes

INGREDIENTS

1 large yellow onion, chopped
2 lb pork shoulder
1 cup tomato sauce
2 red chilis, chopped
1 cup red salsa
Salt and pepper to taste

DIRECTIONS

In your Slow Cooker, stir pork shoulder, tomato sauce, red chilis, onion, red salsa, salt, and pepper. Cover with the lid and cook for 7 hours on Low. Serve warm and enjoy!

307. Citrus Pork Tenderloin

Serves: 6 | Total Time: 7 hours 15 minutes

INGREDIENTS

1 cup vegetable broth
2 lb pork tenderloin
1 orange, thinly sliced
1 cup olive oil
1 tsp black pepper kernels
Salt to taste

DIRECTIONS

In your Slow Cooker, mix pork tenderloin, orange slices, black pepper kernels, olive oil, vegetable broth, salt, and pepper. Cover and cook for 7 hours on Low. Serve sliced and enjoy!

308. Smoky Chipotle Pulled Pork

Serves: 6 | Total Time: 9 hours 15 minutes

INGREDIENTS

2 chipotle peppers in adobo sauce, chopped
6 garlic cloves, minced
2 lb pork butt, trimmed of excess fat
1 cup pineapple juice
1 cup vegetable broth
¼ cup maple syrup
1 tsp chili powder
1 tsp dry mustard
¼ tsp ground cloves
Salt to taste

DIRECTIONS

Combine chili powder, maple syrup, mustard, chipotle peppers, garlic, cloves, and salt in a bowl. Rub the pork with the mixture until well-coated. Transfer it to your Slow Cooker and pour in pineapple juice and broth. Cover with the lid and cook for 9 hours on Low. When done, shred the pork finely using two forks, and serve.

309. Plum-Glazed Pork Chops

Serves: 6 | Total Time: 7 hours 15 minutes

INGREDIENTS

6 pitted plums, chopped
6 pork chops
½ cup apple cider
½ cup chicken broth
1 tbsp red wine vinegar
2 tbsp agave syrup
1-star anise
1 cinnamon stick
1 bay leaf
2 whole cloves
Salt and pepper to taste

DIRECTIONS

In your Slow Cooker, combine plums, apple cider, chicken broth, red wine vinegar, agave syrup, star anise, cinnamon stick, bay leaf, and cloves. Put in pork chops, salt, and pepper. Cover with the lid and cook for 7 hours on Low. Serve topped with sauce and enjoy!

310. Pork & Vegetable Roast

Serves: 6 | Total Time: 8 hours 15 minutes

INGREDIENTS

1 can fire-roasted tomatoes
2 carrots, sliced
2 lb pork loin, cubed
2 celery stalks, sliced
1 large onion, chopped
1 tsp smoked paprika
½ tsp cumin powder
1 bay leaf
1 cup vegetable broth
Salt and pepper to taste

DIRECTIONS

In your Slow Cooker, mix pork loin, tomatoes, carrots, celery, onion, paprika, cumin, bay leaf, vegetable broth, salt, and pepper. Cover with the lid and cook for 8 hours on Low. When done, remove the lid and serve immediately.

311. Cinnamon-Maple Glazed Pork Tenderloin

Serves: 6 | Total Time: 4 hours 15 minutes

INGREDIENTS

1 can condensed cream of mushroom soup
2 lb pork tenderloin
2 tbsp pure maple syrup
1 tbsp soy sauce
1 tsp Tabasco sauce
1 tsp garlic powder
½ tsp ground cinnamon
¼ tsp allspice powder
½ tsp ground ginger
1 tsp salt

DIRECTIONS

Combine maple syrup, soy sauce, Tabasco sauce, garlic powder, ground cinnamon, allspice powder, ginger, and salt in a bowl. Rub pork tenderloin with the spice mixture and massage until well coated. Place marinated pork and mushroom soup in your Slow Cooker. Cover with the lid and cook for 4 hours on High. Serve and enjoy!

312. Herbed Tomato Pork Shoulder

Serves: 6 | Total Time: 7 hours 15 minutes

INGREDIENTS

- 1 large yellow onion, sliced
- 4 garlic cloves, minced
- 2 lb pork shoulder
- 2 leek stalks, sliced
- 2 ripe tomatoes, diced
- ¼ cup red wine
- 1 tsp dried thyme
- 1 rosemary sprig
- Salt and pepper to taste

DIRECTIONS

Combine pork, onion, garlic, leek, tomatoes, wine, thyme, rosemary sprig, salt, and pepper in your Slow Cooker. Cover with the lid and cook for 7 hours on Low. When done, remove the lid and serve warm. Enjoy!

313. BBQ Short Ribs

Serves: 8 | Total Time: 11 hours 15 minutes

INGREDIENTS

- 1 large onion, sliced
- 1 celery stalk, sliced
- 4 garlic cloves, minced
- 5 lb pork ribs
- 2 cups BBQ sauce
- 1 tbsp Dijon mustard
- 1 tsp Tabasco sauce
- 1 tbsp honey
- Salt and pepper to taste

DIRECTIONS

In your Slow Cooker, toss pork ribs, BBQ sauce, onion, celery, mustard, Tabasco sauce, honey, garlic, ¼ cup of water, salt, and pepper. Cover with the lid and cook for 11 hours on Low. Serve and enjoy!

314. Southern-Style Pineapple Pork Ribs

Serves: 4 | Total Time: 6 hours 15 minutes

INGREDIENTS

- 1 cup pineapple juice
- 3 lb pork spare ribs
- 1 tsp salt
- 1 tsp garlic powder
- 1 tbsp honey
- 1 tsp dried thyme

DIRECTIONS

Season spare ribs with salt, garlic powder, honey, and thyme and transfer them to your Slow Cooker. Pour in pineapple juice. Cover with the lid and cook for 6 hours on Low. When done, remove the lid and serve warm.

315. Tasty Pork Ham

Serves: 6 | Total Time: 7 hours 15 minutes

INGREDIENTS

- 1 cup cranberry sauce
- 1 cup pineapple juice
- 2 lb smoked ham
- ½ tsp ground ginger
- ½ tsp ground cinnamon
- 1 cinnamon stick
- 1-star anise
- 1 bay leaf
- Salt and pepper to taste

DIRECTIONS

Mix cranberry sauce, pineapple juice, ground ginger, cinnamon, stick, star anise, bay leaf, salt, and pepper in your Slow Cooker. Add ham on top. Cover with the lid and cook for 7 hours on Low. Serve warm and enjoy!

316. Pork Roast with a Five-Spice Twist

Serves: 8 | Total Time: 6 hours 15 minutes

INGREDIENTS

¼ cup balsamic vinegar
4 lb pork loin, cubed
2 tbsp agave syrup
1 tsp five-spice powder
1 tsp garlic powder
2 tbsp honey
1 tsp hot sauce
Salt and pepper to taste

DIRECTIONS

Mix agave syrup, five-spice powder, garlic powder, honey, and hot sauce in a bowl. Rub pork with the marinade until well coated. Transfer it to your Slow Cooker and pour in balsamic vinegar, salt, and pepper. Cover with the lid and cook for 6 hours on Low. Serve and enjoy!

317. Dallas-Style Pork Spareribs

Serves: 6 | Total Time: 8 hours 15 minutes

INGREDIENTS

½ cup BBQ sauce
1 cup vegetable broth
1 cup apple butter
2 lb pork spareribs
2 tbsp maple syrup
1 tsp garlic powder
1 tsp onion powder
½ tsp red chili flakes
Salt and pepper to taste

DIRECTIONS

In your Slow Cooker, mix apple butter, maple syrup, garlic powder, onion powder, red chili flakes, BBQ sauce, and vegetable broth. Put in pork spareribs and season with salt and pepper. Cover with the lid and cook for 8 hours on Low. When done, remove the lid and serve warm. Enjoy!

318. Dijon-Style Short Ribs

Serves: 6 | Total Time: 6 hours 45 minutes

INGREDIENTS

1 cup ginger beer
½ cup ketchup
2-3 lb pork short ribs
1 tbsp Worcestershire sauce
1 tbsp Dijon mustard
½ tsp red chili flakes
1 tbsp agave syrup
Salt and pepper to taste

DIRECTIONS

In your Slow Cooker, toss pork short ribs, ginger beer, ketchup, Worcestershire sauce, Dijon mustard, red chili flakes, agave syrup, salt, and pepper. Cover with the lid and cook for 6 ½ hours on Low. Serve warm. Enjoy!

319. Sriracha Pork Tenderloin

Serves: 6 | Total Time: 7 hours 15 minutes

INGREDIENTS

4 garlic cloves, minced
1 onion, chopped
2 lb pork tenderloin
¼ cup soy sauce
¼ cup ketchup
2 tbsp smooth peanut butter
1 tbsp honey
1 tbsp Sriracha sauce
¼ cup chicken broth

DIRECTIONS

In your Slow Cooker, stir pork tenderloin, soy sauce, ketchup, onion, peanut butter, honey, sriracha sauce, garlic, and chicken broth. Cover and cook for 7 hours on Low. Serve and enjoy!

320. Pork and Sauerkraut Casserole

Serves: 6 | Total Time: 6 hours 15 minutes

INGREDIENTS

1 large yellow onion, chopped
2 carrots, grated
1 ½ lb sauerkraut, shredded
1 ½ lb pork loin, cubed
1 ½ tsp caraway seeds
¼ tsp red pepper flakes
1 cup chicken broth
1 bay leaf
Salt and pepper to taste

DIRECTIONS

In your Slow Cooker, mix pork loin, sauerkraut, onion, carrots, caraway seeds, red pepper flakes, chicken broth, bay leaf, salt, and pepper. Cover with the lid and cook for 6 hours on Low. Serve warm and enjoy!

321. Cheddar Pork Tenderloin

Serves: 6 | Total Time: 6 hours 15 minutes

INGREDIENTS

¼ cup pine nuts
½ cup chicken broth
½ cup grated cheddar cheese
1 lime, juiced
2 lb pork tenderloin
1 cup chopped parsley
½ cup chopped cilantro
4 basil leaves
Salt and pepper to taste

DIRECTIONS

Blend parsley, cilantro, basil, pine nuts, chicken broth, lime juice, salt, pepper, and cheddar cheese until smooth in a food processor. Add pork tenderloin and herb mixture to your Slow Cooker and toss until well coated. Cover with the lid and cook for 6 hours on Low. Serve and enjoy!

322. Blue Cheese Short Ribs

Serves: 6 | Total Time: 8 hours 30 minutes

INGREDIENTS

2 cups Blue cheese sauce
3 lb pork short ribs
2 tbsp brown sugar
2 tbsp red wine vinegar
1 tsp Worcestershire sauce
1 ½ tsp chili powder
1 tsp cumin powder
Salt and pepper to taste

DIRECTIONS

Combine blue cheese sauce, chili powder, cumin, sugar, vinegar, Worcestershire sauce, salt, and pepper in your Slow Cooker. Place in pork short ribs and toss until well coated. Cover with the lid and cook for 8 hours on Low. When done, remove the lid and serve immediately. Enjoy!

323. Tropical Pork Roast

Serves: 6 | Total Time: 8 hours 15 minutes

INGREDIENTS

2 peaches, peeled and cubed
1 cup pineapple juice
1 cup frozen blueberries
2 lb pork roast
2 tbsp red wine vinegar
1 bay leaf
1 rosemary sprig
Salt and pepper to taste

DIRECTIONS

In your Slow Cooker, toss pork roast, peaches, pineapple juice, blueberries, vinegar, bay leaf, rosemary, salt, and pepper. Cover with the lid and cook for 8 hours on Low. When done, remove the lid and serve right away. Enjoy!

324. Barbecue Pork Ribs

Serves: 6 | Total Time: 8 hours 15 minutes

INGREDIENTS

¼ cup BBQ sauce
1 cup chicken stock
4 lb pork ribs
2 tbsp apricot preserves
2 tbsp honey
1 tbsp maple syrup
1-star anise
1 tsp salt
½ tsp cayenne pepper

DIRECTIONS

In the Slow Cooker, combine apricot preserves, honey, maple syrup, star anise, BBQ sauce, chicken stock, salt, and cayenne pepper. Add pork ribs and toss to coat well. Cover and cook on Low for 8 hours. Serve and enjoy!

325. Mango Chipotle Pulled Pork

Serves: 6 | Total Time: 7 hours 15 minutes

INGREDIENTS

2 lb pork roast, cut into large pieces
1 ripe mango, diced
1 chipotle pepper, chopped
1 cup BBQ sauce
¼ cup rum
1 cup chicken stock
1 tbsp red wine vinegar
Salt and pepper to taste

DIRECTIONS

In the Slow Cooker, combine pork roast, mango, rum, chicken stock, chipotle pepper, red wine vinegar, BBQ sauce, salt, and pepper. Cover and cook on Low for 7 hours. Remove the lid and shred the pork finely using two forks. Serve warm or chilled and enjoy!

326. Blackberry Pork Tenderloin

Serves: 6 | Total Time: 7 hours 15 minutes

INGREDIENTS

2 cups fresh blackberries
2 yellow onions, sliced
2 lb pork tenderloin
½ tsp dried sage
½ tsp dried thyme
2 tbsp agave syrup
1 tbsp balsamic vinegar
½ cup chicken stock
Salt and pepper to taste

DIRECTIONS

In the Slow Cooker, combine blackberries, onions, pork tenderloin, sage, thyme, agave syrup, balsamic vinegar, chicken stock, salt, and pepper. Cook on Low for 7 hours. Slice the tenderloin and drizzle with the sauce to serve.

327. Porto Pork Chops with Mushrooms

Serves: 6 | Total Time: 6 hours 15 minutes

INGREDIENTS

1 can condensed cream of mushroom soup
1 onion, sliced
4 garlic cloves, chopped
2 cups sliced mushrooms
½ cup Porto wine
6 pork chops
2 tbsp all-purpose flour
1 tsp onion powder
Salt and pepper to taste

DIRECTIONS

Season pork chops with onion powder, salt, and pepper. Dredge seasoned pork in flour. In the Slow Cooker, combine floured pork chops, onion, garlic, mushrooms, Porto wine, and cream of mushroom soup. Cover and cook on Low for 6 hours. Drizzle with the sauce to serve. Enjoy!

328. Citrusy Pork Roast

Serves: 6 | Total Time: 6 hours 15 minutes

INGREDIENTS

1 onion, sliced
1 celery stalk, sliced
4 garlic cloves, chopped
2 lb pork roast
½ cup fresh grapefruit juice
1 lime, zested and juiced
1 tsp cumin powder
1 bay leaf
Salt and pepper to taste

DIRECTIONS

Combine pork roast, onion, celery, garlic, grapefruit juice, lime zest, lime juice, cumin, bay leaf, salt, and pepper in your Slow Cooker. Cover and cook on Low for 6 hours. Serve immediately and enjoy!

329. Creamy Pork Shoulder

Serves: 6 | Total Time: 7 hours 15 minutes

INGREDIENTS

1 cup heavy cream
4 garlic cloves, chopped
1 large onion, chopped
4 lb pork tenderloin
2 cups sliced mushrooms
1 cup cauliflower florets
2 tbsp olive oil
2 tbsp Dijon mustard
Salt and pepper to taste

DIRECTIONS

Season pork tenderloin with salt and pepper. In a pan over medium heat, warm olive oil and sear the pork until golden brown and crusty on all sides. Transfer it to your Slow Cooker. Add in garlic, onion, mushrooms, cauliflower, Dijon mustard, and heavy cream. Cook on Low for 7 hours. Drizzle with the sauce to serve.

330. Simple Pork Ragú

Serves: 6 | Total Time: 6 hours 15 minutes

INGREDIENTS

1 lb fresh pork sausages, casings removed
4 garlic cloves, minced
1 can fire-roasted tomatoes
1 cup chicken stock
2 leek stalks, chopped
2 carrots, diced
½ tsp dried basil
1 bay leaf
2 tbsp olive oil
½ tsp red pepper flakes
¼ cup dry white wine
Salt and pepper to taste

DIRECTIONS

In a pan over medium heat, warm olive oil. Add sausages and cook for 2-3 minutes, stirring often. Transfer to the Slow Cooker. Add in leek, carrots, basil, garlic, fire-roasted tomatoes, chicken stock, bay leaf, red pepper flakes, wine, salt, and pepper. Cover and cook on Low for 6 hours. Serve warm and enjoy!

331. Mouth-Watering Tomato Pork Tenderloin

Serves: 8 | Total Time: 8 hours 15 minutes

INGREDIENTS

2 cups tomato sauce
4 lb pork tenderloin
2 bay leaves
2 tbsp tomato paste
1 tsp onion powder
Salt and pepper to taste

DIRECTIONS

In the Slow Cooker, combine pork tenderloin, tomato sauce, tomato paste, onion powder, bay leaves, salt, and pepper. Cover and cook on Low for 8 hours. Serve sliced. Enjoy!

FISH AND SEAFOOD

332. Zesty Cod Fillets

Serves: 4 | Total Time: 4 hours 10 minutes

INGREDIENTS

4 cod fillets
2 tsp grated lemon rind
Salt and black pepper to taste
1 onion, chopped
2 tbsp chopped cilantro
4 lemon slices

DIRECTIONS

Coat the inside of your Slow Cooker with cooking spray. Season the fish fillets with salt and pepper, then place them in the cooker. Put onion, cilantro, and lemon rinds over the fish. Pour in 3 cups of water. Close the lid and cook on Low for 4 hours. Top the fish with lemon slices. Serve and enjoy!

333. Salmon & Mushroom Risotto

Serves: 6 | Total Time: 5 hours 10 minutes

INGREDIENTS

6 salmon fillets
1 ½ cups mushrooms, sliced
2 onions, chopped
3 garlic cloves, minced
2 cups arborio rice, rinsed
1 tsp dried thyme
2 cups kale
2 tbsp butter
½ cup grated Parmesan cheese

DIRECTIONS

In your Slow Cooker, combine mushrooms, onions, garlic, rice, thyme, and 6 cups of water. Mix well. Cover and cook on Low for 4 hours. Add the salmon fillets on top of the rice mixture. Continue cooking for 30-35 minutes until the fish easily flakes with a fork. Gently stir the fish into the risotto. Add kale, butter, and Parmesan cheese. Stir and cook for an additional 10 minutes. Serve and enjoy!

334. Jalapeño Salmon

Serves: 6 | Total Time: 4 hours 15 minutes

INGREDIENTS

6 salmon fillets
1 jalapeño pepper, minced
Salt and black pepper to taste
1 tsp dry dill
¾ cup olive oil
1 fennel bulb, crushed
1 seedless orange, sliced
1 seedless lemon, thinly sliced
2 cups seafood stock

DIRECTIONS

In your Slow Cooker, combine jalapeño, lemon slices, orange slices, crushed fennel, dill, olive oil, salt, and pepper. Stir to mix well. Place the salmon fillets on top and pour in the stock. Cover and cook on High for 4 hours. Enjoy!

335. Salmon & Fennel Casserole

Serves: 4 | Total Time: 6 hours 20 minutes

INGREDIENTS

1 tbsp olive oil
2 (5-oz) cans salmon, flaked
½ fennel bulb, sliced
½ cup heavy cream
4 chopped hard-boiled eggs
Salt and black pepper to taste
2 tbsp blue cheese, crumbled
1 cup sweet corn

DIRECTIONS

Grease your Slow Cooker with olive oil. Add in salmon, fennel, heavy cream, chopped hard-boiled eggs, salt, corn, and pepper. Sprinkle the crumbled blue cheese on top of the mixture and 3 cups of water. Cook on Low for 6 hours. Serve hot and enjoy!

336. Mediterranean Seafood Kakavia

Serves: 6 | Total Time: 8 hours 15 minutes

INGREDIENTS

1 lb skinless cod fillets, cubed
12 oz scallops, thawed
1 (14-oz) can diced tomatoes
2 leeks, thinly sliced
Salt and black pepper to taste
12 mussels
12 clams
1 tsp thyme, dried
2 carrots, chopped
1 tbsp garlic, minced
1 rib celery, chopped
½ cup dry white wine
4 tbsp lemon juice
1 cup seafood stock

DIRECTIONS

In the Slow Cooker, combine diced tomatoes, leeks, mussels, clams, thyme, carrots, garlic, celery, stock, and lemon juice. Close the lid and cook on Low for 4 hours. After 4 hours, add the cod, scallops, salt, and pepper. Continue cooking for an additional 4 hours. Remove bay leaves and discard any unopened clams and mussels. Adjust seasoning if necessary. Serve warm and enjoy!

337. Haddock Ratatouille

Serves: 4 | Total Time: 8 hours 20 minutes

INGREDIENTS

1 eggplant, sliced into rounds
1 cup sliced button mushrooms
1 zucchini, sliced into rounds
2 tomatoes, chopped
1 onion, sliced
1 red bell pepper, chopped
2 garlic cloves, minced
2 tbsp olive oil
1 tsp herbes de Provence
1 lb haddock fillets
1/2 cup black olives, halved
1/4 cup fresh basil leaves, torn

DIRECTIONS

In a bowl, combine olive oil, garlic, tomatoes, onion, and herbes de Provence. Add eggplant, mushrooms, bell peppers, zucchini, olives, and basil; toss to coat. Transfer the mixture to your Slow Cooker. Add in 3 cups of water. Cover and cook on Low for 6 hours. Arrange haddock fillets on top of the vegetables and continue cooking for 2 more hours on Low until the fish is cooked through. Gently stir the fish into the vegetables. Serve and enjoy!

338. Haddock & Vegetable Casserole

Serves: 6 | Total Time: 8 hours 20 minutes

INGREDIENTS

2 lb firm haddock fillets, cubed
2 cups vegetable stock
½ cup dry white wine
Salt and black pepper to taste
1 tbsp orange zest
1 tsp crushed fennel seeds
4 potatoes, chopped
1 cup carrots, chopped
1 cup onion, diced
2 tbsp dill, chopped
3 garlic cloves, minced
3 large tomatoes, chopped

DIRECTIONS

In your Slow Cooker, combine stock, wine, orange zest, fennel seeds, potatoes, carrots, onion, tomatoes, garlic, salt, and pepper. Stir to mix the ingredients and pour in 3 cups of water. Cook on Low for 4 hours. Add the cubed haddock fillets to the cooker. Continue to cook for an additional 4 hours. Garnish with dill. Enjoy!

339. Coconut Salmon

Serves: 4 | Total Time: 5 hours 20 minutes

INGREDIENTS

1 can cream of mushroom soup, condensed
1 can cream of onion soup, condensed
2 crushed chicken bouillon cubes
4 salmon fillets, chopped
6 eggs, well beaten
15 oz tomato sauce
1 tbsp lemon juice
1 green bell pepper, diced
1 cup breadcrumbs
Salt and black pepper to taste
½ cup coconut milk
1 tbsp olive oil

DIRECTIONS

Coat your Slow Cooker with olive oil. Add salmon, beaten eggs, breadcrumbs, cream of onion soup, chicken bouillon, and lemon juice. Close the lid and cook on Low for 5 hours. While the salmon cooks, heat the milk and cream of mushroom soup in a pan over medium heat. Simmer for 5 minutes, stirring often. Once the salmon is ready, serve it with the creamy sauce poured over the top. Enjoy!

340. Cannellini Bean & Tuna Casserole

Serves: 4 | Total Time: 8 hours 10 minutes

INGREDIENTS

2 (5-oz) cans white tuna in water, drained and flaked
1 cup cannellini beans, soaked
2 cups tomatoes, chopped
1 clove garlic, crushed
Salt and black pepper to taste
2 tbsp olive oil
2 tbsp chopped basil

DIRECTIONS

In a pan over medium heat, fry the garlic in oil until it browns. Discard the garlic. Transfer the garlic-flavored oil and beans into your Slow Cooker along with 6 cups of water. Cook on High for the first 2 hours. Switch to Low and continue cooking for an additional 5 hours. Add the tuna, tomatoes, salt, pepper, and basil. Cook for 1 more hour on Low. Serve hot and enjoy!

341. Tuna Loaf with Greek Sauce

Serves: 6 | Total Time: 5 hours 10 minutes

INGREDIENTS

CUCUMBER SAUCE:

1 (14.75-oz) can tuna, drained
1 egg, whisked
1 tbsp dried dill weed
1 tbsp capers
1 tbsp lemon juice
3 green onions, chopped
Salt and black pepper to taste
1 cup breadcrumbs
¼ cup milk

CUCUMBER YOGURT SAUCE:

½ cup Greek yogurt
½ cup cucumber, chopped
½ tsp dill weed
Salt and black pepper to taste

DIRECTIONS

Combine tuna, egg, dill weed, capers, lemon juice, green onions, milk, breadcrumbs, salt, and pepper in a large mixing bowl. Shape the mixture into a loaf. Grease your Slow Cooker and place the salmon loaf inside. Pour in 3 cups of water. Close the lid and cook on Low for 5 hours.

While the loaf cooks, prepare the cucumber yogurt sauce by mixing Greek yogurt, chopped cucumber, dill weed, salt, and pepper in a bowl. After 5 hours, carefully remove the loaf from the slow cooker. Serve at room temperature, generously topped with Yogurt Sauce. Enjoy!

342. Tangy Halibut with Mango Sauce

Serves: 4 | Total Time: 4 hours 10 minutes

INGREDIENTS

FOR THE FISH:

FOR MANGO SAUCE:

FOR THE FISH:

4 halibut fillets
½ tsp cayenne pepper
Salt and black pepper to taste
1 tbsp fresh lemon juice
1 tbsp olive oil

FOR MANGO SAUCE:

3 tbsp grapefruit juice
1 mango, chopped
1 Jalapeno pepper, minced
1 tbsp cilantro, chopped
1 garlic clove, minced
Salt to taste

DIRECTIONS

In a small bowl, combine olive oil, lemon juice, salt, pepper, and cayenne pepper. Rub the mixture onto the halibut fillets. Arrange the seasoned fillets in your Slow Cooker.

In a food processor, blend grapefruit juice, mango, Jalapeno pepper, garlic, and salt until smooth. Stir in the chopped cilantro. Pour the mango sauce over the fillets and add in 3 cups of water. Close the lid and cook on High for 4 hours. Serve warm and enjoy!

343. Authentic Cod Curry

Serves: 6 | Total Time: 4 hours 10 minutes

INGREDIENTS

2 zucchinis, sliced
2 tbsp ginger puree
4 tbsp coconut oil
3 garlic cloves, minced
1 onion, minced
2 tomatoes, diced
1 handful of curry leaves
1 tsp ground cumin
1 tsp ground turmeric
2 chilies, minced
1 ½ cups fish stock
1 cup coconut milk
1 tbsp curry powder
6 cod fillets
1 tsp ground coriander

DIRECTIONS

Heat coconut oil in a pan over medium heat. Fry zucchinis for 2 minutes on each side; set aside. In the same pan, fry onion and chilies with curry leaves for 3 minutes. Add fish and fry for 2 minutes. Transfer all ingredients to your Slow Cooker. Cook on High for 4 hours. Serve hot and enjoy!

344. Orange Salmon

Serves: 4 | Total Time: 4 hours 10 minutes

INGREDIENTS

4 salmon fillets
1 tsp garlic powder
Salt and black pepper to taste
1 tbsp honey
1 tbsp white wine vinegar
1 crushed fennel seeds
½ cup orange juice
2 tbsp olive oil
½ red onions, sliced
2 oranges, sliced
2 tbsp tarragon, chopped

DIRECTIONS

Season salmon fillets with garlic powder, salt, and pepper. Add them to your Slow Cooker. Combine 2 cups of water, honey, white wine vinegar, fennel seeds, and orange juice. Pour the mixture over the salmon. Arrange the red onion and orange slices on top and sprinkle with tarragon. Cook on Low for 6-8 hours. Serve and enjoy!

345. Creamy Trout

Serves: 4 | Total Time: 4 hours 10 minutes

INGREDIENTS

1 cup vegetable stock
½ cup heavy cream
1 lb trout, skinned

DIRECTIONS

Blend the stock and heavy cream in your Slow Cooker. Add in the skinned trout. Close with the lid and cook for 4 hours on Low. Serve and enjoy!

346. Seafood Medley Cassoulet

Serves: 6 | Total Time: 4 hours 15 minutes

INGREDIENTS

6 oz mussels
12 oz crab meat
16 oz shrimp, peeled
12 oz Albacore (tuna)
1 (14-oz) can diced tomatoes
¾ tsp red pepper flakes
Salt and black pepper to taste
1 celery rib, chopped
1 red bell pepper, sliced
2 small onions, chopped
2 garlic cloves, minced
2 tsp Italian seasoning

DIRECTIONS

In your Slow Cooker, mix mussels, crab meat, shrimp, tuna, tomatoes, red pepper flakes, salt, pepper, celery, bell pepper, onions, garlic, and Italian seasoning. Stir to combine. Pour in 2 cups of water. Cook for 4 hours on High.

347. Harissa Cod Fillets

Serves: 4 | Total Time: 4 hours 10 minutes

INGREDIENTS

4 cod fillets
1 tbsp harissa paste
1 Fresno chili, minced
¼ cup olive oil
2 pints cherry tomatoes
¼ tsp ground allspice
2 garlic cloves, minced
1 tbsp red wine vinegar
½ tsp red pepper flakes

DIRECTIONS

In a bowl, combine harissa paste, Fresno chili, olive oil, allspice, garlic, and red pepper flakes. Mix well. Place cod fillets in your Slow Cooker and pour the spice mixture over the fish. Slice cherry tomatoes in half and arrange them on top of the fish. Pour in 2 cups of water. Close the lid and cook on High for 4 hours. Serve and enjoy!

348. Seafood Cioppino

Serves: 6 | Total Time: 8 hours 25 minutes

INGREDIENTS

6 cups fish stock
½ cup dry white wine
1 (14-ounce) can tomato sauce
2 shallots, chopped
1 tsp Italian seasoning
3 garlic cloves, minced
Sea salt and black pepper to taste
1 tsp pepper flakes
2 sea bass fillets, cubed
½ lb shrimp, peeled and deveined
½ lb clams, cleaned and debearded
1 lemon, zested

DIRECTIONS

Combine fish stock, white wine, tomato sauce, shallots, Italian seasoning, garlic, sea salt, and pepper in your Slow Cooker. Sprinkle with red pepper flakes. Close the lid and cook on Low for 4 hours. Stir in sea bass, shrimp, and lemon zest and continue cooking for 30 minutes on High. Serve and enjoy!

349. Herby Salmon Curry

Serves: 6 | Total Time: 4 hours 10 minutes

INGREDIENTS

½ cup chicken broth
2 tsp chopped cilantro
2 tsp chopped parsley
Salt and black pepper to taste
6 salmon fillets
1 tsp cumin powder
1 tsp curry powder
2 tsp ginger, minced
2 carrots, sliced
1 celery stalk, chopped
1 (13.5-oz) can coconut milk
1 tbsp tomato paste

DIRECTIONS

In your Slow Cooker, combine broth, cilantro, parsley, salt, pepper, cumin, curry, ginger, carrots, and celery. Stir well. Add coconut milk and tomato paste. Gently place salmon fillets on top. Cook on High for 4 hours. Serve.

350. Salmon & Potato Chowder

Serves: 4 | Total Time: 4 hours 15 minutes

INGREDIENTS

4 cups fish stock
2 tbsp arrowroot powder
1 cup milk
½ tsp dried thyme
2 tbsp hot sauce
1 tsp Old Bay seasoning
Salt and black pepper to taste
2 potatoes, cut into chunks
1 cup sweet corn
1 onion, chopped
2 salmon fillets, cubed
2 tbsp parsley, chopped

DIRECTIONS

Blend the stock, arrowroot powder, milk, thyme, hot sauce, old bay seasoning, salt, and pepper in your Slow Cooker. Add in potatoes, corn, onion, and salmon. Cook on High for 2 hours. Blend the mixture until smooth. Add the salmon. Continue cooking on High for an additional 2 hours. Serve topped with parsley and enjoy!

351. Lemony Poached Salmon

Serves: 4 | Total Time: 4 hours 15 minutes

INGREDIENTS

4 salmon steaks
½ cup dry red wine
1 bay leaf
Salt and black pepper to taste
1 red onion, sliced thin
½ cup lemon caper sauce

DIRECTIONS

In your Slow Cooker, combine 2 cups of water, onion, wine, salt, pepper, and bay leaf. Cook on High for 2 hours. Add the salmon and continue cooking on High for 2 hours. Top with lemon caper sauce. Enjoy!

352. Mediterranean-Style Salmon

Serves: 4 | Total Time: 6 hours 10 minutes

INGREDIENTS

1 tbsp Mediterranean seasoning
1 yellow bell pepper, chopped
1 tbsp olive oil
1 tomato, sliced
1 tsp onion powder
Salt and black pepper to taste
1 small zucchini, sliced
1 tsp garlic powder
1 lb salmon fillets

DIRECTIONS

In your Slow Cooker, combine seasoning, bell pepper, onion powder, garlic powder, tomato, zucchini, olive oil, salt, and pepper. Place the salmon fillets on top and pour in 3 cups of water. Cook on Low for 6 hours.

MEATLESS RECIPES

353. Three-Bean Veggie Casserole

Serves: 6 | Total Time: 8 hours 30 minutes

INGREDIENTS

½ cup cannellini beans, soaked
½ cup black beans, soaked
½ cup kidney beans, soaked
2 carrots, diced
1 celery stalk, diced
1 onion, chopped
2 garlic cloves, minced
2 tbsp tomato paste
½ cup diced tomatoes
1 bay leaf
½ red chili, sliced
½ tsp cumin powder
2 cups vegetable stock
1 cup water
Salt and pepper to taste

DIRECTIONS

Combine cannellini beans, black beans, kidney beans, carrots, celery, onion, minced garlic, tomato paste, diced tomatoes, bay leaf, red chili, cumin powder, vegetable stock, water, salt, and pepper in your Slow Cooker. Cover and cook for 8 hours on Low. Serve hot and enjoy!

354. Sriracha Kale Rice

Serves: 4 | Total Time: 6 hours 10 minutes

INGREDIENTS

2 tbsp roasted peanuts, chopped
4 kale leaves, cut into thin ribbons
1 cup brown rice
6 cups vegetable broth
1 tbsp tamari sauce
1 sweet onion, chopped
1 tbsp minced ginger
2 tbsp tomato sauce
½ cup peanut butter
1 tsp Sriracha sauce
2 tbsp chopped cilantro
1 lime, cut into wedges

DIRECTIONS

Coat the inside of your Slow Cooker with cooking spray. Add brown rice, 4 cups of vegetable broth, tamari sauce, kale, and chopped onion. Stir to combine.

In a medium bowl, whisk together the remaining vegetable broth, ginger, tomato sauce, peanut butter, and Sriracha. Pour the peanut sauce mixture into the slow cooker. Cover and cook for 6 hours on Low. Serve garnished with chopped cilantro, lime wedges, and roasted peanuts. Enjoy!

355. Cheesy Spinach Lasagna

Serves: 6 | Total Time: 6 hours 30 minutes

INGREDIENTS

6 lasagna noodles
16 oz spinach, torn
2 cups shredded provolone cheese
1 cup ricotta cheese
½ tsp dried oregano
2 garlic cloves, chopped
½ cup grated Pecorino Romano
2 ½ cups marinara sauce
Salt and pepper to taste

DIRECTIONS

Combine spinach, ricotta, oregano, garlic, Pecorino Romano cheese, salt, and pepper in a bowl. In your Slow Cooker, start with a layer of lasagna noodles, followed by a layer of spinach and ricotta filling, and then a layer of marinara sauce. Repeat the process until you run out of ingredients. Finish with a layer of marinara sauce.

Scatter provolone cheese over the top. Pour in 1 cup of water. Cover with the lid and cook for 6 hours on Low. When done, remove the lid and let it sit for a few minutes before serving. Serve and enjoy!

356. Navy Chili with Grits

Serves: 6 | Total Time: 6 hours 45 minutes

INGREDIENTS

2 cups navy beans, soaked
2 cups vegetable stock
2 garlic cloves, chopped
1 carrot, diced
1 onion, chopped
1 celery stalk, diced
1 green chili, chopped
½ tsp cumin powder
1 cup fire-roasted tomatoes
1 bay leaf
2 cups spinach, shredded
1 cup grits
2 cups water
2 cups whole milk
1 cup grated Cheddar
Salt and pepper to taste

DIRECTIONS

Combine navy beans, vegetable stock, water, onion, garlic, carrot, celery, green chili, cumin, fire-roasted tomatoes, bay leaf, salt, and pepper in the Slow Cooker. Sprinkle shredded spinach on top. Cook on Low for 6 ½ hours.

In a separate pot, bring milk to a boil. Stir in grits and cook over Low heat until creamy. Turn off the heat and sprinkle with grated cheese. Divide the cheesy grits between bowls. Once the beans are cooked, remove the Slow Cooker lid, and spoon the white bean chili over the cheesy grits in each bowl. Serve and enjoy!

357. Bean Enchiladas with Spinach

Serves: 6 | Total Time: 3 hours 15 minutes

INGREDIENTS

2 cups spinach, shredded
2 shallots, chopped
2 garlic cloves, chopped
1 can (15 oz) black beans
1 can sweet corn, drained
1 cup vegetable broth
½ tsp chili powder
1 cup red enchilada sauce
2 tbsp olive oil
Salt and pepper to taste
6 corn tortillas
3 tbsp grated Mexican blend cheese

DIRECTIONS

Heat the olive oil in a pan over medium heat and sauté shallots for 2 minutes, stirring frequently. Transfer them to your Slow Cooker. Add in garlic, black beans, corn, spinach, vegetable broth, chili powder, red enchilada sauce, salt, and pepper. Stir to combine. Cover with the lid and cook for 3 hours on High. When done, remove the lid and divide the mixture between corn tortillas. Top with grated Mexican blend cheese. Serve and enjoy!

358. Flavorful Bean Chili with Corn Chips

Serves: 6 | Total Time: 2 hours 45 minutes

INGREDIENTS

3 garlic cloves, chopped
1 can kidney beans, drained
1 can black beans, drained
1 carrot, sliced
1 red bell pepper, diced
1 red onion, chopped
½ red chili, chopped
1 cup diced tomatoes
½ tsp cumin powder
1 cup vegetable stock
1 bay leaf
2 cups corn chips
2 tbsp olive oil
1 tsp smoked paprika
Salt and pepper to taste

DIRECTIONS

In your Slow Cooker, combine garlic, carrot, bell pepper, kidney beans, black beans, red onion, red chili, tomatoes, cumin powder, vegetable stock, bay leaf, salt, and pepper. Cover with the lid and cook for 2 ½ hours on High.

While the chili is cooking, preheat the oven to 400ºF. Lay corn chips on a baking tray, sprinkle with olive oil and smoked paprika, and bake for 10 minutes. Once the chili is ready, remove the bay leaf and adjust the seasoning if needed. Serve in bowls, generously topped with the crispy corn chips. Enjoy!

359. Tomato & Sweet Potato Casserole

Serves: 6 | Total Time: 2 hours 30 minutes

INGREDIENTS

1 lb sweet potatoes, cubed
1 shallot, chopped
2 garlic cloves, minced
2 red bell peppers, diced
1 carrot, diced
½ tsp ground cumin
½ tsp ground turmeric
½ tsp paprika
2 tbsp tomato sauce
1 cup vegetable broth
2 tbsp olive oil
½ cup light coconut milk
1 bay leaf
Salt and pepper to taste

DIRECTIONS

Heat the olive oil in a pan over medium heat and sauté shallot and garlic for 2 minutes until softened. Transfer them to your Slow Cooker. Add in bell peppers, carrot, ground cumin, ground turmeric, paprika, tomato sauce, sweet potatoes, vegetable broth, coconut milk, bay leaf, salt, and pepper. Cook for 2 hours on High or until the sweet potatoes are tender. Remove the bay leaf before serving. Enjoy!

360. Spiced Stuffed Peppers

Serves: 4 | Total Time: 6 hours 10 minutes

INGREDIENTS

8 oz soy chorizo, crumbled
1 tsp olive oil
1 cup cooked black beans, mashed
¼ cup minced onions
1 tsp minced garlic
1 tsp ground cumin
2 tbsp vegan shredded cheese
Sea salt to taste
4 red bell peppers

DIRECTIONS

Coat the inside of your Slow Cooker with olive oil. In a medium bowl, combine soy chorizo, black beans, onions, garlic, cumin, shredded cheese, and salt. Slice the tops off the red peppers and discard the seeds. Spoon the soy chorizo mixture into the peppers and put the lids back on. Arrange the stuffed peppers in your Slow Cooker. and pour in 2 cups of water. Cover and cook for 6 hours on Low until the peppers are tender. Serve and enjoy!

361. Southwestern Bean & Rice Casserole

Serves: 6 | Total Time: 6 hours 15 minutes

INGREDIENTS

1 celery stalk, diced
2 tomatoes, diced
½ cup wild rice
1 can black beans, drained
½ lime, juiced
2 tbsp pine nuts
2 tbsp chopped parsley
2 cups vegetable stock
Salt and pepper to taste

DIRECTIONS

Combine wild rice, white beans, celery, diced tomatoes, pine nuts, vegetable stock, salt, and pepper in your Slow Cooker. Cover and cook for 6 hours on Low. Stir in lime juice and garnish with parsley. Serve warm and enjoy!

362. Vegetable Medley Quiche

Serves: 4 | Total Time: 8 hours 10 minutes

INGREDIENTS

4 bread slices, crusts removed, cubed
1 cup diced bell peppers
8 eggs, beaten
1 tsp fresh basil
Salt and pepper to taste
2 green onions, chopped
2 cups chopped kale
1 cup grated Gruyère cheese

DIRECTIONS

Combine beaten eggs, fresh basil, salt, and pepper in a bowl. Grease the inside of your Slow Cooker. Put in bread cubes, bell peppers, green onions, and kale. Top the ingredients with the egg mixture and stir gently to combine. Pour in 1 cup of water. Cover and cook for 8 hours on Low. Cut into wedges and serve warm. Enjoy!

363. Cabbage and Chickpea Harvest Curry

Serves: 6 | Total Time: 3 hours 15 minutes

INGREDIENTS

½ green cabbage head, shredded
1 green apple, peeled and diced
4 garlic cloves, chopped
2 carrots, sliced
2 shallots, chopped
1 parsnip, diced
1 red bell pepper, diced
2 celery stalks, sliced
1 can (15 oz) chickpeas, drained and rinsed
1 ½ cups broccoli florets
2 cups cauliflower florets
2 tbsp olive oil
1 cup tomato sauce
1 cup vegetable stock
½ tsp chili powder
½ tsp cumin powder
1 tsp curry powder
1 tbsp brown sugar
½ cup coconut milk
Salt and pepper to taste

DIRECTIONS

In your Slow Cooker, warm olive oil and sauté shallots, garlic, carrots, bell pepper, and celery. Cook for 5 minutes until softened. Add in parsnip, green cabbage, green apple, chickpeas, cauliflower florets, broccoli florets, tomato sauce, vegetable stock, chili powder, cumin powder, curry powder, brown sugar, coconut milk, salt, and pepper. Cover with the lid and cook for 3 hours on High. Serve warm in bowls and enjoy!

364. Smoky Roasted Vegetables Cassoulet

Serves: 6 | Total Time: 2 hours 30 minutes

INGREDIENTS

3 roasted red bell peppers, chopped
1 large onion, chopped
3 garlic cloves, minced
1 carrot, grated
1 zucchini, grated
2 tbsp tomato paste
1 cup tomato sauce
2 tbsp olive oil
¼ tsp smoked paprika
¼ tsp dried oregano
1 thyme sprig
Salt and pepper to taste

DIRECTIONS

In a pan, warm olive oil over medium heat and sauté onion, garlic, and grated carrot for 5 minutes until softened. Transfer to your Slow Cooker. Add zucchini, bell pepper, tomato paste, tomato sauce, ½ cup of water, paprika, oregano, thyme, salt, and pepper. Cover and cook for 2 hours on High. Serve immediately and enjoy!

365. Savory Vegetable Harvest Chili

Serves: 6 | Total Time: 2 hours 15 minutes

INGREDIENTS

1 can diced tomatoes
2 garlic cloves, minced
1 can (15 oz) chickpeas
1 red bell pepper, diced
1 bay leaf
1 eggplant, cubed
1 cup vegetable stock
1 celery stalk, diced
1 tsp dried Italian herbs
Salt and pepper to taste

DIRECTIONS

Combine tomatoes, garlic, chickpeas, bell pepper, bay leaf, eggplant, celery, Italian herbs, salt, pepper, and vegetable stock in your Slow Cooker. Cover and cook for 2 hours on High. Serve hot and enjoy!

366. Coco Bean Curry

Serves: 6 | Total Time: 2 hours 15 minutes

INGREDIENTS

2 shallots, chopped
2 garlic cloves, minced
2 cans (15 oz) white beans
1 can diced tomatoes
1 cup coconut milk
½ cup vegetable stock
2 tbsp chopped parsley
1 tsp curry powder
Salt and pepper to taste

DIRECTIONS

Combine shallots, garlic, beans, tomatoes, coconut milk, vegetable stock, curry powder, salt, and pepper in your Slow Cooker. Cover and cook for 2 hours on High. Stir in parsley before serving. Enjoy!

367. Tasty Green Ragú

Serves: 6 | Total Time: 6 hours 15 minutes

INGREDIENTS

2 cans (15-oz) black beans, drained
6 canned artichoke hearts, chopped
1 carrot, sliced
4 garlic cloves, minced
2 sweet potatoes, cubed
1 small fennel bulb, sliced
2 tbsp olive oil
2 leeks, sliced
½ tsp dried basil
1 cup vegetable stock
Salt and pepper to taste

DIRECTIONS

In a pan, warm olive oil over medium heat. Cook leeks for 5 minutes until softened. Transfer to your Slow Cooker. Add sliced carrot, garlic, black beans, sweet potatoes, artichoke hearts, fennel, basil, vegetable stock, salt, and pepper. Cover and cook for 6 hours on Low. Serve warm and enjoy!

368. Poblano Chickpea Curry with Vegetables

Serves: 6 | Total Time: 6 hours 15 minutes

INGREDIENTS

2 sweet potatoes, diced
1 yellow bell pepper, diced
1 poblano pepper, chopped
1 cup chickpeas, rinsed
1 large onion, soaked
1 carrot, sliced
1 tsp curry
1 tsp grated ginger
2 garlic cloves, chopped
1 cup fire-roasted tomatoes
2 cups vegetable stock
1 bay leaf
Salt and pepper to taste
2 tbsp chopped cilantro

DIRECTIONS

In your Slow Cooker, combine sweet potatoes, bell pepper, poblano pepper, chickpeas, onion, carrot, curry, ginger, garlic, fire-roasted tomatoes, vegetable stock, salt, pepper, and bay leaf. Cover with the lid and cook on Low for 6 hours. Once cooked, remove the bay leaf and stir the curry gently. Serve in bowls. Garnish with cilantro. Enjoy!

369. Succulent Veggie & Bean Casserole

Serves: 6 | Total Time: 6 hours 30 minutes

INGREDIENTS

3 garlic cloves, chopped
1 can white beans, drained
1 can navy beans, drained
1 large onion, chopped
2 carrots, diced
2 tbsp olive oil
1 parsnip, diced
1 cup vegetable stock
1 thyme sprig
1 ½ cups diced tomatoes
1 bay leaf
Salt and pepper to taste

DIRECTIONS

In a pan over medium heat, warm the olive oil and sauté onion, carrot, and garlic for 5 minutes until they become tender. Then, transfer this mixture to your Slow Cooker. Add in parsnip, white beans, navy beans, vegetable stock, thyme sprig, tomatoes, bay leaf, salt, and pepper. Cover with the lid and cook on Low for 6 hours. Enjoy!

370. Vegetable Gumbo with Beans

Serves: 6 | Total Time: 8 hours 30 minutes

INGREDIENTS

1 can (15 oz) kidney beans, drained
1 can (15 oz) black beans, drained
1 sweet onion, chopped
1 celery stalk, sliced
2 garlic cloves, chopped
1 red bell pepper, diced
2 tbsp olive oil
2 tbsp all-purpose flour
2 cups vegetable stock
2 cups sliced mushrooms
1 zucchini, cubed
1 cup chopped okra
1 tsp Cajun seasoning
½ cup coconut milk
Salt and pepper to taste

DIRECTIONS

In a pan over medium heat, warm the olive oil and sauté sweet onion, celery, garlic, and bell pepper for 5 minutes until softened. Add all-purpose flour and cook for another minute. Transfer this mixture to your Slow Cooker. Add in vegetable stock, tomatoes, kidney beans, black beans, mushrooms, zucchini, okra, Cajun seasoning, coconut milk, salt, and pepper. Cover the Slow Cooker and cook on Low for 8 hours. Serve immediately and enjoy!

371. Bean & Pumpkin Curry

Serves: 6 | Total Time: 6 hours 30 minutes

INGREDIENTS

1 can (15 oz) white beans, drained
1 cup diced tomatoes
2 shallots, chopped
4 garlic cloves, chopped
4 cups pumpkin cubes
1 cup coconut milk
1 cup vegetable stock
2 cups fresh spinach
2 tbsp chopped parsley
2 tbsp red curry paste
Salt and pepper to taste

DIRECTIONS

In your Slow Cooker, combine shallots, garlic, butternut squash, white beans, tomatoes, coconut milk, vegetable stock, red curry paste, fresh spinach, parsley, salt, and pepper. Cover the Slow Cooker and cook on Low for 6 hours until the butternut squash is tender and the flavors are well combined. Serve warm and enjoy!

372. Rustic Tomato Basil Sauce

Serves: 6 | Total Time: 6 hours 30 minutes

INGREDIENTS

2 lb fresh tomatoes, pureed
2 large onions, chopped
2 carrots, grated
1 celery stalk, diced
4 garlic cloves, minced
½ tsp dried basil
¼ tsp red pepper flakes
2 tbsp tomato paste
3 tbsp olive oil
1 tsp honey
1 tsp sherry vinegar
1 bay leaf
½ cup vegetable stock
Salt and pepper to taste

DIRECTIONS

In a pan, warm olive oil over medium heat and sauté onions and garlic for 5 minutes until softened. Transfer to your Slow Cooker. Add grated carrots, diced celery, dried basil, red pepper flakes, tomato paste, pureed tomatoes, salt, pepper, honey, vinegar, bay leaf, and vegetable stock. Cover and cook for 6 hours on Low. Serve and enjoy!

373. Creamy Mushroom Medley Stroganoff

Serves: 6 | Total Time: 6 hours 15 minutes

INGREDIENTS

1 ½ lb mushrooms, sliced
2 tbsp cornstarch
1 onion, chopped
4 garlic cloves, chopped
½ tsp smoked paprika
2 tbsp olive oil
1 cup heavy cream
½ cup vegetable stock
Salt and pepper to taste

DIRECTIONS

In a pan over medium heat, warm the olive oil and sauté onion and garlic for 2 minutes. Transfer this mixture to your Slow Cooker. Add in mushrooms, cornstarch, smoked paprika, heavy cream, vegetable stock, salt, and pepper. Cover the Slow Cooker and cook on Low for 6 hours until the mushrooms are tender and the sauce is creamy. Serve warm and enjoy!

374. Portobello Bolognese

Serves: 4 | Total Time: 8 hours 10 minutes

INGREDIENTS

1 lb portobello mushrooms, chopped
1 head cauliflower, cut into florets
1 shallot, chopped
2 (14-oz) cans crushed tomatoes
¼ cup vegetable stock
1 tsp garlic powder
1 tsp dried basil
Salt to taste
½ tsp red pepper flakes

DIRECTIONS

In your Slow Cooker, combine portobello mushrooms, cauliflower, shallot, tomatoes, vegetable stock, garlic powder, dried basil, salt, and red pepper flakes. Mix to combine. Cover and cook for 8 hours on Low. When done, remove the lid and use a potato masher to lightly mash the sauce, breaking up the cauliflower. Enjoy!

375. Pesto Chickpea & Tomato Lasagna

Serves: 6 | Total Time: 6 hours 30 minutes

INGREDIENTS

2 summer squashes, cut into strips
4 ripe tomatoes, pureed
1 ½ cups shredded mozzarella cheese
4 tbsp Italian pesto
1 can chickpeas, drained
½ cup green lentils
1 shallot, chopped
½ cup chopped parsley
1 lemon, juiced
½ tsp dried thyme
½ tsp chili flakes
Salt and pepper to taste

DIRECTIONS

Place chickpeas, lentils, parsley, lemon juice, thyme, chili flakes, salt, and pepper in a bowl and mix well. In your Slow Cooker, layer squash slices, brush with Italian pesto, and top with chickpea mixture. Add a spoonful of tomato puree. Repeat until all ingredients are used. Scatter shredded mozzarella cheese on top. Cover and cook for 6 hours on Low. Serve immediately and enjoy!

376. Garden Couscous

Serves: 6 | Total Time: 2 hours 30 minutes

INGREDIENTS

½ head cauliflower, cut into florets
2 yellow bell peppers, diced
2 carrots, diced
1 cup couscous
2 cups vegetable stock
1 lemon, juiced
½ cup chopped parsley
2 tbsp chopped cilantro
Salt and pepper to taste

DIRECTIONS

Combine couscous, vegetable stock, yellow bell peppers, carrots, cauliflower, salt, and pepper in the Slow Cooker. Cover and cook on High for 2 hours. Stir in lemon juice, parsley, and cilantro. Serve and enjoy!

377. Bean and Veggie Chili

Serves: 6 | Total Time: 7 hours 30 minutes

INGREDIENTS

1 can (15-oz) cannellini beans, drained
1 can (15 oz) black beans, drained
4 cups spinach, shredded
1 red bell pepper, diced
1 green bell pepper, diced
1 yellow bell pepper, diced
1 zucchini, cubed
1 carrot, sliced
1 shallot, chopped
4 garlic cloves, chopped
1 sweet potato, peeled and cubed
2 tbsp tomato paste
½ cup diced tomatoes
½ cup butter
1 cup vegetable stock
½ tsp chili powder
1 thyme sprig
Salt and pepper to taste

DIRECTIONS

In a pan over medium heat, melt the butter. Sauté shallot, garlic, and bell peppers for 5 minutes until softened, then transfer this mixture to your Slow Cooker. Add in zucchini, carrot, sweet potato, tomato paste, tomatoes, cannellini beans, black beans, spinach, vegetable stock, chili powder, thyme sprig, salt, and pepper.

Cover with the lid and cook on Low for 7 hours until the vegetables are tender and the flavors meld together. Stir gently and remove the thyme sprig. Serve warm and enjoy!

378. Tofu & Lentil Curry

Serves: 6 | Total Time: 6 hours 30 minutes

INGREDIENTS

12 oz firm tofu, cubed
1 can (15 oz) lentils
1 cup diced tomatoes
1 large onion, chopped
2 garlic cloves, minced
2 cups cauliflower florets
1 sweet potato, cubed
1 tsp curry powder
1 cup coconut milk
1 cup vegetable stock
2 tbsp olive oil
1 kaffir lime leaf
1 tsp grated ginger
Salt and pepper to taste

DIRECTIONS

In a pan, warm olive oil over medium heat. Cook tofu until golden and crusty on all sides. Add curry powder and cook for another minute. Transfer to your Slow Cooker. Add onion, garlic, cauliflower, sweet potato, lentils, tomatoes, coconut milk, vegetable stock, kaffir leaf, ginger, salt, and pepper. Cover and cook for 6 hours on Low.

379. Ceci Comfort Cassoulet

Serves: 6 | Total Time: 6 hours 30 minutes

INGREDIENTS

2 ripe tomatoes, peeled and diced
1 yellow bell pepper, diced
1 sweet potato, peeled and diced
2 /3 cup chickpeas, rinsed
2 cups vegetable stock
4 cups water
1 celery stalk, sliced
1 carrot, diced
1 shallot, chopped
1 tbsp lemon juice
Salt and pepper to taste

DIRECTIONS

Combine chickpeas, stock, water, celery, carrot, shallot, tomatoes, yellow bell pepper, sweet potato, lemon juice, salt, and pepper in the Slow Cooker. Cook on Low for 6 hours. Serve hot and enjoy!

380. Tropical Kidney Bean

Serves: 6 | Total Time: 8 hours 15 minutes

INGREDIENTS

1 cup chopped onion
2 yellow bell peppers, diced
1 cup kidney beans, soaked
2 cups vegetable stock
1 tsp fennel seeds
½ tsp cumin seeds
½ tsp ground coriander
1 tsp sherry wine vinegar
1 can fire-roasted tomatoes
1 green chile, chopped
Salt and pepper to taste

DIRECTIONS

Combine beans, stock, 2 cups of water, onion, bell peppers, fennel seeds, cumin seeds, coriander, sherry vinegar, roasted tomatoes, green chile, salt, and pepper in the Slow Cooker. Cover and cook on Low for 8 hours. Serve.

381. Peppery Vegetarian Curry

Serves: 6 | Total Time: 7 hours 30 minutes

INGREDIENTS

2 red bell peppers, diced
1 ½ lb potatoes, cubed
2 carrots, sliced
1 can (15 oz) chickpeas, rinsed
1 tsp turmeric powder
1 tsp curry powder
½ tsp chili powder
½ tsp red pepper flakes
1 ½ cups coconut milk
½ cup vegetable stock
Salt and pepper to taste

DIRECTIONS

In your Slow Cooker, combine bell peppers, potatoes, carrots, chickpeas, curry powder, chili powder, red pepper flakes, coconut milk, vegetable stock, salt, and pepper. Cover with the lid and cook on Low for 7 hours until the potatoes are tender and the flavors are well blended. Serve immediately and enjoy!

382. Mixed Bean Fajitas

Serves: 6 | Total Time: 6 hours 15 minutes

INGREDIENTS

1 can (15 oz) kidney beans, rinsed
1 can (15 oz) black beans, rinsed
1 yellow bell pepper, diced
4 oz green chilies, chopped
1 small onion, chopped
1 tsp cumin powder
¼ tsp chili powder
½ tsp dried oregano
½ cup vegetable stock
Salt and pepper to taste
Flour tortillas for serving

DIRECTIONS

In your Slow Cooker, combine heirloom tomatoes, green chilies, bell pepper, onion, cumin powder, chili powder, dried oregano, vegetable stock, kidney beans, black beans, salt, and pepper. Cover with the lid and cook on Low for 6 hours until the vegetables are tender and the flavors meld together. Warm the flour tortillas. Spoon the fajita mixture onto warm flour tortillas. Wrap the tortillas and serve. Enjoy!

383. Roasted Tomato Okra Stew

Serves: 6 | Total Time: 2 hours 15 minutes

INGREDIENTS

1 lb fresh okra, trimmed and sliced
1 can (15 oz) fire-roasted tomatoes
1 small red onion, chopped
2 garlic cloves, chopped
½ tsp cumin seeds
½ tsp mustard seeds
¼ tsp smoked paprika
½ cup vegetable stock
Salt and pepper to taste

DIRECTIONS

In your Slow Cooker, combine onion, garlic, cumin seeds, mustard seeds, smoked paprika, sliced okra, fire-roasted tomatoes, vegetable stock, salt, and pepper. Cover and cook for 2 hours on High until the okra is tender and the flavors are well combined. Stir gently before serving. Enjoy!

384. Rice & Lentil Stuffed Bell Peppers

Serves: 6 | Total Time: 6 hours 30 minutes

INGREDIENTS

2 carrots, grated
1 large onion, chopped
6 mixed bell peppers, cored
2 ½ cups cooked red lentils
½ cup brown rice
2 tbsp tomato paste
1 celery stalk, diced
½ tsp dried oregano
½ tsp dried basil
1 pinch nutmeg
1 ½ cups tomato sauce
1 ½ cups vegetable stock

DIRECTIONS

Mix carrots, onion, lentils, brown rice, tomato paste, celery, oregano, basil, nutmeg, salt, and pepper in a bowl. Carefully stuff the bell peppers with the lentil and rice mixture and place them in your Slow Cooker.

In a separate bowl, mix tomato sauce and vegetable stock. Pour the mixture over the stuffed peppers. Cover and cook for 6 hours on Low until the peppers are tender and the filling is cooked through. Serve and enjoy!

385. Twisted Chickpea Dal

Serves: 10 | Total Time: 6 hours 15 minutes

INGREDIENTS

2 cups chickpeas, rinsed
1 sweet onion, chopped
2 garlic cloves, chopped
1 can diced tomatoes
1 tsp grated ginger
1 tsp turmeric powder
¼ tsp ground cardamom
1 bay leaf
4 cups water
½ tsp cumin powder
½ tsp fenugreek seeds
½ tsp mustard seeds
1 tsp fennel seeds
Salt and pepper to taste
1 lemon, juiced for serving
Cooked rice for serving

DIRECTIONS

In a pan over medium heat, toast the fenugreek, mustard, and fennel seeds for 1 minute or until their flavors are released. Combine chickpeas, water, tomatoes, onion, garlic, ginger, turmeric, ground cardamom, bay leaf, cumin, salt, and pepper in your Slow Cooker. Sprinkle the toasted seeds on top. Cover with the lid and cook for 6 hours on Low. Serve over cooked rice, and sprinkle with lemon juice for extra flavor. Enjoy!

386. Herbed Artichokes

Serves: 4 | Total Time: 6 hours 30 minutes

INGREDIENTS

2 garlic cloves, minced
1 shallot, minced
4 large artichokes
1 lemon, juiced
3/4 cup vegetable stock
1 rosemary sprig
1 thyme sprig
Salt and pepper to taste

DIRECTIONS

Peel and rinse the artichokes under water. Place them in your Slow Cooker. Add lemon juice, garlic, shallot, vegetable stock, rosemary, thyme, salt, and pepper. Cover with the lid and cook for 6 hours on Low. When done, remove the lid and serve warm. Enjoy!

387. Spicy Red Curry

Serves: 6 | Total Time: 6 hours 30 minutes

INGREDIENTS

1 can pinto beans, drained and rinsed
1 can (15 oz) chickpeas, rinsed
2 garlic cloves, chopped
1 red onion, chopped
1 tbsp olive oil
1 tsp grated ginger
½ tsp chili powder
½ tsp cumin powder
1 tsp curry powder
1 cup coconut milk
1 cup vegetable stock
2 tbsp tomato paste
1 bay leaf
1 tsp brown sugar
Salt and pepper to taste

DIRECTIONS

In your Slow Cooker, combine pinto beans, chickpeas, olive oil, onion, garlic, ginger, chili powder, cumin, curry, coconut milk, stock, tomato paste, bay leaf, brown sugar, salt, and pepper. Cover with the lid and cook for 6 hours on Low until the flavors meld together and the beans are tender. Remove the bay leaf before serving. Enjoy!

388. Easy Stuffed Zucchini

Serves: 4 | Total Time: 2 hours 30 minutes

INGREDIENTS

1 small eggplant, peeled and diced
2 garlic cloves, chopped
1 carrot, grated
2 zucchini
1 shallot, chopped
2 tbsp tomato paste
1 cup marinara sauce
1 rosemary sprig
Salt and pepper to taste

DIRECTIONS

In your Slow Cooker, add marinara sauce and rosemary sprig. Cut the zucchini in half, scoop out the flesh, and place it in a bowl. Leave a 1/2-inch-thick intact shell. In the same bowl, stir in shallot, garlic, carrot, eggplant, tomato paste, salt, and pepper to create the stuffing mixture. Stuff each zucchini half with the eggplant mixture and place them in the Slow Cooker. Cover and cook for 2 hours on High. Serve and enjoy!

389. Smoked BBQ Tofu

Serves: 4 | Total Time: 2 hours 15 minutes

INGREDIENTS

1 cup Spicy BBQ sauce
1 tsp Worcestershire sauce
4 thick slices firm tofu
1 red onion, sliced
2 garlic cloves, minced
¼ tsp cumin powder
1 pinch smoked paprika
1 thyme sprig

DIRECTIONS

In your Slow Cooker, combine red onion, garlic, Spicy BBQ sauce, Worcestershire sauce, cumin, smoked paprika, water, and thyme. Add the firm tofu slices and toss gently to coat. Cook for 2 hours on High. Serve and enjoy!

390. Fresh Pumpkin Casserole

Serves: 8 | Total Time: 6 hours 30 minutes

INGREDIENTS

2 cups fresh kale
2 shallots, chopped
4 garlic cloves, chopped
1 small pumpkin, cubed
1 cup diced tomatoes
1 tbsp tomato paste
½ tsp cumin seeds
1 pinch paprika
2 tbsp olive oil
1 cup vegetable stock
Salt and pepper to taste

DIRECTIONS

In a pan over medium heat, warm the olive oil. Sauté the shallots and garlic for 2 minutes until softened. Transfer the onion and garlic mixture to your Slow Cooker. Add pumpkin, tomatoes, tomato paste, cumin seeds, paprika, vegetable stock, kale, salt, and pepper. Cover and cook for 6 hours on Low. Serve right away and enjoy!

391. Homemade Puttanesca Pizza

Serves: 6 | Total Time: 2 hours 30 minutes

INGREDIENTS

DOUGH:

2 cups whole wheat flour
1 tsp active dry yeast
2 tbsp olive oil
1 cup warm water
¼ tsp salt

TOPPING:

½ cup crushed fire-roasted tomatoes
12 black olives, sliced
¼ cup green olives, sliced
1 tbsp capers, chopped
½ tsp dried basil
½ tsp dried oregano

DIRECTIONS

Blend olive oil, whole wheat flour, yeast, water, and salt in a bowl. Mix well until a dough forms. Let it rest for 10 minutes. Flatten the dough into a round sheet. Spread crushed fire-roasted tomatoes, black olives, green olives, and capers. Sprinkle with dried basil and oregano. Carefully transfer the pizza into your Slow Cooker. Pour in 1 cup of water. Cover with the lid and cook for 1 ½ hours on High. Serve right away and enjoy!

392. Seitan Jambalaya

Serves: 6 | Total Time: 6 hours 30 minutes

INGREDIENTS

1 red bell pepper, diced
1 celery stalk, sliced
2 shallots, chopped
2 garlic cloves, chopped
8 oz seitan, cubed
2 cups vegetable stock
1 tbsp olive oil
1 tsp miso paste
1 tsp Cajun seasoning
1 cup brown rice
½ tsp turmeric powder
Salt and pepper to taste

DIRECTIONS

Heat olive oil in a pan over medium heat and sauté shallots and garlic for 2 minutes until softened. Transfer to your Slow Cooker. Add in seitan, bell pepper, celery, vegetable stock, miso paste, Cajun seasoning, brown rice, turmeric powder, salt, and pepper. Cover with the lid and cook for 6 hours on Low. Serve warm and enjoy!

393. Spiced Barley Tacos

Serves: 10 | Total Time: 6 hours 15 minutes

INGREDIENTS

10-14 whole wheat taco shells
1 red onion, chopped
1 cup frozen corn
1 can (15 oz) kidney beans, rinsed
1 cup fire-roasted tomatoes
1 cup pearl barley
2 cups vegetable stock
½ tsp chili powder
½ cup chopped cilantro
2 limes for serving
Salt and pepper to taste

DIRECTIONS

Stir red onion, corn, kidney beans, fire-roasted tomatoes, pearl barley, vegetable stock, chili powder, salt, and pepper in your Slow Cooker. Cover with the lid and cook for 6 hours on Low. When done, remove the lid, divide the mixture between whole wheat taco shells, and top with chopped cilantro. Sprinkle with lime juice. Enjoy!

394. Coconut Chickpea Curry

Serves: 6 | Total Time: 4 hours 15 minutes

INGREDIENTS

1 sweet onion, chopped
2 garlic cloves, chopped
1 can (14 oz) chickpeas, rinsed
1 can (14 oz) diced tomatoes
½ tsp grated ginger
½ tsp cumin powder
¼ tsp ground coriander
½ tsp turmeric powder
¼ tsp curry powder
½ cup coconut milk
2 tbsp coconut oil
Salt and pepper to taste

DIRECTIONS

In a pan, melt coconut oil over medium heat and sauté onion and garlic for 2 minutes until softened. Add ginger, cumin, coriander, turmeric, and curry powder; cook for 30 seconds until fragrant. Transfer to your Slow Cooker. Add chickpeas, coconut diced tomatoes, ½ cup of water, coconut milk, salt, and pepper. Cover and cook for 4 hours on Low. Serve immediately and enjoy!

395. Gingery Tofu

Serves: 4 | Total Time: 2 hours 15 minutes

INGREDIENTS

2 garlic cloves, minced
4 slices firm tofu
½ cup hoisin sauce
½ tsp sesame oil
1 tbsp soy sauce
1 tsp grated ginger
1 tsp rice vinegar
1 tsp honey

DIRECTIONS

In your Slow Cooker, combine hoisin sauce, soy sauce, ginger, vinegar, sesame oil, garlic, water, and honey. Add the firm tofu slices and toss gently to coat. Cover with the lid and cook for 2 hours on High. Serve and enjoy!

396. Mushroom Brown Rice Risotto

Serves: 6 | Total Time: 6 hours 30 minutes

INGREDIENTS

2 carrots, diced
2 celery stalks, diced
1 shallot, chopped
1 cup brown rice
3 cups vegetable stock
1 oz dried porcini, crushed
1 cup sliced cremini mushrooms
Salt and pepper to taste

DIRECTIONS

In your Slow Cooker, combine brown rice, vegetable stock, carrots, celery, shallot, crushed porcini, cremini mushrooms, salt, and pepper. Cover and cook for 6 hours on Low. Serve right away and enjoy!

397. Heavy Broccoli Mash

Serves: 4 | Total Time: 4 hours 30 minutes

INGREDIENTS

1 lb potatoes, cubed
2 cups broccoli florets
2 tbsp coconut oil
¼ cup vegetable stock
¼ cup coconut cream
Salt and pepper to taste

DIRECTIONS

In your Slow Cooker, combine potatoes, broccoli, vegetable stock, coconut oil, coconut cream, salt, and pepper. Cover with the lid and cook for 4 hours on Low. Using a potato masher, mash until smooth and creamy. Serve.

398. Smooth Sweet Potato Purée

Serves: 4 | Total Time: 2 hours 30 minutes

INGREDIENTS

1 green onion, chopped
1 garlic clove, minced
1 ½ lb sweet potatoes, cubed
1 cup water
¼ cup coconut cream
Salt and pepper to taste

DIRECTIONS

In your Slow Cooker, combine sweet potatoes, water, salt, and pepper. Cover with the lid and cook for 2 hours on High. After cooking, remove the lid and use a potato masher to mash the sweet potatoes into a puree. Mix in coconut cream, green onion, and minced garlic. Serve right away and enjoy!

399. Tangy Mushrooms in Cream

Serves: 6 | Total Time: 6 hours 15 minutes

INGREDIENTS

1 lb cremini mushrooms, sliced
4 garlic cloves, chopped
2 tbsp cornstarch
2 shallots, chopped
¼ cup vegetable stock
2 tbsp olive oil
1 cup coconut milk
½ cup cream cheese
Salt and pepper to taste

DIRECTIONS

Coat sliced mushrooms with cornstarch. In a pan over medium heat, warm olive oil. Add mushrooms and cook until golden on each side. Transfer them to your Slow Cooker. Add in shallots, vegetable stock, garlic, coconut milk, cream cheese, salt, and pepper. Cover with the lid and cook for 6 hours on Low. Serve and enjoy!

400. Harissa Spiced Mushrooms

Serves: 6 | Total Time: 8 hours 15 minutes

INGREDIENTS

½ cup butter
18 oz mushrooms, sliced
1 cup vegetable stock
1 cup soy sauce
¼ tsp harissa paste
1 tsp rice vinegar

DIRECTIONS

In your Slow Cooker, combine mushrooms, butter, vegetable stock, soy sauce, harissa paste, and rice vinegar. Cover with the lid and cook for 8 hours on Low. Serve warm and enjoy!

401. Lentil & Cauliflower Curry

Serves: 6 | Total Time: 6 hours 15 minutes

INGREDIENTS

2 cups baby spinach leaves
1 can (14 oz) diced tomatoes
1 shallot, chopped
3 garlic cloves, chopped
1 cup red lentils, rinsed
2 cups cauliflower florets
2 carrots, sliced
1 tsp grated ginger
½ tsp cumin powder
1 tsp curry powder
1 tbsp tomato paste
2 cups vegetable stock
1 tsp honey
Salt and pepper to taste

DIRECTIONS

Combine shallot, garlic, lentils, cauliflower, carrots, ginger, cumin powder, curry powder, tomatoes, tomato paste, vegetable stock, honey, baby spinach leaves, salt, and pepper in your Slow Cooker. Cook for 6 hours on Low.

402. Chili Bean & Rice Casserole

Serves: 6 | Total Time: 6 hours 30 minutes

INGREDIENTS

2 garlic cloves, chopped
1 can (10 oz) black beans
1 can diced tomatoes
1 can (10 oz) diced green chilies
1 red bell pepper, diced
1 shallot, chopped
¼ tsp chili powder
½ tsp cumin powder
½ cup wild rice
4 cups vegetable stock
Salt and pepper to taste

DIRECTIONS

Combine black beans, bell pepper, shallot, garlic, green chilies, tomatoes, chili powder, cumin, rice, vegetable stock, salt, and pepper in your Slow Cooker. Cover and cook on Low for 6 hours. Serve warm and enjoy!

403. Tomato Cavatappi with Vegetables

Serves: 6 | Total Time: 5 hours 30 minutes

INGREDIENTS

2 large zucchinis, peeled and cubed
1 sweet onion, chopped
2 garlic cloves, chopped
½ tsp dried thyme
½ tsp dried oregano
2 tbsp olive oil
½ cup sun-dried tomatoes
½ cup cavatappi pasta
Salt and pepper to taste

DIRECTIONS

Combine zucchini, sweet onion, garlic, dried thyme, dried oregano, olive oil, sun-dried tomatoes, 2 cups of water, cavatappi pasta, salt, and pepper in your Slow Cooker. Cover and cook on Low for 5 hours. Serve and enjoy!

404. Mediterranean Vegetable Medley

Serves: 6 | Total Time: 6 hours 30 minutes

INGREDIENTS

1 large yellow squash, cubed
2 cups sliced bell mushrooms
3 ripe tomatoes, diced
2 red bell peppers, diced
1 tbsp olive oil
1 large onion, chopped
4 garlic cloves, chopped
1 large zucchini, cubed
½ cup vegetable stock
1 thyme sprig
Salt and pepper to taste

DIRECTIONS

Combine onion, olive oil, garlic, yellow squash, zucchini, bell mushrooms, tomatoes, red bell peppers, vegetable stock, thyme, salt, and pepper in your Slow Cooker. Cover and cook on Low for 6 hours. Serve and enjoy!

405. Garlicky Chickpeas

Serves: 6 | Total Time: 2 hours 15 minutes

INGREDIENTS

1 cup diced tomatoes
1 cup tomato sauce
2 cans chickpeas, drained
2 shallots, chopped
1 red bell pepper, diced
½ leek stalk, diced
3 garlic cloves, minced
1 tbsp chopped parsley
Salt and pepper to taste

DIRECTIONS

Blend chickpeas, shallots, bell pepper, leek, garlic, tomatoes, tomato sauce, parsley, salt, and pepper in your Slow Cooker. Cover with the lid and cook for 2 hours on High. Serve warm and enjoy!

406. Cheesy Potato Bake

Serves: 6 | Total Time: 6 hours 30 minutes

INGREDIENTS

2 zucchinis, sliced
4 garlic cloves, minced
2 ½ lb potatoes, sliced
2 large onions, sliced
1 ½ cups tomato sauce
½ tsp dried oregano
½ cup vegetable stock
Salt and pepper to taste
1 cup shredded mozzarella cheese

DIRECTIONS

Arrange zucchini and potatoes in your Slow Cooker and top with a single layer of zucchini. In a bowl, combine garlic, tomato sauce, oregano, vegetable stock, salt, and pepper, then pour it over the vegetables. Sprinkle with shredded mozzarella on top. Cover with the lid and cook for 6 hours on Low. Serve immediately and enjoy!

407.Simple Stuffed Bell Peppers

Serves: 6 | Total Time: 6 hours 30 minutes

INGREDIENTS

1 can (15 oz) kidney beans, rinsed
1 shallot, chopped
1 carrot, grated
6 red bell peppers, cored
½ cup tomato sauce
2 cups cooked wild rice
1 ½ cups vegetable stock
1 sprig of rosemary
Salt and pepper to taste

DIRECTIONS

Mix tomato sauce, kidney beans, cooked wild rice, shallot, grated carrot, salt, and pepper in a bowl. Place the mixture into the red bell peppers in your Slow Cooker. Pour in vegetable stock and add a sprig of rosemary. Cover with the lid and cook for 6 hours on Low. Serve warm and enjoy!

408. Kiddo Vegetable Purée

Serves: 6 | Total Time: 6 hours 15 minutes

INGREDIENTS

1 head broccoli, cut into florets
1 shallot, chopped
1 tsp minced garlic
2 lbs sweet potatoes, cubed
1 cup vegetable stock
Salt and pepper to taste

DIRECTIONS

Combine broccoli florets, peeled and cubed sweet potatoes, shallot, minced garlic, vegetable stock, salt, and pepper in your Slow Cooker. Cover and cook for 6 hours on Low. When done, remove the lid and mash the mixture until smooth using a potato masher. Serve warm and enjoy!

409. Classic Mushroom Risotto

Serves: 6 | Total Time: 4 hours 15 minutes

INGREDIENTS

2 ½ cups sliced mushrooms
1 shallot, chopped
1 tsp minced garlic
1 cup arborio rice
2 tbsp olive oil
¼ cup white wine
1 ½ cups vegetable stock
Salt and pepper to taste

DIRECTIONS

Blend olive oil, mushrooms, shallot, garlic, arborio rice, white wine, vegetable stock, salt, and pepper in your Slow Cooker. Cover with the lid and cook for 4 hours on Low. When done, remove the lid and serve warm. Enjoy!

410. Daily Tomato Sauce

Serves: 10 | Total Time: 8 hours 15 minutes

INGREDIENTS

2 onions, chopped
4 garlic cloves, chopped
1 large fennel bulb, chopped
1 can (14 oz) crushed tomatoes
2 tbsp tomato paste
2 tbsp olive oil
1 cup tomato sauce
1 cup vegetable stock
1 bay leaf
1 tsp dried thyme leaves
Salt and pepper to taste

DIRECTIONS

Heat the olive oil in a pan over medium heat and sauté onions and garlic for 5 minutes until softened and caramelized. Transfer to your Slow Cooker. Add chopped fennel, crushed tomatoes, tomato paste, tomato sauce, vegetable stock, bay leaf, dried thyme, salt, and pepper. Cover and cook for 8 hours on Low. Serve and enjoy!

411. Broccoli & Chickpea Casserole

Serves: 8 | Total Time: 8 hours 30 minutes

INGREDIENTS

1 head broccoli, cut into florets
1 can diced tomatoes
2 large onions, chopped
4 garlic cloves, chopped
1 celery stalk, sliced
1 zucchini, diced
¼ tsp cumin seeds
½ tsp fennel seeds
½ tsp ground ginger
2 tbsp olive oil
1 pinch cinnamon powder
2 cups chickpeas, soaked
3 cups vegetable stock
1 thyme sprig
Salt and pepper to taste

DIRECTIONS

In a pan over medium heat, warm the olive oil and sauté the onions, garlic, celery, and zucchini for 5 minutes until softened. Transfer the sautéed mixture to your Slow Cooker. Add in cumin seeds, fennel seeds, ginger, cinnamon powder, chickpeas, broccoli, tomatoes, vegetable stock, thyme, salt, and pepper. Cover with the lid and cook for 8 hours on Low. Serve immediately and enjoy!

412. Butternut Squash Mash with Lentils

Serves: 6 | Total Time: 6 hours 15 minutes

INGREDIENTS

1 teaspoon minced garlic
1 lb butternut squash, cubed
1 shallot, chopped
2/3 cup red lentils, rinsed
2 cups vegetable stock
Salt and pepper to taste
¼ tsp cumin seeds
1 pinch chili powder

DIRECTIONS

Combine butternut squash, red lentils, shallot, garlic, vegetable stock, cumin seeds, chili powder, salt, and pepper in your Slow Cooker. Cover and cook for 6 hours on Low. When done, remove the lid and, using a potato masher, mash until smooth. Serve warm and enjoy!

413. Roasted Tomato and Bean Chili

Serves: 6 | Total Time: 8 hours

INGREDIENTS

1 lb fresh tomatoes, halved
1 can (15 oz) kidney beans, rinsed
2 red onions, sliced
2 red bell peppers, sliced
1 tsp dried thyme
2 tbsp olive oil

1 tsp chili powder
½ tsp cumin powder
½ tsp ground coriander
1 cup vegetable stock
Salt and pepper to taste

DIRECTIONS

Preheat the oven to 400°F. Combine fresh tomatoes, red onions, red bell peppers, olive oil, and dried thyme on a baking sheet. Sprinkle with salt and pepper and roast for 30 minutes. When done, transfer everything to your Slow Cooker. Add kidney beans, chili powder, cumin powder, ground coriander, vegetable stock, salt, and pepper. Cover and cook for 7 hours on Low. When done, remove the lid and serve immediately. Enjoy!

414. Layered Vegetable Rice Casserole

Serves: 6 | Total Time: 6 hours 30 minutes

INGREDIENTS

1 ½ cups grated cheddar cheese
1 large zucchini, cut into ribbons
1 large eggplant, cut into ribbons
1 can diced tomatoes
1 cup wild rice
1 celery stalk, diced
½ tsp dried oregano
2 cups vegetable stock
Salt and pepper to taste

DIRECTIONS

Create ribbons from the eggplant and zucchini using a vegetable peeler. Set aside. In a bowl, combine tomatoes, wild rice, celery, oregano, salt, and pepper. In your Slow Cooker, start with a layer of vegetable ribbons, followed by a layer of the rice mixture, and then another layer of veggie ribbons. Repeat the layering process until all ingredients are used. Pour vegetable stock over the layers. Top with grated cheese. Cook for 6 hours on Low.

415. Herby Sweet Potato Bake

Serves: 6 | Total Time: 4 hours 15 minutes

INGREDIENTS

2 lbs sweet potatoes, cubed
4 cups spinach
1 shallot, chopped
2 garlic cloves, chopped
¼ tsp cumin powder
¼ tsp coriander powder
¼ tsp fennel seeds
1 tsp dried thyme leaves
2 tbsp olive oil
1 cup vegetable stock
Salt and pepper to taste

DIRECTIONS

Heat the olive oil in a pan over medium heat and sauté shallot and garlic for 2 minutes until softened. Sprinkle with cumin, coriander, and fennel seeds; toast for 30 seconds to release flavors. Transfer everything to your Slow Cooker. Add sweet potatoes, spinach, vegetable stock, salt, pepper, and dried thyme leaves. Cover with the lid and cook for 4 hours on Low. Serve warm and enjoy!

416. Pineapple Teriyaki Tofu

Serves: 6 | Total Time: 2 hours 15 minutes

INGREDIENTS

1 can (20 oz) pineapple chunks, drained
1 ½ lb firm tofu, cubed
1 ½ cups vegetable broth
1 tbsp tamarind paste
1 tbsp mirin
1 tsp sesame oil
2 tbsp brown sugar
1 tsp grated ginger
2 tbsp soy sauce
3 cups cooked rice

DIRECTIONS

Place tofu, pineapple chunks, vegetable broth, tamarind paste, mirin, brown sugar, sesame oil, ginger, and soy sauce in your Slow Cooker. Stir to combine. Cover and cook for 2 hours on High. Serve over cooked rice.

417. Sticky BBQ Lentils

Serves: 6 | Total Time: 2 hours 15 minutes

INGREDIENTS

1 cup green lentils
¼ cup black lentils
1 cup BBQ sauce
1 ½ cups vegetable stock
2 shallots, chopped
1 carrot, diced
1 red bell pepper, diced
3 garlic cloves, chopped
1 tbsp apple cider vinegar
½ tsp mustard seeds
½ tsp cumin seeds
Salt and pepper to taste

DIRECTIONS

Mix shallots, carrot, red bell pepper, garlic, apple cider vinegar, mustard seeds, cumin seeds, green lentils, black lentils, BBQ sauce, vegetable stock, salt, and pepper in your Slow Cooker. Cover with the lid and cook for 2 hours on High. Serve right away and enjoy!

418. Lemony Sweet Potato Curry

Serves: 6 | Total Time: 4 hours 30 minutes

INGREDIENTS

2 yellow bell peppers, diced
1 ½ lbs sweet potatoes, cubed
1 shallot, chopped
2 garlic cloves, chopped
1 cup diced tomatoes
1 cup vegetable stock
½ celery stalk, diced
1 tbsp red curry paste
1 tbsp tomato paste
½ lemongrass stalk, crushed
Salt and pepper to taste
2 tbsp chopped cilantro

DIRECTIONS

Mix sweet potatoes, shallot, garlic, yellow bell peppers, celery, red curry paste, tomato paste, tomatoes, vegetable stock, lemongrass, salt, and pepper in your Slow Cooker. Cover with the lid and cook for 4 hours on Low. When done, remove the lid and top with cilantro to serve. Enjoy!

419. Indian-Inspired Lentils

Serves: 6 | Total Time: 6 hours 15 minutes

INGREDIENTS

1 tsp minced garlic
1 sweet onion, chopped
1 cup red lentils, rinsed
1 medium butternut squash, cubed
1 cup tomato sauce
2 cups vegetable stock
2 tbsp olive oil
¼ tsp chili powder
½ tsp turmeric powder
½ tsp garam masala
½ tsp grated ginger
Salt and pepper to taste

DIRECTIONS

Stir garlic, sweet onion, olive oil, red lentils, butternut squash, chili powder, turmeric powder, garam masala, tomato sauce, vegetable stock, grated ginger, salt, and pepper in your Slow Cooker. Cover with the lid and cook for 6 hours on Low. When done, remove the lid and serve warm. Enjoy!

420. Gruyère Barley Risotto

Serves: 6 | Total Time: 6 hours 15 minutes

INGREDIENTS

1 carrot, diced
1 cup pearl barley
1 shallot, chopped
1 leek, chopped
1 garlic clove, minced
2 cups vegetable stock
¼ cup grated Gruyère cheese
2 tbsp olive oil
Salt and pepper to taste

DIRECTIONS

Heat olive oil over medium heat and sauté leek, shallot, and garlic cook for 2 minutes until softened. Transfer to your Slow Cooker with barley, carrot, vegetable stock, thyme, salt, and pepper. Cover with the lid and cook for 6 hours on Low. Stir in grated Gruyère cheese and serve immediately. Enjoy!

421. Seitan Kurma with a Twist

Serves: 6 | Total Time: 8 hours 15 minutes

INGREDIENTS

2 cups broccoli florets
1 cup diced tomatoes
8 oz firm seitan, cubed
2 red bell peppers, diced
1 carrot, diced
½ celery stalk, diced
2 tbsp olive oil
½ tsp grated ginger
½ tsp turmeric powder
¼ tsp chili powder
½ tsp curry powder
1 cup vegetable broth
½ cup coconut milk
Salt and pepper to taste

DIRECTIONS

In a pan over medium heat, warm olive oil. Add seitan and cook until it's golden and crispy on all sides. Transfer it to your Slow Cooker. Add in bell peppers, carrot, celery, broccoli florets, tomatoes, ginger, turmeric powder, chili powder, curry powder, vegetable broth, coconut milk, salt, and pepper. Cover with the lid and cook for 8 hours on Low. Serve warm and enjoy!

422. Vegetarian Shepherd's Pie

Serves: 6 | Total Time: 7 hours 30 minutes

INGREDIENTS

1 lb potatoes, cubed
½ lb sweet potatoes, cubed
1 cup frozen green peas
1 cup frozen corn
2 large carrots, diced
2 cups sliced mushrooms
1 ½ cups vegetable broth
½ tsp dried thyme
1 tbsp cornstarch
Salt and pepper to taste

DIRECTIONS

Cook potatoes and sweet potatoes in a pot of salted boiling water until tender. Mash them until smooth, adding some cooking liquid. In a bowl, mix green peas, corn, carrots, mushrooms, cornstarch, dried thyme, salt, and pepper. Transfer the vegetable mixture to your Slow Cooker. Pour vegetable broth over the vegetables and top with the mashed potato puree. Cover and cook for 7 hours on Low. Serve warm and enjoy!

423. Easy Tacos with Beans & Orzo

Serves: 6 | Total Time: 8 hours 15 minutes

INGREDIENTS

1 can (15 oz) kidney beans
1 large onion, chopped
2 carrots, diced
1 leek stalk, diced
1 cup orzo
1 cup diced tomatoes
2 cups vegetable stock
2 tbsp tomato paste
2 tbsp olive oil
2 tbsp chopped cilantro
Salt and pepper to taste
Flour tortillas for serving

DIRECTIONS

In a pan over medium heat, warm olive oil and sauté onion, carrots, and leek cook 5 minutes until softened. Transfer to your Slow Cooker. Add in orzo, tomatoes, kidney beans, vegetable stock, tomato paste, salt, and pepper. Cover and cook for 8 hours on Low. Divide the mixture between tortillas and top with cilantro. Serve.

424. Bourbon Glazed Black Beans

Serves: 6 | Total Time: 10 hours 15 minutes

INGREDIENTS

1 lb canned black beans, rinsed
1 cup BBQ sauce
2 cups vegetable stock
1 tbsp bourbon
¼ cup maple syrup
½ cup ketchup
1 tsp mustard seeds
1 tbsp molasses
1 tsp smoked paprika
1 tbsp apple cider vinegar
1 tsp Worcestershire sauce
Salt and pepper to taste

DIRECTIONS

Combine black beans, bourbon, maple syrup, BBQ sauce, vegetable stock, ketchup, mustard seeds, molasses, apple cider vinegar, Worcestershire sauce, salt, pepper, and smoked paprika in your Slow Cooker. Cover with the lid and cook for 10 hours on Low. When done, remove the lid and serve warm. Enjoy!

425. Milky Sweet Corn

Serves: 6 | Total Time: 3 hours 15 minutes

INGREDIENTS

1 cup shredded mozzarella cheese
½ cup whole milk
2 cans (15 oz) sweet corn
1 cup cream cheese
Salt and pepper to taste
1 pinch nutmeg

DIRECTIONS

In your Slow Cooker, combine sweet corn, cream cheese, mozzarella cheese, whole milk, nutmeg, salt, and pepper. Stir well. Cover and cook for 3 hours on Low. Serve immediately and enjoy!

426. Delicious Barley with Asparagus & Peas

Serves: 6 | Total Time: 5 hours 15 minutes

INGREDIENTS

1 bunch asparagus, chopped
1 cup split peas
1 small shallot, chopped
1 celery stalk, sliced
1 cup barley
2 cups vegetable stock
2 tbsp olive oil
½ lemon, juiced
Salt and pepper to taste

DIRECTIONS

In your Slow Cooker, combine olive oil, shallot, celery, barley, vegetable stock, asparagus, split peas, salt, and pepper. Mix well. Cover and cook for 5 hours on Low. Squeeze in the juice of half a lemon. Serve and enjoy!

427. Holiday Squash Bites

Serves: 6 | Total Time: 2 hours 30 minutes

INGREDIENTS

1 can diced tomatoes
1 cup vegetable stock
1 butternut squash, shredded
1 cup cooked quinoa
1 garlic clove, minced
1 small onion, chopped
½ tsp ground cumin
½ tsp dried thyme
Salt and pepper to taste

DIRECTIONS

In your Slow Cooker, combine tomatoes and vegetable stock. In a bowl, add butternut squash, quinoa, garlic, onion, ground cumin, thyme, salt, and pepper. Mix well. Form small balls from the mixture and place them in the pot. Cover and cook for 2 hours on High. Serve warm with cooked rice or potato purée. Enjoy!

428. Creamy Tofu & Mushroom Stroganoff

Serves: 6 | Total Time: 6 hours 30 minutes

INGREDIENTS

1 can condensed cream of mushroom soup
1 oz dried porcini mushrooms, chopped
2 Portobello mushrooms, sliced
1 cup tofu cream
1 tsp Worcestershire sauce
1 large onion, chopped
½ cup penne pasta
Salt and pepper to taste

DIRECTIONS

In your Slow Cooker, combine Portobello mushrooms, porcini mushrooms, onion, mushroom soup, tofu cream, Worcestershire sauce, 1 ½ cup of water, salt, pepper, and penne pasta. Cover and cook for 6 hours on Low. Serve

429. Apple Pumpkin Medley

Serves: 6 | Total Time: 6 hours 30 minutes

INGREDIENTS

2 red apples, peeled and cubed
4 cups pumpkin cubes
½ cinnamon stick
2 onions, chopped
2 garlic cloves, minced
2 ripe tomatoes, diced
¼ cup cranberry juice
2 tbsp olive oil
1 cup vegetable stock
1 thyme sprig
Salt and pepper to taste

DIRECTIONS

In your Slow Cooker, combine red apples, pumpkin cubes, cinnamon stick, onions, garlic, tomatoes, cranberry juice, olive oil, vegetable stock, thyme, salt, and pepper. Cover and cook for 6 hours on Low. Serve and enjoy!

430. Mom´s Lentils

Serves: 6 | Total Time: 7 hours 15 minutes

INGREDIENTS

1 sweet potato, diced
1 carrot, diced
1 cup black lentils
2 ripe tomatoes, diced
2 cups vegetable stock
½ tsp ground cumin
½ red chili, chopped
Salt and pepper to taste

DIRECTIONS

Place black lentils, sweet potato, carrot, tomatoes, vegetable stock, ground cumin, red chili, salt, and pepper in your Slow Cooker and mix well. Cover and cook for 7 hours on Low. Serve hot and enjoy!

431. Smoky Eggplant Meal

Serves: 4 | Total Time: 2 hours 15 minutes

INGREDIENTS

1 large eggplant, peeled and cubed
¼ cup hoisin sauce
½ cup almond milk
3 tbsp coconut oil
1 tbsp soy sauce
1 tsp smoked paprika

DIRECTIONS

In a pan over medium heat, melt the coconut oil. Cook the eggplant until golden brown on all sides. Transfer the eggplant to your Slow Cooker. Add hoisin sauce, soy sauce, almond milk, and smoked paprika. Cover and cook for 2 hours on High. Serve hot and enjoy!

432. Tomato & Quinoa Chili

Serves: 6 | Total Time: 6 hours 15 minutes

INGREDIENTS

1 can (15 oz) kidney beans
1 can fire-roasted tomatoes
1 sweet onion, chopped
2 garlic cloves, chopped
½ cup quinoa, rinsed
1 ½ cups vegetable stock
¼ tsp red chili flakes
¼ tsp cumin powder
Salt and pepper to taste

DIRECTIONS

In your Slow Cooker, combine kidney beans, fire-roasted tomatoes, sweet onion, garlic, quinoa, vegetable stock, red chili flakes, cumin, salt, and pepper. Cover and cook for 6 hours on Low. Serve hot and enjoy!

433. Tofu & Vegetables Quinoa with Pesto

Serves: 6 | Total Time: 6 hours 15 minutes

INGREDIENTS

1 cup cauliflower florets
1 cup broccoli florets
6 oz firm tofu, cubed
½ cup quinoa, rinsed
1 celery stalk, sliced
1 potato, diced
1 carrot, diced
½ cup sweet corn
1 tbsp Pesto sauce
2 tbsp green lentils
1 cup vegetable stock
Salt and pepper to taste

DIRECTIONS

Combine tofu, quinoa, sliced celery, potato, carrot, sweet corn, cauliflower florets, broccoli florets, pesto sauce, green lentils, vegetable stock, salt, and pepper in your Slow Cooker. Cover with the lid and cook for 6 hours on Low. Serve immediately and enjoy!

434. Vegetable Pot Pie

Serves: 6 | Total Time: 6 hours 30 minutes

INGREDIENTS

1 can (14 oz) diced tomatoes
1 onion, chopped
1 celery stalk, diced
1 carrot, diced
6 oz biscuit dough
½ tsp dried oregano
1 tbsp all-purpose flour
1 cup green peas
1 cup chopped green beans
1 tsp dried thyme leaves
1 cup vegetable stock
Salt and pepper to taste

DIRECTIONS

Mix tomatoes, celery, carrot, onion, dried oregano, and flour until well combined in a bowl. Pour the mixture into your Slow Cooker. Add green peas, beans, vegetable stock, salt, pepper, and thyme leaves. Place biscuit dough on top. Cover with the lid and cook for 6 hours on Low. Serve warm and enjoy!

435. Sweet Chole

Serves: 6 | Total Time: 8 hours 15 minutes

INGREDIENTS

2 cups vegetable stock
½ cup tomato sauce
1 cup coconut milk
1 ½ cups dried chickpeas
1 lb sweet potatoes, cubed
½ tsp chili powder
1 tsp curry powder
½ tsp garam masala
2 tbsp tomato paste
½ tsp ground coriander
1 stalk lemongrass, crushed
2 kaffir lime leaves
1 lime, juiced
2 tbsp chopped cilantro
Salt and pepper to taste

DIRECTIONS

Mix chickpeas, sweet potatoes, chili powder, curry powder, garam masala, tomato paste, tomato sauce, ground coriander, vegetable stock, coconut milk, lemongrass, kaffir lime leaves, salt, and pepper in your Slow Cooker. Cover with the lid and cook for 8 hours on Low. Sprinkle with lime juice and cilantro to serve. Enjoy!

436. Asian-Style Meatless Bolognese

Serves: 6 | Total Time: 8 hours 15 minutes

INGREDIENTS

1 can (15 oz) diced tomatoes
1 lb soy ground meat
2 large onions, chopped
6 garlic cloves, minced
2 celery stalks, diced
2 carrots, grated
2 tbsp olive oil
1 parsnip, grated
1 tsp dried basil
1 tsp dried oregano
2 tbsp marinara sauce
1 cup vegetable stock
2 tbsp lemon juice
Salt and pepper to taste

DIRECTIONS

In a pan over medium heat, warm olive oil and sear soy meat for 2-3 minutes until golden and crispy on all sides. Transfer it to your Slow Cooker. Add in onions, garlic, celery, carrots, parsnip, basil, oregano, marinara sauce, tomatoes, vegetable stock, lemon juice, salt, and pepper. Cook for 8 hours on Low. Serve and enjoy!

437. Coconut-Mango Curry

Serves: 6 | Total Time: 3 hours 15 minutes

INGREDIENTS

1 ripe mango, cubed
8 oz firm tofu, cubed
2 onions, chopped
2 garlic cloves, minced
¼ tsp cayenne pepper
¼ tsp garam masala
¼ tsp ground ginger
¼ tsp ground cumin
1 bay leaf
1 cup coconut milk
2 tbsp olive oil
2 tbsp tomato paste
1 cup vegetable stock
Salt and pepper to taste

DIRECTIONS

In a pan over medium heat, warm olive oil. Cook tofu until golden and crispy on all sides. Transfer to your Slow Cooker. Add onions, garlic, cayenne pepper, garam masala, ground ginger, ground cumin, bay leaf, coconut milk, mango, tomato paste, vegetable stock, salt, and pepper. Cover and cook for 3 hours on High. Serve hot and enjoy!

438. Tofy With Lentils & Chickpeas

Serves: 6 | Total Time: 6 hours 15 minutes

INGREDIENTS

1 can chickpeas, drained and rinsed
2 tbsp olive oil
8 oz firm tofu, cubed
1 cup red lentils
2 cups vegetable stock
2 tbsp tomato paste
2 tbsp red curry paste
1 bay leaf
½ lemongrass stalk, crushed
½ tsp grated ginger
Salt and pepper to taste

DIRECTIONS

Heat the olive oil in a pan over medium heat and sear tofu until golden brown and crispy on all sides. Add it to your Slow Cooker. Add in red curry paste, lentils, vegetable stock, chickpeas, tomato paste, bay leaf, lemongrass, ginger, salt, and pepper. Cover with the lid and cook for 6 hours on Low. Serve warm and enjoy!

439. Effortless Zucchini Rolls

Serves: 8 | Total Time: 7 hours

INGREDIENTS

1 large eggplant, cut into sticks
2 carrots, cut into matchsticks
2 parsnips, cut into matchsticks
1 cup marinara sauce
2 large zucchinis, sliced into ribbons
1 cup vegetable stock
1 tsp dried thyme
½ tsp dried oregano
Salt and pepper to taste

DIRECTIONS

Create zucchini ribbons with a vegetable peeler and place them on a cutting board. Top each zucchini ribbon with eggplant sticks, carrot matchsticks, and parsnip matchsticks, then roll them up. Place the vegetable rolls in your Slow Cooker. Pour marinara sauce, vegetable stock, thyme, oregano, salt, and pepper over the rolls. Cover with the lid and cook for 6 hours on Low. Serve warm and enjoy!

440. Cauliflower & Rice Tofu

Serves: 6 | Total Time: 4 hours 15 minutes

INGREDIENTS

1 head cauliflower, cut into florets
8 oz firm tofu, cubed
1 cup jasmine rice
¼ cup white wine
2 cups vegetable stock
2 tbsp olive oil
1 tbsp lemon juice
¼ tsp garlic powder
¼ tsp onion powder
½ tsp dried oregano
Salt and pepper to taste

DIRECTIONS

In a pan over medium heat, warm olive oil. Add tofu and cook until golden on all sides. Transfer it to your Slow Cooker. Add in cauliflower florets, jasmine rice, white wine, vegetable stock, lemon juice, garlic powder, onion powder, dried oregano, salt, and pepper. Cover with the lid and cook for 4 hours on Low. Enjoy!

441. Olive Tapenade with Eggplant & Artichokes

Serves: 6 | Total Time: 4 hours 15 minutes

INGREDIENTS

1 large eggplant, peeled and diced
1 cup green olives, sliced
½ cup Kalamata olives, sliced
1 can fire-roasted tomatoes
2 artichoke hearts, diced
1 cup vegetable stock
1 tbsp olive oil
¼ tsp dried oregano
Salt and pepper to taste

DIRECTIONS

In your Slow Cooker, combine eggplant, olive oil, green olives, Kalamata olives, tomatoes, artichoke hearts, vegetable stock, oregano, salt, and pepper. Cover and cook on Low for 2 hours, then switch to High and cook for an additional 2 hours. Serve warm and enjoy!

442. Mung Bean Risotto

Serves: 6 | Total Time: 6 hours 15 minutes

INGREDIENTS

1 carrot, diced
2 ripe tomatoes, diced
1 cup mung beans, rinsed
½ cup Arborio rice
3 cups vegetable stock
1 celery stalk, sliced
½ tsp dried thyme
½ tsp dried basil
¼ tsp ground cumin
¼ tsp smoked paprika
Salt and pepper to taste

DIRECTIONS

Combine mung beans, Arborio rice, vegetable stock, celery, carrot, tomatoes, dried thyme, dried basil, ground cumin, smoked paprika, salt, and pepper in your Slow Cooker. Cover and cook for 6 hours on Low. Serve.

443. Paprika Chickpea Bake

Serves: 6 | Total Time: 8 hours 15 minutes

INGREDIENTS

1 can fire-roasted tomatoes
1 ½ cups chickpeas, soaked
2 onions, chopped
1 celery stalk, diced
1 tsp dried oregano
2 cups vegetable stock
½ tsp garlic powder
¼ tsp smoked paprika
Salt and pepper to taste

DIRECTIONS

In your Slow Cooker, combine chickpeas, onions, celery, fire-roasted tomatoes, oregano, vegetable stock, garlic powder, smoked paprika, salt, and pepper. Cover and cook for 7 hours on Low. Serve hot and enjoy!

444. Meatless Stew

Serves: 6 | Total Time: 2 hours 15 minutes

INGREDIENTS

1 lb frozen split peas
1 cup diced tomatoes
2 onions, chopped
1 celery stalk, sliced
1 red bell pepper, diced
1 carrot, diced
1 cup vegetable stock
2 tbsp olive oil
Salt and pepper to taste

DIRECTIONS

In a pan over medium heat, warm olive oil and sauté onions until softened, about 2 minutes. Transfer to your Slow Cooker. Add celery, bell pepper, carrot, split peas, diced tomatoes, stock, salt, and pepper. Cook for 2 hours on High.

445. Marinara Cauliflower

Serves: 4 | Total Time: 6 hours 15 minutes

INGREDIENTS

1 cup marinara sauce
1 head cauliflower
¼ tsp garlic powder
¼ tsp onion powder
½ tsp dried thyme
¼ tsp salt
1 pinch paprika
½ cup vegetable broth

DIRECTIONS

Add cauliflower to your Slow Cooker. Place cauliflower florets in your Slow Cooker. In a bowl, whisk together marinara sauce, garlic powder, onion powder, dried thyme, salt, paprika, and vegetable broth. Pour the sauce mixture over the cauliflower into the pot. Cover and cook for 6 hours on Low. Serve warm and enjoy!

DESSERTS

446. Decadent Strawberry Chocolate Brownies

Serves: 6 | Total Time: 2 hours 15 minutes

INGREDIENTS

1 ½ cups fresh strawberries, halved
1 cup dark chocolate chips
2 eggs
½ cup butter, cubed
½ cup sugar
½ cup unsweetened applesauce
¼ cup cocoa powder
½ cup flour

DIRECTIONS

In a heatproof bowl over a pot of boiling water, melt butter and dark chocolate chips, stirring until smooth. Remove from heat and let it cool slightly. Stir in sugar and applesauce into the melted chocolate mixture. Add eggs one at a time, mixing gently. Mix in cocoa powder and flour until well incorporated. Spoon the batter into your Slow Cooker. Arrange strawberries on top. Cook for 2 hours on High. Serve cold slices into small squares.

447. Cinnamon-Spiced Apple Butter

Serves: 6 | Total Time: 8 hours 15 minutes

INGREDIENTS

4 lb Granny Smith apples, peeled and cored
2 lb Honeycrisp apples, peeled and cored
2 cups sugar
1 cup fresh apple juice
1 ½ tsp ground cinnamon
½ tsp ground ginger

DIRECTIONS

Combine the apples, sugar, apple juice, cinnamon, and ginger in your Slow Cooker. Cover with the lid and cook for 8 hours on Low. Remove the lid and use a hand blender to puree the mixture until smooth.Transfer the apple butter into sealable jars and store it in your storage space for up to 2-3 months. Enjoy!

448. Raspberry Crumble

Serves: 6 | Total Time: 2 hours 15 minutes

INGREDIENTS

¼ cup brown sugar
1 ½ lb fresh raspberries
2 tbsp arrowroot powder
1 tsp lemon zest
1 cup flour
½ cup cold butter, solid

DIRECTIONS

Blend raspberries, arrowroot powder, brown sugar, and lemon zest in your Slow Cooker. In a bowl, mix flour and cold butter until sandy and crumbly. Pour the crumble mixture over the berry mixture. Cover with the lid and cook for 2 hours on High. Let cool the crumble to room temperature before serving.

449. Tropical Cake

Serves: 6 | Total Time: 2 hours 45 minutes

INGREDIENTS

1 cup crushed pineapple, drained
1 cup grated carrots
½ cup chopped almonds
½ cup canola oil
1 ½ cups flour
1 cup sugar

12 eggs
1 tsp vanilla extract
1 tsp baking powder
½ tsp ground ginger
1 tsp cinnamon powder
¼ tsp cardamom powder

DIRECTIONS

Combine canola oil, sugar, eggs, and vanilla extract until creamy. Add flour, baking powder, ground ginger, cinnamon powder, and cardamom powder in a bowl. Mix until well combined. Fold in grated carrots, crushed pineapple, and chopped almonds. Pour the mixture into your Slow Cooker. Cook for 2 ¼ hours on High.

450. Cinnamon Pear Cake with White Chocolate

Serves: 6 | Total Time: 6 hours 30 minutes

INGREDIENTS

4 pears, peeled, cored, and sliced
½ cup white chocolate chips
5 eggs, separated
¾ cup sugar
½ cup butter, melted
½ cup milk
1 cup flour
1 tsp baking powder
½ tsp ground cinnamon

DIRECTIONS

Beat egg yolks and half of the sugar in a bowl until it increases in volume. Mix in butter and milk until smooth. Add flour and baking powder. Mix to combine. In another bowl, whisk egg whites until soft peaks form. Gradually add the remaining sugar and continue whisking until stiff peaks form.

Fold the whipped egg whites into the flour mixture until well combined. Fold in white chocolate chips. Transfer the mixture to your Slow Cooker and top with pear slices and ground cinnamon. Cook for 6 hours on Low.

451. Berry Rum Muffin Cake

Serves: 6 | Total Time: 6 hours 20 minutes

INGREDIENTS

1 tsp dark rum
1 tbsp butter, melted
3 cups flour
½ cup Greek yogurt
¼ cup sugar
3 large eggs
2 tsp grated lemon zest
1 ½ tsp baking powder
1 tsp almond extract
½ tsp baking soda
1 cup mixed fresh berries

DIRECTIONS

Combine dark rum, butter, flour, Greek yogurt, sugar, eggs, lemon zest, baking powder, almond extract, and baking soda in a bowl. Whisk with a hand mixer until well blended. Carefully fold in the mixed fresh berries. Grease your Slow Cooker with butter. Pour in the batter. Cover and cook for 6 hours on Low or until a cake tester inserted in the center comes out clean and dry. Let it cool to room temperature before serving. Enjoy!

452. Apricot Cobbler

Serves: 6 | Total Time: 6 hours 30 minutes

INGREDIENTS

2 lb apricots, pitted and sliced
1 tbsp arrowroot powder
4 tbsp sugar
¼ cup sugar
1 ½ cups flour
½ cup cold butter, cubed
2/3 cup milk, chilled
½ tsp baking powder

DIRECTIONS

Mix the apricots, arrowroot powder, and 2 tbsp of sugar sugar in your Slow Cooker. In a bowl, whisk flour, baking powder, remaining sugar, and butter until sandy. Pour in milk and mix until slightly crumbly. Top the apricots with the flour mixture. Cook for 6 hours on Low. Serve warm or chilled. Enjoy!

453. Almond Butter Chocolate Bliss Cake

Serves: 6 | Total Time: 2 hours 15 minutes

INGREDIENTS

¼ cup milk
1 cup flour
¼ cup cocoa powder
2 eggs
¼ cup canola oil
½ cup smooth almond butter
¾ cup brown sugar
1 tsp orange zest
1 tsp baking powder

DIRECTIONS

Mix canola oil, brown sugar, almond butter, orange zest, and eggs in a bowl. Stir in milk, flour, cocoa powder, and baking powder until well combined. Pour the batter into your Slow Cooker. Cover with the lid and cook for 2 hours on High. Let cool before serving. Enjoy!

454. Rich Mocha Cake

Serves: 6 | Total Time: 4 hours 15 minutes

INGREDIENTS

2 eggs
1 cup milk
1 ½ cups sugar
1 ½ cups flour
½ cup cocoa powder
½ cup sunseed oil
½ cup brewed coffee
1 tsp baking powder
1 tsp almond extract

DIRECTIONS

Beat sugar, flour, cocoa powder, baking powder, eggs, milk, sunseed oil, almond extract, and coffee until smooth with an electric mixer. Transfer the batter to your Slow Cooker. Cook for 4 hours on Low. Serve cool.

455. Stuffed Apple with Honey & Raisins

Serves: 6 | Total Time: 4 hours 15 minutes

INGREDIENTS

6 apples, cored
1 cup sultana raisins
¼ cup cold butter, cubed
1 cup rolled oats
¼ cup flour
½ cup orange juice
2 tbsp honey
1 tsp orange zest

DIRECTIONS

Combine raisins, butter, flour, rolled oats, orange zest, and honey until crumbly in a bowl. Fill the cored apples with the raisin mixture. Place the stuffed apples into your Slow Cooker. Pour orange juice over the apples. Cover with the lid and cook for 4 hours on Low. Serve chilled and enjoy!

456. Spiced Poached Pears

Serves: 6 | Total Time: 6 hours 30 minutes

INGREDIENTS

1-inch ginger, sliced
¾ cup sugar
6 firm pears, peeled and cored
2 cups red grape juice
1 ½ cups water
1 star anise
4 whole cloves
2 cinnamon sticks

DIRECTIONS

Add ginger, sugar, pears, red grape juice, water, star anise, cloves, and cinnamon sticks to your Slow Cooker. Stir gently. Cover and cook for 6 hours on Low. Serve chilled and enjoy!

457. Cinnamon Peach Brioche

Serves: 6 | Total Time: 6 hours 30 minutes

INGREDIENTS

4 peaches, cubed
16 oz brioche bread, cubed
1 cup evaporated milk
1 cup condensed milk
1 cup oat milk
4 eggs
1 tsp cinnamon powder
½ tsp ground ginger
2 tbsp sugar

DIRECTIONS

Place brioche bread, peaches, cinnamon powder, ground ginger, and sugar in your Slow Cooker. In a bowl, whisk evaporated milk, condensed milk, and oat milk until well combined. Beat in eggs until smooth. Pour the mixture over the bread and peaches in the Slow Cooker. Cook for 6 hours on Low. Serve cool.

458. Vanilla-Chocolate Chip Cake

Serves: 6 | Total Time: 4 hours 15 minutes

INGREDIENTS

½ cup dark chocolate chips
1 cup flour
½ cup butter, softened
½ cup smooth peanut butter
½ cup sugar
3 eggs
1 tsp vanilla extract
1 tsp baking powder

DIRECTIONS

Combine butter, peanut butter, and sugar until creamy in a bowl. Add eggs, one at a time, and vanilla extract. Mix until well combined. Mix in flour,and baking powder until a smooth batter forms. Fold in chocolate chips. Transfer the batter to your Slow Cooker. Cook for 4 hours on Low. Let cool before slicing to serve. Enjoy!

459. Chocolate Cherry Cola Cake

Serves: 6 | Total Time: 4 hours 15 minutes

INGREDIENTS

2 cups pitted Amarena cherries
½ cup milk
1 ½ cups flour
¼ cup cocoa powder
½ cup butter, melted
1 cup cola
¼ cup cherry preserves
1 tsp vanilla extract
½ tsp baking powder

DIRECTIONS

Mix cola, cherry preserves, butter, vanilla extract, and milk. Add flour, cocoa powder, and baking powder in a bowl. Mix until well combined. Fold in pitted Amarena cherries. Pour the mixture into your Slow Cooker. Cover and cook for 4 hours on Low. Serve chilled and enjoy!

460. Cuban Brioche Pudding

Serves: 6 | Total Time: 6 hours 30 minutes

INGREDIENTS

4 eggs, beaten
2 cups whole milk
10 oz brioche bread, cubed
¼ cup rum
½ cup light brown sugar
1 tsp vanilla extract

DIRECTIONS

Place brioche bread in your Slow Cooker. In a bowl, combine eggs, milk, rum, sugar, and vanilla extract until smooth and pour it over the bread. Cover with the lid and cook for 6 hours on Low. Serve and enjoy!

461. Zesty Orange Cheesecake

Serves: 6 | Total Time: 7 hours 30 minutes

INGREDIENTS

6 oz graham crackers, crushed
½ cup butter, melted
1 cup heavy cream
4 eggs
20 oz cream cheese
1 tbsp arrowroot powder
1 tsp grated ginger
1 tsp grated orange zest
½ cup sugar

DIRECTIONS

Combine graham crackers, butter, and orange zest until crumbly in your Slow Cooker and press down firmly to form the crust. In a bowl, combine cream cheese, heavy cream, eggs, arrowroot powder, ginger, and sugar. Mix until creamy. Pour the cheese mixture over the crust. Cook for 7 hours on Low. Serve and enjoy!

462. Luscious Lemon Cheesecake

Serves: 6 | Total Time: 6 hours 15 minutes

INGREDIENTS

4 eggs
24 oz cream cheese
½ cup buttermilk
1 lemon, zested and juiced
2/3 cup sugar
2 tbsp arrowroot powder
1 tsp vanilla extract

DIRECTIONS

Beat cream cheese, buttermilk, eggs, arrowroot powder, lemon zest, lemon juice, sugar, and vanilla extract until smooth and creamy in a bowl. Grease the pot of your Slow Cooker and pour in the batter. Cook for 6 hours on Low. Serve chilled and enjoy!

463. Maple-Glazed Cherry Crumble

Serves: 6 | Total Time: 4 hours 30 minutes

INGREDIENTS

1 lb cherries, pitted
4 tbsp honey
2 tbsp arrowroot powder
1 tbsp lemon juice
½ cup unsweetened milk
½ cup cold butter, cubed
1 ¼ cups flour
2 tbsp sugar

DIRECTIONS

Toss cherries, honey, arrowroot powder, and lemon juice in your Slow Cooker. In a bowl, combine flour, butter, and sugar until sandy. Pour in milk and stir until well combined. Pour the crumble mixture over the fruits. Cook for 4 hours on Low. Serve chilled and enjoy!

464. Pecan Apple Strudel

Serves: 4 | Total Time: 4 hours 30 minutes

INGREDIENTS

4 large apples, peeled and cubed
½ cup golden raisins
1 tsp ground cinnamon
½ cup chopped pecans
1 cup flour
2 tbsp melted butter
2 tbsp flour
2 tbsp sugar

DIRECTIONS

Combine apples, golden raisins, and cinnamon in your Slow Cooker. In a bowl, whisk together pecans, flour, butter, flour, and sugar until crumbly. Pour the nut topping mixture over the fruits. Cook for 4 hours on Low.

465. Fragrant Ginger Rice Pudding

Serves: 6 | Total Time: 4 hours 15 minutes

INGREDIENTS

1 cup Arborio rice
3 cups milk
½-inch ginger, sliced
½ cup brown sugar
1 cinnamon stick
1-star anise
2 whole cloves
½ tsp rose water

DIRECTIONS

Combine Arborio rice, brown sugar, milk, cinnamon stick, star anise, cloves, sliced ginger, and rose water in your Slow Cooker. Cover with the lid and cook for 4 hours on Low. Once cooked, chill in the refrigerator. Enjoy!

466. Cranberries & Dark Chocolate Bread Pudding

Serves: 6 | Total Time: 5 hours 30 minutes

INGREDIENTS

1 cup dried cranberries, diced
1 cup dark chocolate chips
8 cups bread cubes
2 cups milk
1 cup heavy cream
4 eggs
1 tsp vanilla extract
1 tsp orange zest
½ cup white sugar

DIRECTIONS

Combine bread cubes, cranberries, and dark chocolate chips in your Slow Cooker. In a bowl, whisk together milk, heavy cream, eggs, vanilla extract, orange zest, and sugar. Pour the mixture over the bread and ingredients in the slow cooker. Cover with the lid and cook on Low for 5 hours. Serve and enjoy!

467. Chocolate Cheesecake

Serves: 6 | Total Time: 6 hours 30 minutes

INGREDIENTS

1 ½ cups crushed graham crackers
½ cup butter, melted
20 oz cream cheese
4 eggs
½ cup sugar
½ cup smooth peanut butter
½ cup chocolate sauce
1 tbsp cornstarch
1 tsp vanilla extract

DIRECTIONS

Combine crackers and butter until crumbly, transfer it to your Slow Cooker, and press down on the bottom in a bowl. In a separate bowl, beat peanut butter, chocolate sauce, cream cheese, eggs, cornstarch, vanilla extract, and sugar until smooth and pour it over the crust. Cook for 6 hours on Low. Enjoy!

468. Velvety Caramel Infusion Custard

Serves: 6 | Total Time: 6 hours 15 minutes

INGREDIENTS

4 cups whole milk
1 cup heavy cream
1 cup sugar for caramelizing
2 egg yolks
4 eggs
2 tbsp vanilla sugar

DIRECTIONS

In a pan over high heat, caramelize 1 cup of sugar until it turns amber in color. Pour the caramel into your Slow Cooker and swirl to coat the bottom. In a bowl, whisk together milk, heavy cream, egg yolks, eggs, and vanilla sugar until smooth. Pour the custard mixture over the caramel. Cook for 6 hours on Low.

469. Traditional Crème Brulee

Serves: 4 | Total Time: 6 hours 15 minutes

INGREDIENTS

2 egg yolks
2 whole eggs
2½ cups milk
1 ½ cups heavy cream
1 tsp vanilla extract
2 tbsp maple syrup
2 tbsp agave syrup
1 cup sugar for topping

DIRECTIONS

Whisk together milk, heavy cream, egg yolks, whole eggs, vanilla extract, agave syrup, and maple syrup in a bowl until well combined. Divide the mixture evenly among 4 ramekins and place them in your Slow Cooker. Add enough water to the Slow Cooker to cover 3/4 of the height of the ramekins. Cook for 6 hours on Low. Sprinkle the tops with sugar. Caramelize the sugar using a torch until golden and crispy. Serve and enjoy!

470. Nutty Apple Crisp

Serves: 6 | Total Time: 4 hours 30 minutes

INGREDIENTS

1 lb apples, peeled, cored, and sliced
6 tbsp sugar
1 tsp ground cinnamon
1 tbsp lemon juice
1 tbsp arrowroot powder
1 cup chopped walnuts
¼ cup butter, melted
½ cup flour
Caramel sauce for serving

DIRECTIONS

Combine apples, 4 tbsp of sugar, ground cinnamon, lemon juice, and arrowroot powder in your Slow Cooker. In a bowl, mix walnuts, butter, flour, and remaining sugar until crumbly. Sprinkle the nutty topping over the apple mixture. Cook for 4 hours on Low. Sprinkle with caramel sauce. Enjoy!

471. Double Chocolate Coffee Bread Pudding

Serves: 6 | Total Time: 4 hours 30 minutes

INGREDIENTS

2 tsp instant coffee dissolved in 2 tbsp hot water
1 cup white chocolate chips
1 ½ cups milk
8 cups brioche bread cubes
1 cup heavy cream
1 cup dark chocolate chips
4 eggs
¼ cup sugar
1 tsp orange zest

DIRECTIONS

In a pot over medium heat, melt white chocolate chips with milk, stirring until smooth. Remove from heat and set aside. In a large bowl, combine brioche bread cubes, dark chocolate chips, and melted white chocolate mixture.

In another bowl, whisk eggs, instant coffee, sugar, and orange zest. Pour the egg mixture over the bread mixture. Transfer the combined mixture to your Slow Cooker. Cook for 4 hours on Low. Serve and enjoy!

472. Spiced Pumpkin Cheesecake

Serves: 6 | Total Time: 6 hours 30 minutes

INGREDIENTS

½ cup butter, melted
8 oz graham crackers, crushed
1 ½ cups pumpkin puree
24 oz cream cheese
3 eggs
2 tbsp arrowroot powder
½ cup sugar
½ tsp ground cinnamon
½ tsp ground ginger

DIRECTIONS

Combine butter and graham cracker crumbs until well combined in a bowl. Press the mixture into the bottom of your Slow Cooker. In another bowl, combine pumpkin puree, cream cheese, eggs, arrowroot powder, sugar, cinnamon, and ginger. Mix until well combined. Pour the filling over the crust. Cook for 6 hours on Low.

473. Maple Cinnamon Streusel

Serves: 6 | Total Time: 4 hours 30 minutes

INGREDIENTS

CINNAMON STREUSEL:

½ cup all-purpose flour
½ cup light brown sugar
1 cup chopped almonds
1 tsp cinnamon powder
2 tbsp maple syrup

CAKE:

1 ½ cups all-purpose flour
1 cup sour cream
3/4 cup butter, softened
3/4 cup sugar
4 eggs
1 ½ tsp baking powder

DIRECTIONS

Combine almonds, flour, sugar, cinnamon, and maple syrup for the streusel mixture in a bowl. Using an electric mixer, beat butter and sugar until creamy. Mix in eggs one by one. Add in the flour, baking powder, and sour cream. Pulse for 2 minutes until well combined. Pour half of the batter into your Slow Cooker, add the maple mixture, and top with the remaining batter. Cook for 4 hours on Low. Let cool before serving.

474. Festive Spice Gingerbread

Serves: 6 | Total Time: 2 hours 30 minutes

INGREDIENTS

½ cup raisins
½ cup whole milk
1¼ cups all-purpose flour
3/4 cup butter, softened
½ cup white sugar
½ cup dark brown sugar
3 eggs
1 tsp vanilla extract
1 tbsp cocoa powder
1 tsp ground ginger
1 tsp cinnamon powder
¼ tsp ground cloves
1 tsp baking powder
¼ tsp baking soda

DIRECTIONS

Beat butter, white, and brown sugar until creamy in a bowl. Add eggs one at a time, followed by vanilla extract, and mix until well combined. Incorporate milk, flour, cocoa powder, ginger, cinnamon powder, cloves, baking powder, baking soda, and raisins into the mixture, stirring until well combined. Pour the batter into your Slow Cooker. Cover and cook for 2 hours on High. Once cooked, let it cool and then chill in the refrigerator.

475. Milky Poached Pears

Serves: 6 | Total Time: 6 hours 15 minutes

INGREDIENTS

2 cups milk
3/4 cup sugar
6 pears, peeled and cored
2 cups water
1 cinnamon stick
1 star anise
1 whole clove
2 orange rings

DIRECTIONS

Place pears, milk, water, cinnamon stick, star anise, clove, sugar, and orange rings in your Slow Cooker. Cover and cook for 6 hours on Low. Let cool before serving. Enjoy!

476. Easy Grand Marnier Soufflé

Serves: 6 | Total Time: 2 hours 30 minutes

INGREDIENTS

1 large orange, zested
¼ cup Grand Marnier
8 egg yolks
10 egg whites
Butter to grease the pot
¼ cup butter, softened
2/3 cup sugar
1 cup milk
½ cup flour

DIRECTIONS

Grease the pot of your Slow Cooker with butter. In a bowl, combine orange zest and sugar to release the flavor. Bring orange zest, sugar, and milk to a boil in a pot over high heat. In a separate bowl, beat egg yolks and flour until creamy. Gradually add the hot milk mixture, stirring frequently. Reduce heat and cook for 2-3 minutes until the mixture thickens, stirring often. Remove from heat, mix in butter and Grand Marnier. Set aside to cool.

In another bowl, whisk egg whites until stiff peaks form. Gently fold the whipped egg whites into the orange mixture. Pour the batter into your greased Slow Cooker. Cover with the lid and cook for 2 hours on High.

477. Mother´s Biscotti Cheesecake

Serves: 6 | Total Time: 6 hours 30 minutes

INGREDIENTS

6 oz Biscotti cookies, crushed
¼ cup butter, melted
4 eggs
24 oz cream cheese
½ cup sour cream
½ cup brown sugar
1 tbsp vanilla extract
1 tbsp Amaretto liqueur

DIRECTIONS

Mix crushed Biscotti cookies and butter until crumbly. Press the mixture into your Slow Cooker. In a separate bowl, whisk together cream cheese, sour cream, eggs, sugar, vanilla extract, and Amaretto liqueur until smooth. Pour the creamy mixture over the crust. Cover with the lid and cook on Low for 6 hours. Serve and enjoy!

478. Divine Dulce de Leche Pie

Serves: 6 | Total Time: 2 hours 30 minutes

INGREDIENTS

¼ cup chilled milk
½ cup cold butter, cubed
1 cup all-purpose flour
¼ tsp baking powder
2 tbsp vanilla sugar
2 cups milk chocolate chips
1 can (14 oz) dulce de leche

DIRECTIONS

Combine butter, flour, baking powder, and sugar until sandy in your blender. Pour in milk and pulse until combined. Put the dough on a floured surface, roll it into a round, and place it on the bottom of your Slow Cooker. Pour dulce de leche over the crust and scatter with milk chocolate chips. Cook for 2 hours on High.

479. Lemon Berry Cake

Serves: 6 | Total Time: 4 hours 30 minutes

INGREDIENTS

1 cup fresh mixed berries
4 eggs
1 cup all-purpose flour
1 cup butter, melted
1 cup brown sugar
1 tsp vanilla extract
2 tsp lemon zest
1 tsp baking powder

DIRECTIONS

Beat butter, sugar, and vanilla extract until creamy with an electric mixer. Pour in eggs, one by one, and lemon zest and pulse for 1 minute at high speed. Add in flour and baking powder and pulse to combine. Transfer the batter to your Slow Cooker and top with fresh mixed berries. Cook for 4 hours on Low. Let cool before serving. Enjoy!

480. Pumpkin Cheesecake

Serves: 6 | Total Time: 6 hours 30 minutes

INGREDIENTS

1 ¼ cups crushed chocolate cookies
½ cup butter
½ cup light brown sugar
¼ cup canola oil
1 cup pumpkin puree
24 oz cream cheese
4 eggs
1 tsp cinnamon powder
1 tsp ground ginger
1 tsp ground nutmeg
½ tsp cardamom powder

DIRECTIONS

Melt the butter in a pan over medium heat until it turns golden. Set it aside to cool. In a bowl, combine crushed cookies and butter until it becomes crumbly. Press the crumbly mixture into the Slow Cooker to form the crust.

In a separate bowl, mix together the pumpkin puree, canola oil, cream cheese, eggs, brown sugar, nutmeg, cinnamon, ginger, and cardamom. Pour the filling over the crust. Cook for 6 hours on Low. Enjoy!

481. Spiced Fruit Dessert

Serves: 6 jars | Total Time: 6 hours 30 minutes

INGREDIENTS

4 ripe pears, peeled, cored, and sliced
3 banans, sliced
1 ½ cups fresh apple juice
1 cup white sugar
1 cup light brown sugar
1 cinnamon stick
1 whole clove
4 cardamom pods, crushed

DIRECTIONS:

In your Slow Cooker, combine pears, banans, apple juice, white sugar, light brown sugar, cinnamon stick, clove, and crushed cardamom pods. Cover with the lid and cook for 6 hours on Low, allowing the fruits and spices to meld together. Once cooked, remove the cinnamon stick, whole clove and cardamom pods. Blend the mixture until smooth using an immersion blender or a regular blender. Divide between jars and let it cool before sealing.

482. Crazy Chocolate Cake

Serves: 6 | Total Time: 4 hours 30 minutes

INGREDIENTS

1 cup crushed graham crackers
6 oz dark chocolate, melted
3/4 cup brown sugar
2 eggs
3/4 cup all-purpose flour
½ cup butter, melted
½ cup mini marshmallows
½ cup mixed nuts, chopped
½ cup milk chocolate chips
½ cup unsalted pretzels, chopped
1 tsp baking powder

DIRECTIONS

Mix melted chocolate and butter until smooth in a bowl. Stir in sugar and eggs until well combined. Add flour and baking powder; stir until thoroughly incorporated. Pour the batter into your Slow Cooker. Sprinkle crushed graham crackers, marshmallows, nuts, milk chocolate chips, and pretzels on top. Cook for 4 hours on Low. Serve.

483. Pear Cake with Caramel Sauce

Serves: 6 | Total Time: 4 hours 30 minutes

INGREDIENTS

4 ripe pears, cored and sliced
3/4 cup caramel sauce
2/3 cup all-purpose flour
1 tsp baking powder
¼ cup butter, melted
½ cup brown sugar
½ tsp cinnamon powder
¼ cup milk

DIRECTIONS

Whisk flour, baking powder, brown sugar, and cinnamon powder in a bowl. Pour in milk and melted butter and toss to combine. Place sliced pears in your Slow Cooker, top with the flour mixture, and drizzle with caramel sauce. Cover with the lid and cook for 4 hours on Low. Serve chilled and enjoy!

484. Chocolate & Rum Fondue

Serves: 6 | Total Time: 2 hours 15 minutes

INGREDIENTS

10 strawberries
1 cup heavy cream
¼ cup condensed milk
¼ cup buttermilk
1 ½ cups chocolate chips
2 tbsp dark rum

DIRECTIONS

Blend the heavy cream, condensed milk, buttermilk, chocolate chips, and rum in your Slow Cooker. Cover with the lid and cook for 2 hours on Low. When done, remove the lid and serve with the dipping strawberries. Enjoy!

485. Choco Pecan Bread

Serves: 6 | Total Time: 2 hours 30 minutes

INGREDIENTS

1 cup pecans, chopped
1 cup all-purpose flour
1 cup whole milk
3 eggs
¼ cup sour cream
½ cup olive oil
½ cup light brown sugar
½ cup cocoa powder
1 tsp baking powder

DIRECTIONS

In a bowl, whisk milk, eggs, olive oil, and sour cream until creamy. Add sugar, flour, cocoa powder, and baking powder; mix until well combined. Gently fold in pecans and pour the mixture into your Slow Cooker. Cover and cook for 2 hours on High. Serve and enjoy!

486. Cocoa Plum Crumble

Serves: 6 | Total Time: 4 hours 30 minutes

INGREDIENTS

6 plums, sliced
¼ cup light brown sugar
1 tbsp cornstarch
3/4 cup all-purpose flour
½ cup cocoa powder
½ cup cold butter, cubed
½ tsp baking powder
1 tsp lemon zest

DIRECTIONS

In your Slow Cooker, plums apples, sugar, and cornstarch. In a separate bowl, mix flour, cocoa powder, lemon zest, and baking powder. Add cold butter to the dry mixture and toss until crumbly. Sprinkle the crumble mixture over the plums. Cover with the lid and cook for 4 hours on Low. Serve chilled and enjoy!

487. Caribbean Fruit Compote

Serves: 6 | Total Time: 6 hours 30 minutes

INGREDIENTS

2 red apples, peeled, cored, and sliced
½ cup dried cranberries, halved
2 ripe pears, peeled and cubed
1 pineapple, cubed
3 kiwis, cubed
1 cup fresh orange juice
3 tbsp light brown sugar
1-star anise
2 whole cloves

DIRECTIONS

In your Slow Cooker, combine apples, cranberries, pears, pineapple, kiwi, fresh orange juice, sugar, 2 cups of water, star anise and cloves. Cover with the lid and cook for 6 hours on Low. Let cool before serving.

488. Brown Rice Pudding with Vanilla

Serves: 6 | Total Time: 4 hours 15 minutes

INGREDIENTS

1 vanilla pod, cut in half lengthwise
4 cups whole milk
1 ½ cups brown rice
¼ cup cold water
½ cup sugar
2 tbsp cornstarch
1 tsp cinnamon powder
1 tsp nutmeg

DIRECTIONS

Combine rice, milk, vanilla pod, nutmeg, and sugar in your Slow Cooker. Cover and cook for 3 hours on Low. In a bowl, whisk cornstarch and water until smooth, then pour it over the rice. Cover again and cook for 1 more hour on Low, allowing the pudding to thicken. Dust with cinnamon before serving. Enjoy!

489. Choco-Caramel Cake

Serves: 6 | Total Time: 2 hours 30 minutes

INGREDIENTS

1 cup caramel sauce
1 cup all-purpose flour
¼ cup cocoa powder
½ cup butter, melted
4 eggs
1 tsp vanilla extract
1 tsp baking powder

DIRECTIONS

Beat eggs, melted butter, vanilla, and caramel sauce in a bowl until creamy. Add flour, cocoa powder, and baking powder; mix until well combined. Transfer the batter to your Slow Cooker. Cook for 2 hours on High.

490. Easy Tiramisu Bread Pudding

Serves: 6 | Total Time: 4 hours 15 minutes

INGREDIENTS

½ cup mascarpone cheese
1 ½ cups milk
6 cups brioche cubes
¼ cup brown sugar
2 eggs
2 tsp coffee powder
2 tbsp Kahlua
2 tbsp cocoa powder

DIRECTIONS

Place bread cubes in your Slow Cooker. In a bowl, whisk together sugar, coffee powder, Kahlua, mascarpone cheese, milk, and eggs until smooth. Pour the mixture over the bread cubes in the Slow Cooker. Sprinkle the top with cocoa powder. Cover and cook for 4 hours on Low. Serve and enjoy!

491. Red Velvet Milky Way Brioche Pudding

Serves: 6 | Total Time: 5 hours 30 minutes

INGREDIENTS

½ cup Milky Way chocolate, chopped
5 cups brioche cubes
2 cups whole milk
1 cup cream cheese
3 eggs
½ cup white sugar
1 tsp vanilla extract
1 tsp red food coloring

DIRECTIONS

Put brioche cubes and chopped chocolate in your Slow Cooker. In a bowl, whisk together milk, cream cheese, red food coloring, eggs, sugar, and vanilla extract until smooth. Pour the mixture over the bread. Cover with the lid and cook for 5 hours on Low, allowing the flavors to meld. Serve and enjoy!

492. Chocolate Chip Walnut Bars

Serves: 6 | Total Time: 2 hours 45 minutes

INGREDIENTS

½ cup ground walnuts
½ cup dark chocolate chips
1 cup all-purpose flour
1 cup butter, softened
¼ cup buttermilk
1 cup powdered sugar
2 egg yolks
½ tsp baking powder

DIRECTIONS

In a bowl, cream together softened butter and powdered sugar until creamy. Add egg yolks, ground walnuts, flour, baking powder, and buttermilk; mix until well combined. Gently fold the dark chocolate chips into the batter. Transfer the batter to your Slow Cooker, spreading it evenly. Cook for 2 ½ hours on High. Enjoy!

493. Butterscotch Chocolate Cake

Serves: 6 | Total Time: 4 hours 30 minutes

INGREDIENTS

1 cup butterscotch chocolate chips, melted
½ cup milk
½ cup butter, softened
½ cup brown sugar
1 ½ cups all-purpose flour
1 tsp baking powder

DIRECTIONS

Blend butter and sugar with an electric mixer, until creamy, about 5 minutes. Add melted butterscotch chips, milk, and 1 cup of hot water. Pulse until well combined. Add flour and baking powder; mix until smooth. Pour the batter into your Slow Cooker, spreading it evenly. Cover with the lid and cook for 4 hours on Low.

494. Dark Bread Pudding with Cranberries

Serves: 6 | Total Time: 6 hours 30 minutes

INGREDIENTS

6 cups bread cubes
¼ cup dried cranberries
½ cup dark chocolate chips
¼ cup butter, melted
4 eggs
1 ½ cups milk
½ cup heavy cream
1 pinch cinnamon powder
2 tbsp dark rum

DIRECTIONS

Place bread cubes, dried cranberries, and dark chocolate chips in your Slow Cooker. In a bowl, whisk together butter, eggs, milk, heavy cream, cinnamon powder, and dark rum until smooth. Pour the liquid mixture over the bread and other ingredients, ensuring even distribution. Cook for 6 hours on Low. Enjoy!

495. Orange Pots de Crème

Serves: 6 | Total Time: 2 hours 15 minutes + chilling time

INGREDIENTS

1 (14 oz) can sweetened condensed milk
4 egg yolks, whisked
3 tbsp canola oil
½ cup fresh orange juice
2 tsp orange zest
1 tbsp orange liqueur

DIRECTIONS

Coat 6 ramekin with canola oil. Blend the egg yolks and condensed milk in a bowl. Stir in orange juice, orange zest, and orange liqueur. Divide the mixture between the ramekins.

Put a towel in your Slow Cooker and arrange ramekins, and add warm water until halfway up the sides. Cook for 2 hours on High. Let the creme child to room temperature, then place in the fridge for at least 3 hours before serving. Enjoy!

496. Chocolate Cheesecake Soufflé

Serves: 6 | Total Time: 2 hours 30 minutes

INGREDIENTS

1 ½ cups dark chocolate chips, melted
1 ½ cups cream cheese, softened
Butter to grease the pot
4 egg whites
4 egg yolks
1 tsp vanilla extract

DIRECTIONS

Whisk egg whites in a bowl until stiff peaks form. Set aside. In another bowl, mix chocolate chips, cream cheese, egg yolks, and vanilla until smooth. Gently fold the whites into the chocolate mixture until well combined. Grease your Slow Cooker with butter. Pour the soufflé mixture into the Slow Cooker. Cook for 2 hours on High.

497. Butterscotch Pudding

Serves: 6 | Total Time: 2 hours 15 minutes

INGREDIENTS

1 cup brown sugar
1 ½ cups all-purpose flour
½ cup butter, melted
1 cup whole milk
1 tsp vanilla extract
3/4 cup whitesugar
2 tbsp butter
2 cups hot water

DIRECTIONS

Combine butter, milk, vanilla extract, brown sugar, and flour until smooth. Pour the mixture into your Slow Cooker. In a pot over medium heat, cook white sugar, water, and butter for 5-6 minutes until thickens. Set aside. Sprinkle the butterscotch mixture over the batter. Cook for 2 hours on High. Serve and enjoy!

498. Basic Almond Cheesecake

Serves: 6 | Total Time: 4 hours 15 minutes

INGREDIENTS

1 ½ cups crushed almond cookies
½ cup butter, melted
4 eggs
½ cup sugar
12 oz cream cheese
12 oz sour cream
1 tbsp cornstarch
1 tbsp vanilla extract
½ tsp almond extract

DIRECTIONS

Combine almond cookies and melted butter until sandy; transfer into your Slow Cooker and press down for the crust. In a bowl, mix cream cheese, sour cream, eggs, sugar, cornstarch, vanilla extract, and almond extract until smooth. Pour the filling over the crust. Cover with the lid and cook for 4 hours on Low. Let cool before slicing.

499. Lovely Chocolate Chip Brownies

Serves: 6 | Total Time: 6 hours 30 minutes

INGREDIENTS

1 cup all-purpose flour
½ cup cocoa powder
½ cup butter
2 cups semi-sweet chocolate chips
3 eggs
½ cup sugar

DIRECTIONS

Melt butter and 1 ¼ cups of chocolate chips in a heatproof bowl over boiling water until smooth. Remove the bowl. Mix in eggs, sugar, brown sugar, flour, and cocoa powder until smooth. Fold in the remaining chocolate chips and pour the batter into your Slow Cooker. Cover with the lid and cook for 4 hours on Low. Enjoy!

500. Dark Chocolate Rice Pudding

Serves: 6 | Total Time: 8 hours 15 minutes + chilling time

INGREDIENTS

1 (14-oz) can sweetened condensed milk
1 tbsp butter, softened
1 cup rice
3 cups heavy cream
8 oz dark chocolate, chopped
1 tbap lemon zest
1 tbsp ground cinnamon

DIRECTIONS

Grease your Slow Cooker with butter. In a bowl, place the condensed milk, rice, heavy cream, dark chocolate, and lemon zest. Stir to combine and pour the mixture into the cooker. Cook 8 hours on Low. Serve the pudding cold topped with ground cinnamon. Enjoy!

Made in the USA
Las Vegas, NV
19 November 2023